Affinity Photo Workbook

Take your photo editing to new levels
with Affinity Photo

By the Affinity Team

Foreword

The Affinity Photo Workbook has certainly been long awaited and anticipated, so it's an absolute pleasure to be able to take this book to print. Brought together over many painstaking months, we hope you'll find the Affinity Photo Workbook the perfect companion to Affinity Photo.

With the same high-production values as its sister publication, the Affinity Designer Workbook, this book unlocks the power and diverse feature set of Affinity Photo. You'll discover 'hands-on' projects created by contributors whose work we think you'll love!

I also want to take this opportunity to thank you for coming on this journey with us. The Affinity vision was to create a trio of apps encompassing graphic design, image editing and layout which would not only develop into class-leaders in their own right, but also work together in a way never seen before. The launch of Affinity Publisher in 2019, and the unique integration between the different strands of the Affinity package, represent the culmination of the first part of our journey.

All of this is made possible for us because of creative people like you who have supported our vision by buying our software and our Workbooks, as well as acting as evangelists for us online and in the real world. Thank you, we really appreciate your part in our ongoing success.

Ash Hewson
Managing Director

Contributors from Team Affinity

This book has been conceived and created by the following members of the Affinity team.

Editor	Andy Capstick
Technical Writers	Andy Capstick and James Ritson
Art Direction	Neil Ladkin and Ian Cornwall
Artworkers	Ian Cornwall and Ian Upcott

Workbook contributors

The strength of the Affinity Photo Workbook is that its content is created by photo enthusiasts, professional retouchers and digital artists. We've hand-picked the following contributors (in order of appearance) based on the quality of their work and their excellent understanding of Affinity Photo's editing techniques and principles.

A big thank you to all contributors!

James Ritson—As an in-house Serif contributor, you may be familiar with James's hugely popular Video Tutorials at affin.co/phototuts. His love of photography, Affinity Photo and a great empathy with users makes him an ideal candidate to explore enthusiast techniques. He is based in Nottingham, England and is Serif's Affinity Educator.

Check out his tutorials in the Enthusiast Projects chapter (from p. 139).

Steven Randolph—Florida-based and with an interest in getting 'up close and personal' with macro photography. Spiders, butterflies, ladybirds and flowers all appear as subjects in his work.

Learn how focus merging can overcome focal challenges in macro photography in his project Mother of Millions on p. 248. To see more of Steven's work, visit flickr.com/photos/thelostvertex/

Mark Ivkovic—As a professional Fashion & Beauty photographer, Mark uses Affinity Photo for retouch work with a big emphasis on subtlety and naturalness.

Catch up with Mark at his studio in Huddersfield, England, as he retouches a model portrait in the project Elegance on p. 266. See more of his portfolio at his company's website bangphoto.co.uk

Timothy Poulton—Working out of Sydney, Australia, Tim is a premier landscape photographer whose travel company offers photo adventures in Antarctica, Norway, Chile, Japan, and more.

Learn how Tim takes an already stunning landscape panorama to a new level in the project Torres Del Paine on p. 290. Follow Tim's adventures over at the website oneofakind.photography

Bodo Bertuleit—Bodo is an accomplished designer of paperback cover artwork for crime and suspense thrillers. He chooses Affinity Photo as his 'go-to' app.

As well as printing his Search the Woods project (p. 314) in high resolution, he intelligently repurposes content to output equivalent e-book covers. Catch up with Bodo at bodobe.de

Jordan Gaunce—Jordan is Digital Imaging Artist / Picture Hacker at Bruton Stroube Studios. His retouch work is of the very highest order, as shown in the Grilled Cheese Pull project on p. 340.

Find out more about this creative Studio, based out of St Louis, MO, USA, at brutonstroube.com

Emi Haze—An Italian Digital Artist with a real love of the double exposure effect. As a professional freelance Digital Artist, Emi will walk you through the steps in The Snow Queen project on p. 366.

A lovely portfolio of his work can be found at emihaze.com

Johny Åkerlund—With an idea to combine the dispersion effect with motion, Johny perfectly captures a Speed Skater racing for glory.

See the Pure Gold project on p. 388.

Neil Ladkin—Digital artist and designer, heads up all things creative at Affinity on both desktop and iPad platforms.

Join Neil in the creative projects Chameleon and Discovery on p. 406 and p. 424 where he'll explore image styles and tackle pro compositing. You can also see more of Neil's design and illustration work at behance.net/neilladkin

Paolo Limoncelli—Italian-based Paolo (ux-designstudio.com) is a UX/UI Designer and Illustrator. He also creates brush sets under the brand **DAUB® Brushes**.

His Cologne project (p. 448) explores the powerful Affinity brush engine so you can create your very own custom raster brushes, using hair brush creation as an example—followed up by some portrait retouch work.

TABLE OF CONTENTS

Welcome

Chapter 1 : Interface Tour

Chapter 2 : Core Skills

Chapter 3 : Enthusiast Projects

*Project and imagery by James Ritson

Inserts

Chapter 4 : Commercial Projects

Chapter 5 : Creative Effects & Techniques

Index

WELCOME

Affinity Photo Workbook

Welcome to the Affinity Photo Workbook. This workbook has been created with a host of contributors to help you either get started with Affinity Photo, or to further develop your photo editing skills using the app.

In this introductory section, learn more about us and how to get the most out of your experience with Affinity.

ABOUT AFFINITY

Affinity is revolutionising design, photography and publishing with a trio of powerful, professional apps which work together in a unique way. Created to harness the full power of the latest hardware, their development has been driven by the demands of real-life work environments. Affinity is fast becoming a new global standard with more than 1.5 million users and over 10,000 5-star reviews worldwide.

Our trio of apps comprises:

- **Affinity Designer**—professional graphic design software, available on Mac, Windows and iPad

- **Affinity Photo**—professional photo editing software, available on Mac, Windows and iPad

- **Affinity Publisher**—professional desktop publishing, available on Mac and Windows

Designed for cross-platform creatives

Affinity software is developed with full feature parity and total cross-platform compatibility in mind. Every Affinity file you create can be opened by any app in the Affinity suite, and on any of our supported platforms. That extends to shared history too!

True multi-discipline, mixed-media designing is finally here. It's how we think a creative software suite should be.

Designer
for Mac

2014

The story so far

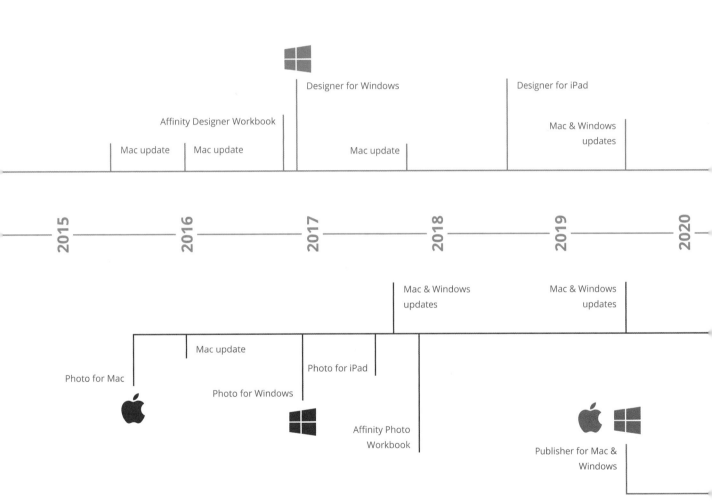

ABOUT
AFFINITY PHOTO

Although a relative newcomer to the photo editing market, Affinity Photo has been attracting admirers who want to own an app that offers a state-of-the-art professional photo-editing experience.

The Affinity team are overwhelmed with the success of Affinity Photo, but its story is still being written and, with big plans for the future, we hope that you share its exciting journey with us.

Be sure to review the subsequent features list to get more of an understanding of Affinity Photo. This represents just the key features of an already comprehensive feature set.

AFFINITY
Photo

KEY FEATURES

Powerful editing experience

Comprehensive layer functionality is backed by a lean, fast rendering engine that gives you realtime previews and feedback of every operation you perform. Build up huge, complex layer stacks whilst maintaining rock solid performance and stability. Edit massive images without lag and fuss on the largest, newest 5K DCI-P3 screens.

It's fast. Really fast

Pan and zoom at 60fps and see all adjustments, effects, transformations and brushes in realtime.

Professional colour format support

Operate in 8-bit, 16-bit and 32-bit unbounded colour formats for incredible precision. RGB, CMYK and LAB are all supported. What's more, most filters and adjustments are not restricted by colour format, and Affinity Photo also ships with full OpenColorIO integration.

Unsurpassed file compatibility

The best PSD import engine available and full support for opened EPS, PDF, and PDF/X files means injecting Affinity Photo into your workflow is painless.

Dedicated raw processing

Edit RAW images in a fully-featured, lossless workspace. Make colour adjustments, push and pull tones, apply noise reduction and sharpening; recover highlights and perform lens corrections.

Swap your workspaces

With focused workspaces, Affinity Photo lets you work how you want—Personas let you jump into the workspace you need, when you need it, while context toolbars offer options specific to the selected tool.

Powerful selection tools

Fast and intelligent selection tools, including brush, freehand and marquee tools, help to create sharp, accurate selections for composite work and selective adjustments. The Selection brush and supporting refinement tools extract the most complex subjects from their backgrounds perfectly.

Non-destructive adjustments

With a huge library of adjustment layers for tonal and colour correction—combined with automatic masking from selections—Affinity Photo offers the most versatile adjustment control that never destroys your base image. You can return to your adjustment at any time to either modify or remove it.

Live filter layers

Add a huge variety of filters for blurring, sharpening, distorting, and more. Like adjustments, filters can be non-destructive and can be previewed in realtime.

Creative and correctional filters

Haze Removal to bring back clarity to landscapes; Lighting to rebalance or completely alter lighting in your images; try equations for advanced transformations.

Live blend modes

Blend modes preview directly on the document as you jump between each blend mode option.

Retouching

Classic Dodge, Burn, and Sponge tools, as well as Healing, Patch and Blemish Removal tools cover most retouching cases, along with the Clone tool which uses the current or a separate image to clone from. Use the Frequency Separation filter for skin retouch of model portraits.

Colour picker

The Colour Picker Tool samples colour under the cursor or average over a sampled region. Colour mode aware with pickup from current or all layers.

Panoramas

Stitch your images with precise image alignment and intelligent cropping; remove leftover transparent regions using automatic inpainting.

HDR Merging

Combine images of different exposures to a 32-bit document with optional tone mapping.

Focus merging

For a greater depth of field, stack and merge images of varying focal points.

Stacking

Stack different images of the same scene for noise reduction, object removal, exposure merging or creative compositing effects.

Automated workflows

Use preset macros or record your very own custom macros for automated operations; all macros offer user interactivity. Batch process all your images to apply a macro, resize, resample, or swap formats.

Natural brushwork

Use Force Touch, stylus pressure, tilt and other controls for natural-looking raster brushwork. Use brush presets, create your own custom brushes, or import .abr brushes. Paint and Erase brush tools work in tandem with brushes from natural, texture, spray, effect, and watercolour categories.

Liquify, mesh warp and perspective

Liquify tools are perfect for subtle model retouch or for more creative warping; use the node-based Mesh Warp Tool for image deformation, while a Perspective Tool warps along single or dual planes.

Extensive Channels support

Manipulate channels with ease—copy them, clear them, load them into other channels. Use Apply Image to calculate channel operations for finer colour and alpha control.

Powerful export

In Export Persona you get a complete workspace dedicated to image export. Select areas, layers or slices to export, controlling each item's output settings independently.

Common Affinity file format

Mixed discipline design is as it should be with a shared file format across Affinity apps. Open any native Affinity file in any Affinity app and just keep working—benefit from shared history, undo options and seamless app switching.

Realtime embedded document editing

Embed other Affinity files in your current design and view results in realtime when editing embedded documents.

Supporting vector tools

A diverse set of shapes come with on-screen controls for adjusting geometry with corner settings and node movement. The Pen Tool lays down Bézier curves which can be converted to masks or selections.

Just your type

Add artistic text for headlines, text frames for paragraph text. Apply sophisticated styling and ligatures, previewing all your available fonts and style sets in on-screen panels. All the controls you need are built in, including leading, kerning, baseline shift, tab stops—as well as the convenience of spell checking and quickly adding placeholder text.

Fully customisable user interface

Panels reorder into any arrangement, while tool sets can be tailored to how you work. Enhance productivity with a huge library of keyboard shortcuts for tools, menu functions, view and controls—and choose your own.

Intelligent editing history

With savable undo history, you can step back to older revisions of your work. You can even save history in your document permanently. Any history step can be tagged as a named snapshot and be restored to at a later date.

Design aids

To improve your editing accuracy, try snapping to align images to the page or other layer content. Fixed grids or guides combined with snapping can help layouts, while Rotate canvas comes in handy when painting brush strokes.

GET THE MOST OUT
OF THIS WORKBOOK

To use this workbook, you must have Affinity Photo installed on your PC or Mac. You can buy Affinity Photo from the Mac App Store or from affinity.serif.com

For full system requirements, please visit affin.co/photofeatures

Be familiar with the Interface

The projects in this book assume that you have a working knowledge of the interface of Affinity Photo already, or that you have read and understood the Interface Tour (p. 13).

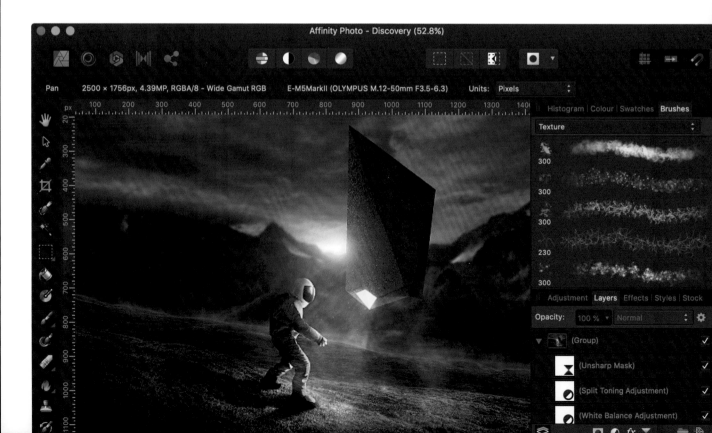

Master the Core Skills

The projects in this book also assume that you have mastered the core skills of Affinity Photo, or that you have understood the principles outlined in Core Skills (p. 87). At the beginning of most projects, core skills that you'll need will be referenced.

Use the Defaults

The projects in this workbook assume that you are using the default settings of Affinity Photo. See Interface Tour (p. 13) to find out how to reset to the default workspace.

Keyboard Shortcuts

At the back of this book you can find some handy pull-out keyboard cheat sheets to help you learn the default keyboard shortcuts.

You can also learn about customising the keyboard shortcuts to your liking in the Interface Tour referenced above.

Project Resources

At the beginning of each project you'll be provided with a link to download all the contributor's resources for that project, e.g.

https://affin.co/mamtor

On later pages, you may see references to downloaded resources (as above) that you can use to follow along with the project.

Snapshots are different saved stages in every project that the user can restore back to, and use as a reference. To view your snapshots, switch on the **Snapshots Panel** (**View > Studio**) and select a snapshot as suggested to you in your workbook project (example at top of page).

Restore Snapshot

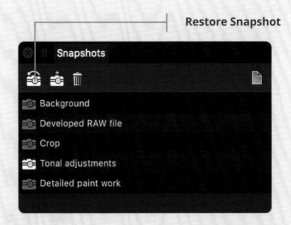

JOIN OUR COMMUNITY

Access our latest news and updates, plus get more resources

We are delighted to provide a wealth of help and support to our growing Affinity community. We do this in a number of ways…

Keep up to date and get support

Our **Twitter**, **Facebook** and **Instagram** pages are great places to get up to date news, exclusives and sneak peeks. Plus, you can sign up to our newsletter to get all the latest news, offers and competitions via email, and we promise to never send you spam, ever.

For in-depth questions and technical support, our **forums** are the best place to go. Our developers play an active role on our forums, so you can get help and updates straight from the source. This is also the place to take part in our free customer betas, so you can try out all our new features first.

Get inspired

Affinity Spotlight is a free, online resource created to share inspirational creative work we love, as well as important advice from professionals. From in-depth interviews with Affinity all-stars, to behind-the-scenes looks at projects created in Affinity to learning resources such as tutorials and explanations of technical concepts, it's all in one place. Visit affinityspotlight.com to find out more.

Keep on learning

Affinity products are backed up by an impressive selection of video tutorials—all recorded in 4k. You can access them from the Welcome screen in the app by clicking **View Tutorials**. They'll help you to learn our software and develop your creative skill set and are intended for beginners and advanced users equally. We'll keep adding more tutorials as we develop more features.

Join our mailing list to get the latest Affinity news and updates at
affin.co/subscribe

 Learn how to use the Affinity suite with our comprehensive video tutorials at
vimeo.com/affinitybyserif and at affin.co/youtube

 Get news, updates, support and take part in our competitions by following us on Twitter
@affinitybyserif

 Get news, updates, support and take part in our competitions by liking us on Facebook
@affinitybyserif

 Share your work tagged with #madeinaffinity for a chance to be featured on our Instagram page
@affinitybyserif

 Get news, learning resources and inspiration from the award-winning Affinity team
affinityspotlight.com

 Take part in our free customer betas and get in-depth support from all our team—including our developers—on our forums at affin.co/forum

CHAPTER 1

Interface Tour

The Affinity Photo interface brings together industry standard concepts such as toolbars and Studio panels, but also offers a context-driven approach where specific tools and their options are available only when needed.

In this chapter, you will be introduced to the workspace of Affinity Photo and see how this well-designed interface is both easy and efficient for your workflow.

AFFINITY PHOTO

The Interface Explained

Toolbar
Use to switch Personas and access commonly used controls and options. These differ depending on the currently active Persona but include viewing, ordering and alignment controls.

Context Toolbar
Dynamically updates according to the selected tool or object so you only get the relevant options as you need them.

Tools Panel
Hosts all the tools relevant to the currently active Persona. The tool set will update when you switch Personas.

*Go to **View Menu > Toggle UI** to toggle your interface on and off. This is useful when you want to look at your document without any distraction.*

Menu Bar
Provides commands and options via multiple menus.

Studio Panels
Gives you control over your document and aids your project workflow. Some panel settings support the current tool.

Document View
This displays your canvas where you can develop, manipulate and enhance your photographs, as well as paint and get creative.

Status Bar
Provides handy tips and shortcuts about the currently active tool.

TOOLS PANEL

The **Tools Panel** hosts a comprehensive set of tools for the currently selected persona.

Some tools are grouped together and are accessible via a flyout menu. Grouped tools can be displayed by clicking the grey marker on an icon's bottom, right corner. Each time you select a new tool, the context toolbar shows the commands and options relevant to the selected tool.

> The tools on this page are available across all personas in Affinity Photo.

View Tool

This tool is used to move the visible portion of your document in the **Document View**. If you double-click on the View Tool's icon on the **Tools Panel**, the zoom will be set to 'Fit'.
Keyboard shortcut: H
Hot key panning: Spacebar

Zoom Tool

The **Zoom Tool** is used to change the zoom level of your page in the Document View. If you double-click on the Zoom Tool's icon on the **Tools Panel**, the zoom will be set to 100%.
Keyboard shortcut: Z

PERSONAS

Think of Personas as different ways of working within your application:

Photo Persona – for image editing using tools, adjustments and filters.

Tone Mapping Persona – for remapping image tones in HDR images.

Liquify Persona – for mesh distortion and warping tools.

Export Persona – to output from your projects as various image file formats.

Develop Persona – for developing raw files.

Each Persona comes with its own specific tools and Studio panels, whilst the top toolbar and menu bar update to show features and options appropriate to the Persona you are in.

Photo Persona will display as default when creating a new document or when opening a saved project or non-raw image. For image editing, the majority of your time will be spent in this Persona.

Develop Persona will display automatically when opening a raw file, while the **Tone Mapping Persona** is activated after an HDR merge. These Personas, plus **Liquify Persona**, can be accessed at any time for any selected RGB pixel layer.

Switching Personas

When you wish to swap your way of working, simply select a different Persona from the **Toolbar** and continue working with a new tool set. Switching between Personas will result in the current workspace changing to display appropriate tools, toolbars, panels and menu options.

PHOTO PERSONA TOOLS

Move Tool

Lets you move, rotate, resize, transform and copy layer contents.
Keyboard shortcut: V

Colour Picker Tool

Samples a colour from your document either directly under the cursor or averaged from an area directly around the cursor.
Keyboard shortcut: I

Crop Tool

Removes areas of an image for practical reasons or to improve composition.
Keyboard shortcut: C

Selection Brush Tool

Selects a region of your image by painting. By simply dragging on your image, you can add or remove regions from a selection. The selection will grow or shrink depending on the brush settings.
Keyboard shortcut: W
*(cycles with the **Flood Select Tool**)*

Flood Select Tool

Selects similar coloured areas of your document with a single click (or drag to grow selection). You can set the tool to select pixels only within the same area or across your entire document.
Keyboard shortcut: W
*(cycles with the **Selection Brush Tool**)*

Photo Persona is where you'll be doing the bulk of your image editing work. It's the default Persona where you'll find all of your brush, selection, fill, healing, gradient and vector tools.

 ## Marquee Selection Tools

Selects parts of your image using various shapes. There is also a **Freehand Selection Tool** to make a selection from a drawn outline (Freehand, Polygonal or Magnetic).
Keyboard shortcut: M
*(cycles through **Rectangular**, **Elliptical**, **Column**, and **Row**).* The **Freehand Selection Tool** uses L by default.

 ## Flood Fill Tool

Fills areas of your page, selection, or object with a colour in a single click. It works by replacing the colour of pixels on the current layer with the **Fill** colour set on the **Colour Panel**.
Keyboard shortcut: G
*(cycles with the **Gradient Tool**)*

 ## Gradient

Applies highly customisable smooth colour gradients when using toning, vector overlays, vector backgrounds, masks and fill layers.
Keyboard shortcut: G
*(cycles with the **Flood Fill Tool**)*

 ## Painting Tools

These tools place coloured pixels on raster layers. The **Paint Brush Tool** lays down natural media brush strokes, while the **Pixel Tool** draws pixel-aligned, hard-edged lines.
Keyboard shortcut: B
*(cycles through **Paint Brush Tool**, **Pixel Tool**, **Colour Replacement Brush Tool** and **Smudge Tool**)*

 ## Paint Mixer Brush

The **Paint Mixer Brush** blends the colour on the brush with coloured pixels on the underlying raster layer, simulating the mixing of wet paint from a paintbrush with paint already on a canvas.

Erase Tools

In contrast to the painting tools, the erase tools remove unwanted pixels from raster layers. They also hide painted areas of previously created vector layers.

Keyboard shortcut: E
*(cycles through **Erase Brush Tool**, **Background Erase Brush** and **Flood Erase Tool**)*

Tonal Brush Tools

With these tools you can precisely lighten, darken, saturate or desaturate areas of your image. The effect of these brushes is cumulative—the more you paint, the more pronounced the effect will be.

Keyboard shortcut: O
*(cycles through **Dodge Brush Tool**, **Burn Brush Tool** and **Sponge Brush Tool**)*

Clone Brush Tool

The **Clone Brush Tool** paints samples from one part of an image onto another or from global sources. Useful for removing defects, retouching and duplicating parts of an image.

Keyboard shortcut: S

Undo Brush Tool

This tool can be used to selectively undo modifications to individual pixels, restoring them to a previous history state or a saved snapshot.

Blur and Sharpen Brush Tools

Use these tools to blur hard edges within an image, increase the contrast of neighbouring pixels, apply clarity and unsharp mask sharpening, and smudging pixel colours. Tools include the **Blur Brush Tool**, **Sharpen Brush Tool**, **Median Brush Tool** and **Smudge Brush Tool**.

Retouch Tools

These tools allow you to repair, tidy up and enhance photographs.

Keyboard shortcut: J
*(cycles through **Healing Brush Tool**, **Blemish Removal Tool**, **Patch Tool**, **Red Eye Removal Tool** and **Inpainting Brush Tool**)*

Vector Line Tools

The **Pen Tool** allows you to quickly create clean, crisp Bézier curves. The **Node Tool** is its perfect partner, allowing you to modify previously drawn curves and shapes (created using the shape tools) with superior precision.
Keyboard shortcut: P
*(cycles through **Pen Tool** and **Node Tool**)*

Shape Tools

These tools allow you to add complicated geometric shapes to your document with little effort. They are highly adaptable and editable and come in a variety of shapes including rectangles, stars, an ellipse and the multifaceted cog.
Keyboard shortcut: U
*(cycles through the **Rectangle Tool**, **Ellipse Tool**, and **Rounded Rectangle Tool**)*

Text Tools

The **Artistic Text Tool** and **Frame Text Tool** allow you to add text to your document from single words to full page stories.
Keyboard shortcut: T
*(cycles through **Artistic Text Tool** and **Frame Text Tool**)*

Warp Tools

The **Mesh Warp Tool** allows you to distort an image (or portion of an image) using a highly customisable grid comprising of nodes and lines. Alternatively, the **Perspective Tool** allows you to modify the perspective of your image.

LIQUIFY PERSONA TOOLS

Push Forward Tool

Shifts pixels in the direction of the stroke.
Keyboard shortcut: P

Push Left Tool

Shifts pixels 90° to the left of the stroke direction. This spreads and compresses edges along the stroke. The option ⌥ key (Mac) or alt key (Win) shifts pixels in the opposite direction.
Keyboard shortcut: L

Twirl Tool

Applies a clockwise rotational distortion under the stroke. The option ⌥ key (Mac) or alt key (Win) applies the warping rotation in the opposite direction.
Keyboard shortcut: T

Pinch Tool

Applies a spherical distortion under the stroke, thereby spreading pixels at the centre outward. The option ⌥ key (Mac) or alt key (Win) applies a 'punch' distortion.
Keyboard shortcut: U

Punch Tool

Applies a spherical distortion under the stroke, thereby compressing pixels at the centre and pushing them inward. The option ⌥ key (Mac) or alt key (Win) applies a 'pinch' distortion.
Keyboard shortcut: N

Turbulence Tool

Applies a crumbling distortion under the stroke which compacts some mesh lines together while expanding others.
Keyboard shortcut: B

Liquify Persona is a dedicated workspace for performing mesh-based distortion operations on a specific, selected RGB pixel layer. The Liquify tools listed below can be used in isolation or combination to allow you to warp an image as appropriate.

 ### Mesh Clone Tool

Paints samples from one part of the mesh onto another. Ideal for applying previously set mesh adjustments to another area of the image. The option ⌥ key (Mac) or alt key (Win) sets the sample area.
Keyboard shortcut: C

Reconstruct Tool

Reduces the warp effect applied to an image using the Liquify tools. With the appropriate number of applications, the area will return to its original, unwarped state.
Keyboard shortcut: R

 ### Freeze Tool

Applies a mask to protect areas of the image from any warp effects applied using the Liquify tools.
Keyboard shortcut: F

 ### Thaw Tool

Removes the current mask from protected areas of the image to allow warping to be applied using the Liquify tools.
Keyboard shortcut: W

DEVELOP PERSONA TOOLS

Develop Persona is a dedicated studio for developing raw files.

 Red Eye Removal Tool

Fixes the red eye effect in your photos and preserves the detail of the eye.
Keyboard shortcut: R

 Blemish Removal Tool

Removes small imperfections from images.
Keyboard shortcut: L

 Overlay Paint Tool*

Paints an overlay to which adjustments can be applied.
Keyboard shortcut: B

Overlay Erase Tool*

Paints away areas of the overlay applied with Overlay Paint Tool.
Keyboard shortcut: E

* Available in **Tone Mapping Persona**.

 Overlay Gradient Tool*

Applies a linear, elliptical, or radial opacity gradient to which adjustments can be applied. Drag on your image to define the gradient length and direction.
Keyboard shortcut: G

Crop Tool

Removes areas of an image to remove unwanted content or improve composition.
Keyboard shortcut: C

 White Balance Tool

Sets the White Balance of the image depending on the colour of the pixel clicked or pixels selected by dragging (averaged colour).
Keyboard shortcut: W

EXPORT PERSONA TOOLS

Export Persona provides the perfect environment for exporting particular areas, layers or your entire document in a variety of sizes and formats.

Slice Tool

The **Slice Tool** allows you to draw, move and resize slices placed on top of your document in readiness for exporting. Slices allow you to export drawn portions of your document as individual graphics.
Keyboard shortcut: S

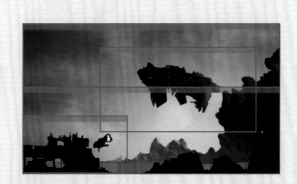

Slice Selection Tool

The **Slice Selection Tool** lets you select groups and layers so you can create slices from them.
Keyboard shortcut: L

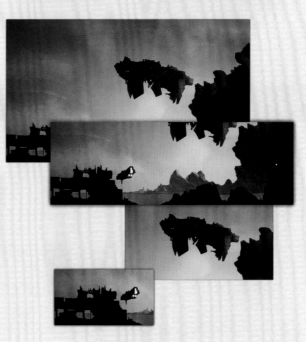

TOOLBAR

The Persona icons precede a mix of icons that give you access to commonly used controls and options. These differ depending on the currently active Persona.

Icons in Liquify Persona include mesh and mask controls, while Develop Persona's Toolbar includes before/after and clipping warning options. Most Personas also give you quick access to split view controls. Icons found on Photo Persona's Toolbar are annotated below.

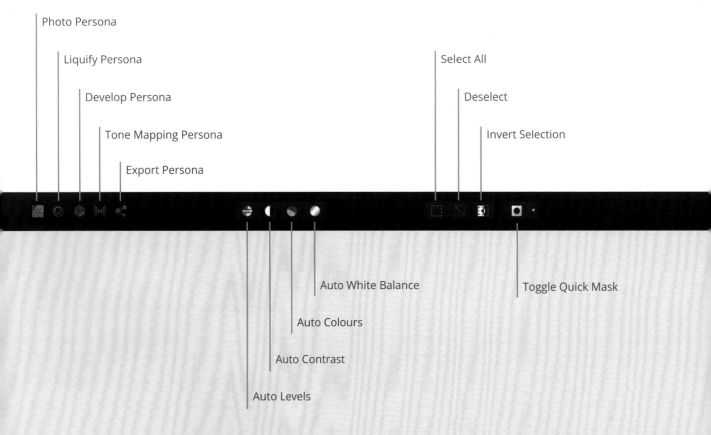

Photo Persona

Liquify Persona

Develop Persona

Tone Mapping Persona

Export Persona

Select All

Deselect

Invert Selection

Auto White Balance

Auto Colours

Auto Contrast

Auto Levels

Toggle Quick Mask

Force Pixel Alignment

Move by Whole Pixels

Snapping

Assistant Options

Alignment

Insert behind the selection

Insert at the top of the layer

Insert inside the selection

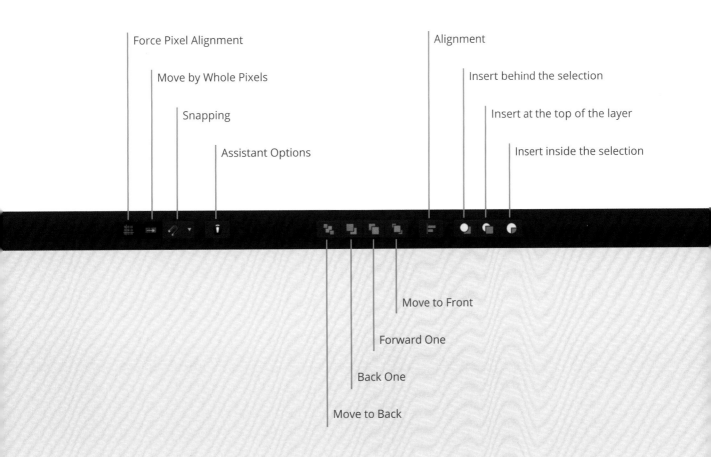

Move to Front

Forward One

Back One

Move to Back

CONTEXT TOOLBAR

As the name implies, the options on the context toolbar will update depending on the currently selected tool. Regardless of the tool you switch to, you'll have quick access to appropriate options while you edit.

For example, the toolbars for the **Paint Brush Tool** (below) and **Clone Brush Tool** (opposite) differ. The screenshot opposite also shows the toolbar's location above an image.

When the **Move Tool** and text, curves or vector shapes are selected, the context toolbar provides editing options for those objects. For example, for a selected curve:

When the **Move Tool** is selected, but no objects are selected, the context toolbar will give you access to the **Preferences** dialog.

STUDIO PANELS

Layer content can be affected in a variety of ways using options which appear on the **Studio Panels**.

The panels also offer tool options, layer control and image information (e.g., channels and histograms).

Although the same named panels may appear in different **Personas**, they may have subtly different options and may function in a slightly different way. Which panels you use will vary depending on your style of working and the aim of the project.

It's also worth knowing that not all panels are displayed by default, as some panels are for less common workflows. Go to **View Menu > Studio** to turn individual panels off and on and use **Reset Studio** to only show the default Studio panels for the Persona you are in.

Histogram Panel

The **Histogram Panel** shows the distribution of Red, Green, Blue, and Luminance values for the image, layer, or current marquee selection.

> In LAB or CMYK colour modes, channels for that mode are displayed instead of Red, Green and Blue (RGB).

The panel gives a graphical representation of the colours and tones present in your image and helps you decide if your image needs correction.

Colour distribution statistics can be presented at the bottom of the panel to provide further colour information. Your cursor can be moved around the histogram, displaying the pixel count at the colour level your cursor is currently placed at.

Layer
Limits the scope of the histogram to the selected layer.

Panel Preferences
Click **Advanced** to display colour statistics information at the bottom of the panel.

Channels
Sets the panel to displays all the channels in the histogram simultaneously or display just a single channel.

Marquee
Limits the scope of the histogram to the area within the current selection marquee.

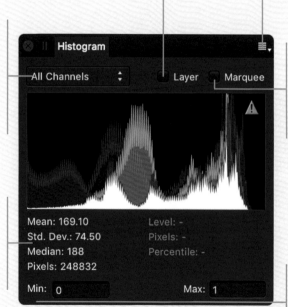

Histogram

All Channels

Layer   Marquee

Mean: 169.10   Level: -
Std. Dev.: 74.50   Pixels: -
Median: 188   Percentile: -
Pixels: 248832

Min: 0   Max: 1

Colour statistics
Activated via panel preferences, this section provides additional colour distribution statistics.

Min/Max
Constrain or expand the tonal range represented in the histogram.

Scope Panel (View > Studio)

The **Scope Panel** provides a variety of charts which allow you to examine the distribution of luminance and chrominance in the current image.

Chart

Sets the chart currently displayed in the panel.

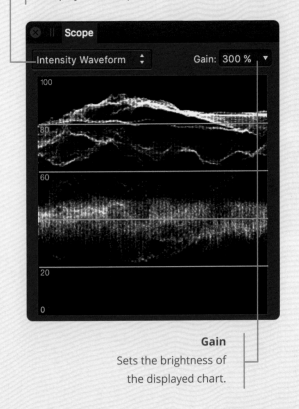

Gain

Sets the brightness of the displayed chart.

Colour Panel

The **Colour Panel** is used to choose colour for various tools and vector objects. A pop-up version of the Colour Panel may appear when choosing colour from within other dialogs.

The Colour Panel can operate in several colour modes—HSL, RGB, CMYK and LAB—and has various ways of defining colour—colour wheel (HSL only), colour boxes and colour sliders. Colour tints can also be applied from within the panel.

By default, the panel shows colours represented by two solid colour selectors indicating your Primary Colour and Secondary Colour.

The panel can take on different appearances depending on the selected tool. For example, the **Gradient Tool** changes the appearance of the Colour Panel by displaying only one colour selector.

None

Removes colour from the active selector.

Swap

Switches the colours applied to the selectors.

Colour picker and **picked colour swatch**

Allows colour sampling from individual pixels and application to active selector.

Lock colourspace

Prevents the colour space from changing with your selection or Swatches panel use.

Panel Preferences

Change colour selection preferences, models and modes.

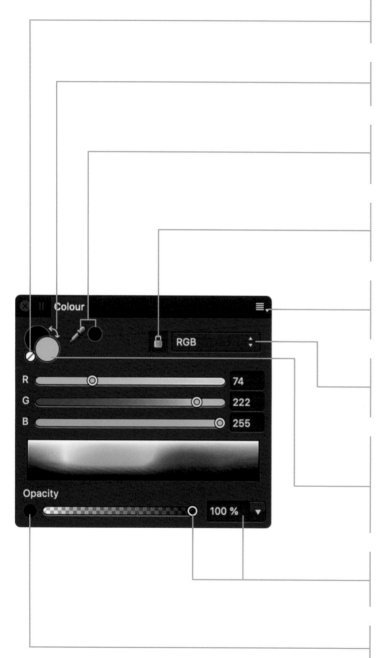

Colourspace

Swap between RGB, CMYK, HSL, Lab and Greyscale colour spaces.

Primary/Secondary Colour

The active colour selector is shown at the front of the two colour selectors. Choosing a new colour will apply it to the active colour selector.

Opacity/Noise Controls

Sets the opacity and/or noise of the active colour.

Opacity/Noise

Click to switch between Opacity and Noise.

Swatches Panel

The **Swatches Panel** stores your recently used colours and lets you access a range of pre-defined palettes, each containing solid or gradient fill swatches. These can be selected for use with various tools and for applying directly to vector objects. You can also create and store your own swatches as custom colour palettes either for the document or application (system-wide for Mac version).

As well as accessing palettes, you can create global and spot colours, and make colours overprint. Your registration colour can also be customised.

Like the Colour Panel, the Swatches Panel has different states depending on the selected tool.

The panel also shows **None**, **Black**, **Mid-grey** and **White** swatches, recently used colours and an opacity control. Swatches are organised into colour palettes by category.

In contrast to the Colour Panel, use this panel if you'd rather select colours from a pre-defined palette. You can choose colours from a temporary (**Recent**) palette as well as from custom and pre-defined palettes such as **PANTONE®** colours.

Search

Overprint Colour

Global Colour

Registration Colour

Spot Colour

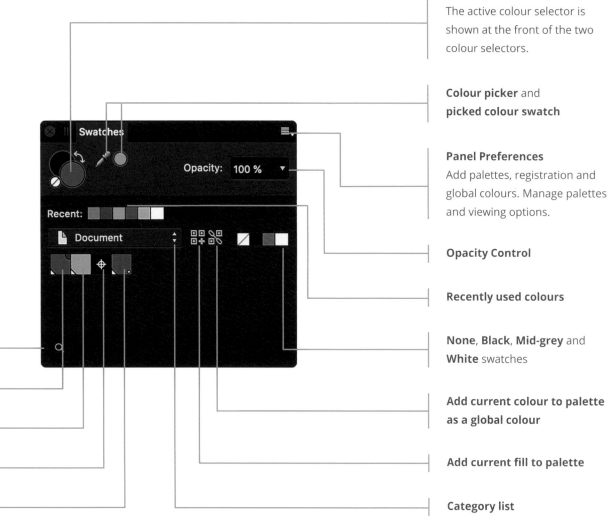

Primary/Secondary colour
The active colour selector is shown at the front of the two colour selectors.

Colour picker and **picked colour swatch**

Panel Preferences
Add palettes, registration and global colours. Manage palettes and viewing options.

Opacity Control

Recently used colours

None, **Black**, **Mid-grey** and **White** swatches

Add current colour to palette as a global colour

Add current fill to palette

Category list

Brushes Panel

The **Brushes Panel** hosts a selection of brush presets which can be selected for use with any of the Brush tools. As well as the pre-designed brushes provided, any custom brushes you create can be saved to your own category.

Edit
Loads the selected brush in the Brush Editor, allowing it to be customised and saved as a new brush preset.

Panel Preferences
Create, rename and delete categories. Import brushes (including ABR format) and export brushes.

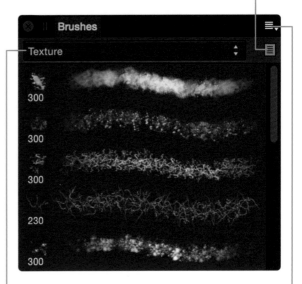

You can create custom brushes such as:

- **New Intensity Brush**
  Creates a brush based on the lightness (intensity) of a raster image.

- **New Round Brush**
  Creates a brush with a soft, feathered edge.

- **New Square Brush**
  Creates a brush with a hard, square edge.

- **New Image Brush**
  Creates a brush based on an image.

Category Menu
Select a category to load the brushes for that category.

Adjustment Panel

The **Adjustment Panel** allows you to apply colour and tonal corrections to your image non-destructively, i.e., without making permanent changes to the underlying image.

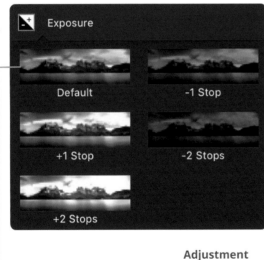

Adjustment
Select an adjustment to display thumbnail adjustment preset(s) and custom settings.

Thumbnail
Click an adjustment thumbnail to apply the preset to the image.

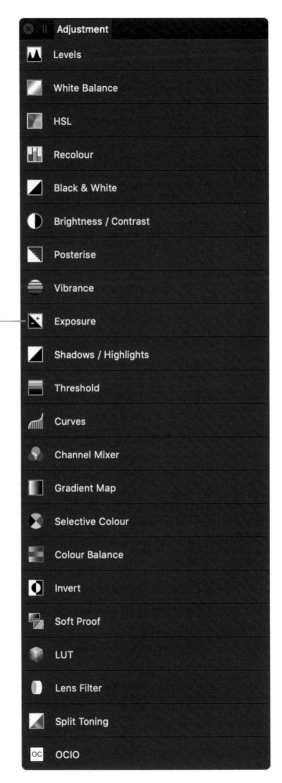

EXIF Panel (View > Studio)

EXIF information is written into image files automatically when taken on a digital camera. It records camera details as well as exposure and aperture settings, and more. This information is displayed in the **EXIF Panel**.

EXIF List

Shows a summary, all EXIF data or raw EXIF data.

EXIF		
Summary		🗑
Camera	DMC-GH4	
Maker	Panasonic	
Lens	LUMIX G VARIO 12-35/F2.8	
Date shot	2014-05-23T17:45:34	
Size	n/a	
Exposure	1/250	
Aperture	8.0	
ISO	200	
Exp. bias	0.0	
Exp. prog	Manual exposure	
Metering	Pattern	
Flash	False	
Author	n/a	
Copyright	n/a	
Description		

Delete EXIF Data

Removes all EXIF data from the document.

Layers Panel

The **Layers Panel** controls the stacking order (Z-order) of layers in your document, helps you organise your layers and controls layer visibility, locking, opacity and blending. It provides information about a layer, such as its type and whether it has effects applied.

Layer

Created layer showing a thumbnail of contents, layer name, type (in parenthesis) and if locked or Layer Effect is applied.

Edit All Layers

Allows editing across all layers (rather than just the current layer).

Mask Layer

Creates a layer mask on the current layer to selectively paint in or out portions of underlying layer(s).

Adjustments

Adds an adjustment layer to the current layer for tonal and colour correction.

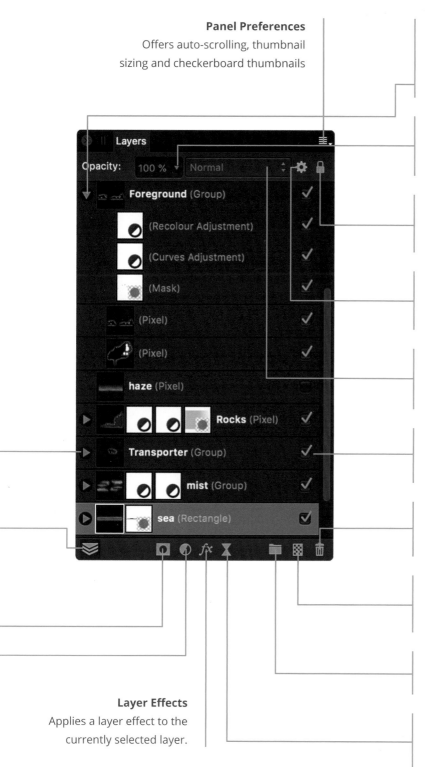

Panel Preferences
Offers auto-scrolling, thumbnail sizing and checkerboard thumbnails

Expand/Collapse
Click to expand the layer, revealing nested or grouped content. Click again to collapse.

Opacity
Adjusts the transparency of the selected layer.

Lock/Unlock
Click to prevent or allow layer contents from being moved or transformed.

Blend Ranges
Access settings for blend ranges, blend gamma and antialiasing.

Blend Mode
Changes how the current layer's colours interact with colours on the layers below.

Hide/Show
Uncheck to hide the layer; check to make it visible again.

Remove Layer
Deletes the currently selected, layer or group.

Add Pixel Layer
Creates an empty pixel layer above the currently selected layer.

Group Layers
Groups the currently selected layers.

Live Filters
Applies a non-destructive filter layer to add creative effects.

Layer Effects
Applies a layer effect to the currently selected layer.

Effects Panel

The **Effects Panel** lets you apply and modify layer effects such as blurs, shadows, glows, and more.

Layer effects can be applied to the currently selected layer's content. These effects are also completely non-destructive so you can change them at any time.

Outer Shadow
Adds a shadow outside layer content's edges.

Outer Glow
Adds a colour glow outside layer content's edges.

Outline
Adds an outline to the layer content's edge.

Bevel/Emboss
Adds rounded edges and shadows to edges for a 3D effect.

Gradient Overlay
Applies a linear, elliptical, radial or conical gradient to layer contents.

Fill Opacity
Alters the opacity of layer content without altering the opacity of the applied layer effect(s).

Gaussian Blur
Blurs the layer content.

Inner Shadow
Adds a shadow inside layer content's edges.

Inner Glow
Adds a colour glow inside layer content's edges.

3D
Adds lighting to give a 3D appearance.

Colour Overlay
Applies a solid colour to layer content.

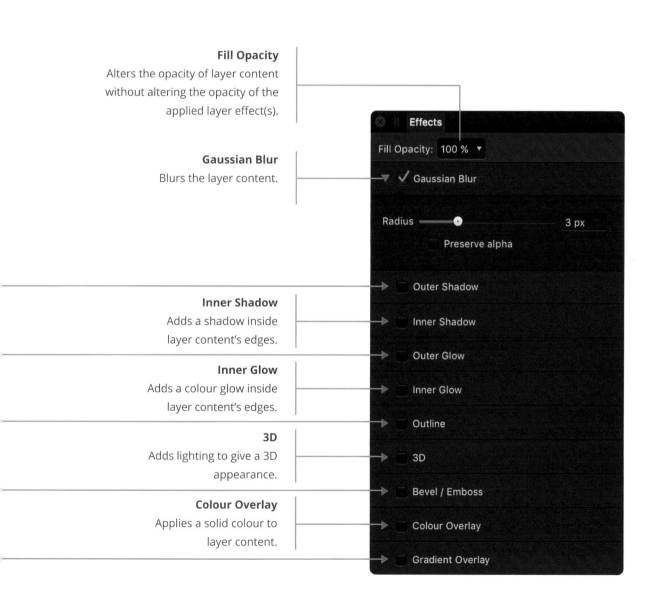

Effects

Fill Opacity: 100 % ▼

☑ Gaussian Blur

Radius ─────●──── 3 px
⬤ Preserve alpha

◻ Outer Shadow

◻ Inner Shadow

◻ Outer Glow

◻ Inner Glow

◻ Outline

◻ 3D

◻ Bevel / Emboss

◻ Colour Overlay

◻ Gradient Overlay

41

Styles Panel

The **Styles Panel** lets you apply pre-designed styles to your layers. Styles are made up of effects, stroke properties, or text attributes and combinations of these. You can apply them easily by drag-and-drop or selecting a layer and clicking on a panel thumbnail. You can also save any layer's style to the panel for future use.

Panel Preferences
Add, remove and rename style categories. Import and export styles. Save a new style to the category based on the current selection.

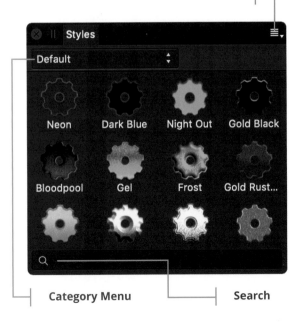

Category Menu   **Search**

Stock Panel

The **Stock Panel** is an in-app image browser which displays content from free and royalty-free photo providers. Search and browse images, then add them to the document by drag and drop.

Archive   **Search**
Sets the provider from which to search.

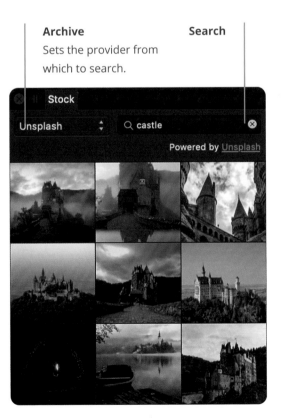

Navigator Panel

This panel allows you to pan and zoom around your Document View and set up specific **View Points** so you can zoom into chosen areas of your project repeatedly.

Panel Preferences
Displays the **View Point Menu** and options.

Zoom
Use the slider, buttons or the percentage display to zoom in or out.

View Rectangle
Pan around your document by dragging the view rectangle around the panel. The area enclosed within the rectangle is your Document View.

View Point Menu
Select a named View Point to jump to a previously saved zoomed-in area.

View Point Options
Add, remove and rename View Points.

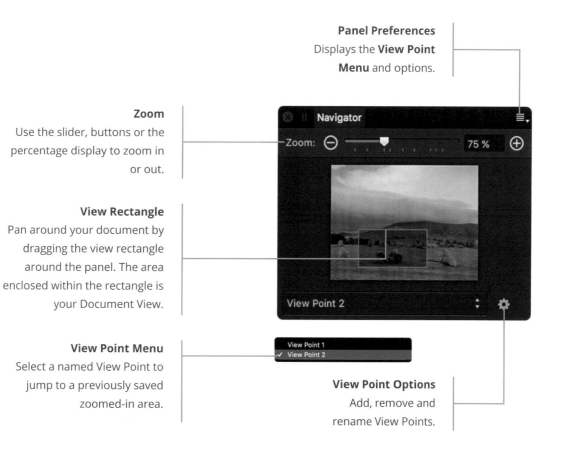

Transform Panel

The **Transform Panel** allows you to edit with the utmost precision by controlling the horizontal (X) and vertical (Y) position of any layer in your document, as well as its overall width (W) and height (H). Rotate and shear options complete the panel. All transforms are carried out in relation to a defined anchor point—corner, edge or centre.

X—Horizontal position
Adjusts the horizontal position of the layer in relation to the selected anchor point.

Y—Vertical position
Adjusts the vertical position of the layer in relation to the selected anchor point.

Anchor point selector
Transforms are carried out from the selected anchor point. Click on an anchor point to select.

R—Rotation
Rotates the layer by a specified number of degrees in relation to the selected anchor point.

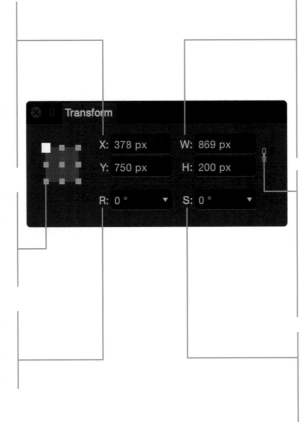

W—Width
Adjusts the layer width in relation to the selected anchor point.

H—Height
Adjusts the layer height in relation to the selected anchor point.

Link
When enabled, width and height are adjusted in proportion to each other, maintaining the current aspect ratio. When deselected, they can be adjusted independently.

S—Shear
Shears the layer by a specified number of degrees in relation to the selected anchor point.

History Panel

The **History Panel** stores changes and shows each state as a labelled entry in a list, allowing you to return to earlier points in time. The oldest state is the topmost in the list, and when edits are made, new states are added to the bottom of the list. If you click on an earlier state and then make a different change, any states that originally came after it are deleted.

A document's history can be saved along with the document by enabling **Save History With Document** in the **File Menu**, so a previous session's edits can be returned to even if the document is closed and reopened.

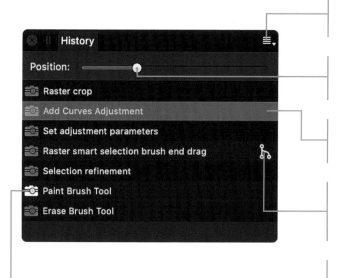

Panel Preferences—Click **Advanced** to show history states with thumbnails and date/time.

Position—Drag the slider left to undo a change, right to redo a change.

State—gives a brief description of the edit made to the document. Click a state to jump to that edit.

Cycle futures—Click to reinstate your 'lost' redo history after making an edit at a state in your undo history.

Set Undo Brush Source
Click to set the history step that the Undo Brush Tool will use to 'paint back' to.

Unless you choose to save the document's history, the undo states listed in the **History Panel** are cleared when the document is closed.

Snapshots Panel (View > Studio)

Snapshots let you define a stage in your session from which you can restore. You might do this in advance of carrying out more complex operations where you might need to restore back to a previous point in time (if things don't go to plan!).

Once a snapshot has been created, it can become the starting point of a new document.

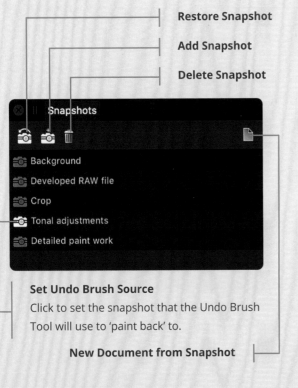

Restore Snapshot

Add Snapshot

Delete Snapshot

Set Undo Brush Source
Click to set the snapshot that the Undo Brush Tool will use to 'paint back' to.

New Document from Snapshot

Channels Panel

The **Channels Panel** displays the colour channels and alpha channel for the whole image and selected layer. The current pixel selection is also shown.

The panel also lets you create and manipulate selections from channels and store selections as channels.

Channel Thumbnail
Displays the colour channel, mask, pixel selection or spare channel as a thumbnail.

Channel Type

Toggle Quick Mask
Toggles between displaying entry as a pixel selection and a Quick Mask.

Document Colour Format and ICC Profile

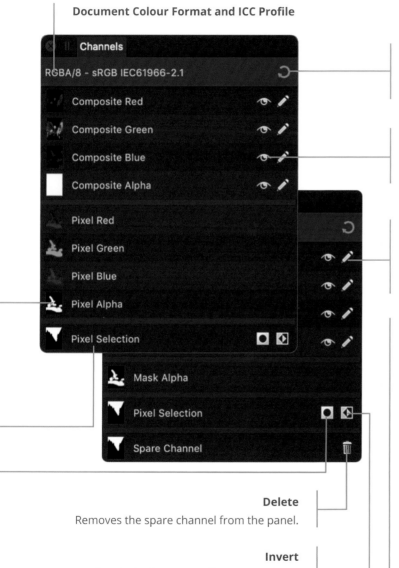

Reset

Reverts the channel settings back to default.

Visible

Toggles between showing and hiding the channel.

Editable

Toggles between allowing the channel to be editable or protecting it from changes.

Option ⌥ click (Mac) or right-click (Win) on panel entries offer the following options:

- Create selections from channels.

- Add to, subtract from, and intersect channel with current selection.

- Create greyscale and mask layers.

- Retrieve stored selections and load selections to current layer channel, mask, adjustment layer, or filter layer.

- Invert selections, layer channels and masks.

Delete

Removes the spare channel from the panel.

Invert

Reverses the pixel selection so all areas which are not selected become selected (or vice versa). Opacity values of selected pixels are also inverted.

Info Panel (View > Studio)

The **Info Panel** provides continuous data readings using one or more samplers. These can sample from the cursor's current position or from a placed target position.

Colour Model
Sets the colour model, or total ink coverage, to be tracked.

Cursor
Presents data sampled from under the current cursor position.

Target
Presents data sampled from under a placed target on the document. Drag from the icon to the document to add a target.

Panel Preferences
Add new samplers or remove selected samplers.

Tracked Data

- Colour values (based on a chosen model) or total ink level.

- Horizontal and vertical position.

- Relative height, width, distance and angle.

- Document colour format and ICC profile.

- Memory information.

Info				
R:	90	C:	65%
G:	187	M:	0%
B:	96	Y:	85%
A:	255	K:	0%

X: 398 px   W: --   D: --
Y: 619 px   H: --   A: --

RGBA/8 - sRGB IEC61966-2.1
Memory pressure: 0%
Memory efficiency: 73%

32-bit Preview Panel (View > Studio)

The **32-bit Preview Panel** provides configurable exposure and gamma controls to preview the vast tonal range of a 32-bit document without tonally modifying it. This is especially useful for floating point lossless workflows where edits need to be made to the image without sacrificing the available tonal range through tonal compression or adjustments.

Exposure

Previews exposure changes to better visualise the highlight or shadow tonal ranges.

Gamma

Sets the gamma correction value of the preview.

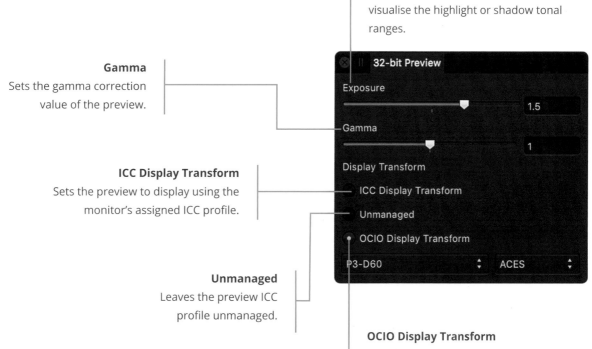

ICC Display Transform

Sets the preview to display using the monitor's assigned ICC profile.

Unmanaged

Leaves the preview ICC profile unmanaged.

OCIO Display Transform

Sets the preview to display with the selected OpenColorIO colour space.

Macro Panel (View > Studio)

Macros are a series of recorded operations that can be quickly reproduced and applied as actions to speed up and aid workflows. The **Macro Panel** provides the means of recording, saving, exporting and importing macros.

Start recording

Stop recording

Play
Runs the list of recorded actions.

Add To Library
Saves the current macro to the Library Panel for future use in any document.

Export
Exports the current macro to an .afmacro file for sharing or storage.

Import
Imports a previously exported macro (.afmacro file).

Edit
Edit the settings of the action via a pop-up dialog.

Toggle Action
Toggle between including or excluding the action from the playback.

Reset
Removes all recorded actions.

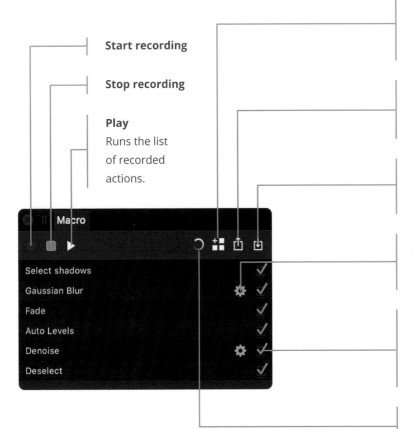

Library Panel (View > Studio)

The **Library Panel** stores pre-supplied, custom and imported macros. These macros can be applied to the current document via a single click.

Panel Preferences
Add new categories and import macros.

Category Options Menu
Rename, delete, move up or down the category. Also allows exporting of macros.

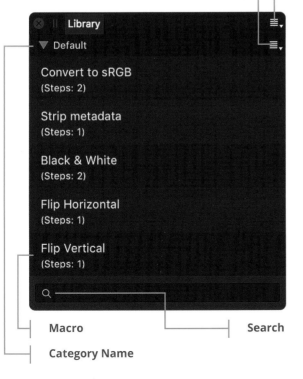

Macro

Search

Category Name

Batch Panel (View > Studio)

Batch jobs allow you to process a number of source files and then save them as afphoto project files or export them to a variety of file formats. Batch jobs can be used in conjunction with macros to boost workflow efficiency.

The **Batch Panel** appears automatically when a batch job is activated and lists all the images being processed and its processing stage.

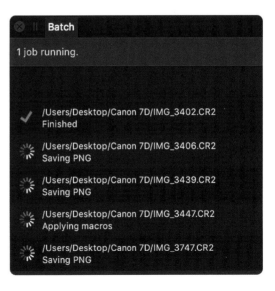

51

Assets Panel

Assets are archived layer content which can be accessed from any open Affinity Photo document. They are conveniently stored in the Assets Panel.

Assets are created by selecting layer content and then from a subcategory's options menu, selecting **Add from Selection**.

Assets are added to a document by simply dragging it from the Assets Panel onto your page.

Asset categories and subcategories can be created at any time to help you organise your assets. They are then listed in the pop-up Category Menu at the top of the Assets Panel. Each category can accommodate an unlimited number of subcategories.

Assets in the panel can be displayed as thumbnails in a grid (default) or as a named list. Tooltips display the name of an asset.

Category Menu
Select a category to load assets within subcategories.

Subcategory
Click to expand to reveal hosted assets. Click again to collapse.

Search

Panel Preferences
Allows you to create, rename and delete categories and add subcategories. Also gives you access to importing and exporting assets and panel display options.

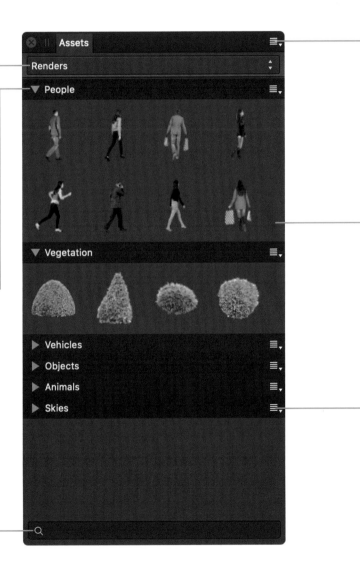

Assets
Displayed as a thumbnail (default) or as a named list.

Subcategory Options Menu
Allows you to rename or delete the subcategory as well as move it up or down within the category. Also allows you to add new assets based on the current page selection.

Assets

Renders

▼ People

▼ Vegetation

▶ Vehicles
▶ Objects
▶ Animals
▶ Skies

Font
Sets the typeface for the selected text.

Font Style
Controls which typeface style is applied to the selected text.

Collection
Filters the list of available fonts in the **Font** pop-up menu.

Font Size
Controls the point size of characters.

Character Panel (View > Studio)

The **Character Panel** allows you to apply local formatting to individual letters, words, sentences and paragraphs as well as entire stories.

Text Style
Allows a character text style to be applied to selected text.

Decorations
Applies underline, strikethrough or outline attributes with colour options.

Kerning
Controls the distance between two characters. **Auto** will give default kerning. Positive values give expanded kerning, negative values give condensed kerning.

Tracking
Controls the spacing between characters throughout a word.

Baseline
Controls the position of the bottom of text characters. Increasing the value lowers the baseline, decreasing the value raises the baseline.

Leading Override
Applies local override to selected text to increase the leading with regard to the paragraph's leading.

Font colour
Sets the colour of the text.

Background colour
Sets the colour applied behind the selected text (i.e., creating a highlight effect).

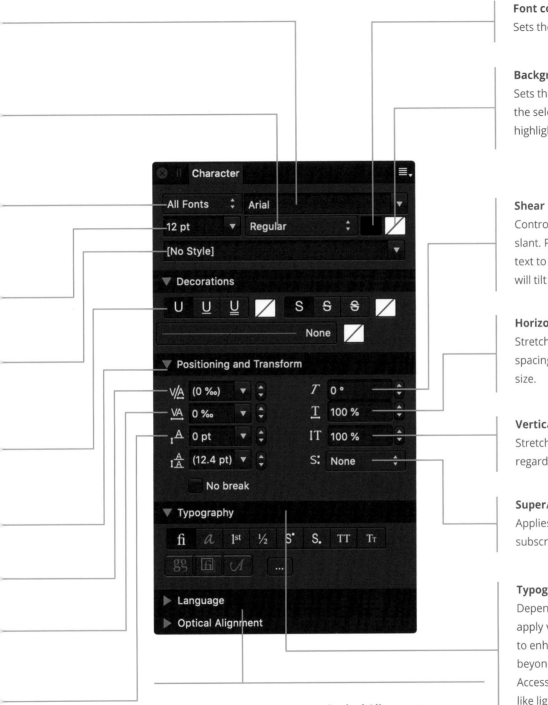

Shear
Controls the extent of text slant. Positive values will tilt text to the left, negative values will tilt text to the right.

Horizontal Scale
Stretches the characters and spacing with regard to point size.

Vertical Scale
Stretches the characters with regard to point size.

Super/Subscript
Applies either a superscript or subscript attribute.

Typography
Depending on your font, you can apply various typographic options to enhance your characters beyond their standard attributes. Access OpenType font features like ligatures, alternates, stylistic sets and more.

Language
Sets the languages for the dictionary (for spell checking), hyphenation and typography.

Optical Alignment
Controls the alignment of dashes, punctuation or any character you choose at the start of paragraphs.

Paragraph Panel (View > Studio)

The **Paragraph Panel** gives you full control over paragraph-level formatting options. Paragraph formatting is applied to the entire paragraph in which selected text is located or to a paragraph in which the caret is located.

Alignment
Select from **Left**, **Centre**, **Right**, **Justify Left**, **Justify Centre**, **Justify Right** or **Justify All** (Force-Justified). The Justify options define what happens to the final sentence.

Text Style
Applies the selected paragraph text style.

First Line Indent
Controls the indent applied to the first line of the paragraph.

Paragraph Leading
Controls the distance between text baselines (vertical gap between lines) within the paragraph.

Space Above/Below Management
Controls how space above/below settings work together.

Tab Stops
Create, position and align paragraph tab stops.

Left Indent

Controls the left indent applied to the entire paragraph (excluding the first line).

Right Indent

Controls the right indent applied to the entire paragraph.

Space Before Paragraph

Controls the vertical gap which precedes the paragraph.

Space After Paragraph

Controls the vertical gap which succeeds the paragraph.

Bullets and Numbering

Creates bulleted lists using any glyph or numbered lists using a choice of number schemas.

⊗ | Paragraph

Bullet 1

▼ Spacing

6.4 mm   6.4 mm   0 mm

[12.4 pt]   0 pt   12 pt

Use space before: Only Between Par...

Sum space before and after

Ignore space for same styles

▶ Tab Stops

▶ Justification

▼ Bullets and Numbering

Type: Bullet   Level: 1

Text: ◼ »   More...

Tabstop: 6.4 mm

Justification

For justified paragraphs, you can control letter and word spacing.

Text Styles Panel (View > Studio)

A text style is a set of one or more attributes which can be applied to text in bulk. Later, if you chose to modify a text style, any text which uses that style will update to conform to the changes you've made. The **Text Styles Panel** enables you to create, apply and manage text styles within your design.

Current Formatting
Displays the formatting applied to the current selection or caret position. Click arrow to show more details.

Text Style
Entry includes name, preview of its formatting, its predominant type and its shortcut keys.

Create
Launches the Edit Text Style dialog ready for creating a new paragraph, character or group text style, respectively, from scratch.

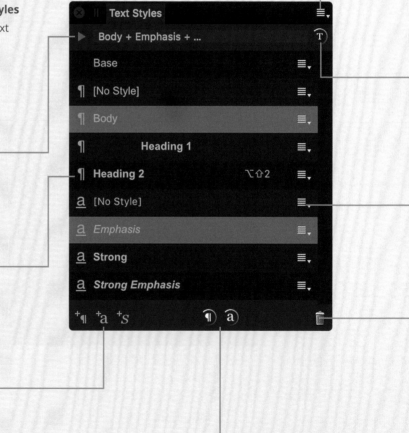

Panel Preferences

Gives you options for displaying and sorting the text styles in the panel as well as detaching all text styles then deleting them, setting a text style as a default for future text and importing text styles.

Reset Formatting

Removes overrides and local formatting applied to the currently selected text but leaves applied text styles in place.

Options menu

Access application, creation, deletion and editing options for individual text styles.

Delete Style

Removes the selected text style from the document and any instances of its application.

Update

Revises the current paragraph or character style, respectively, to conform to the local formatting of the selected text.

Glyph Browser (View > Studio)

The Glyph Browser lets you navigate glyphs or Unicode characters available with your currently installed fonts.

By first choosing a font or using the Search option, you can apply a specific glyph to a selected character (or at an insertion point) by double-clicking.

Panel Preferences

Sorts glyphs by glyph or Unicode value, and sets glyph display size.

Character set

Select a glyph or Unicode character set, e.g. Cyrillic.

Search   **Recent glyphs**

Lock Fonts and Traits

When unlocked, the font shown in the panel changes with the selected text's font; when locked, the font selected in the panel remains unchanged.

Sources Panel (View > Studio)

Stores multiple images for use as global sources during cloning or healing. After a Focus Merge or HDR Merge (without tone mapping), the panel will automatically appear with each contributing image available as an individual source to clone from.

Source Thumbnail

Pickup area indicator
Shows the source point that Clone Brush or Healing Brush tools will clone from.

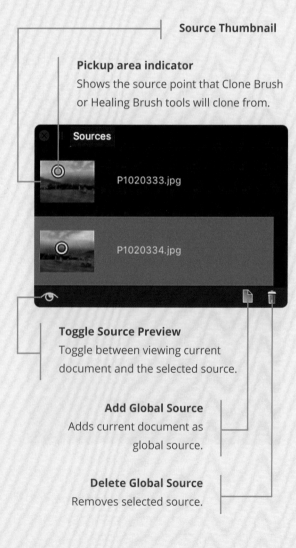

Toggle Source Preview
Toggle between viewing current document and the selected source.

Add Global Source
Adds current document as global source.

Delete Global Source
Removes selected source.

Mesh Panel (Liquify Persona)

In Liquify Persona, the **Mesh Panel** defines and manages the mesh grid overlaid over the image. Manipulation of the grid, using Liquify tools, warps the image.

Divisions
Sets the size of the squares displayed in the mesh.

Colour
Click the swatch to define the colour of the displayed mesh.

Reconstruct Mesh
Sets the strength of the overall warp effect across the entire grid. 0% will remove any currently applied effect from the image.

Load Mesh
Applies a previously saved mesh.

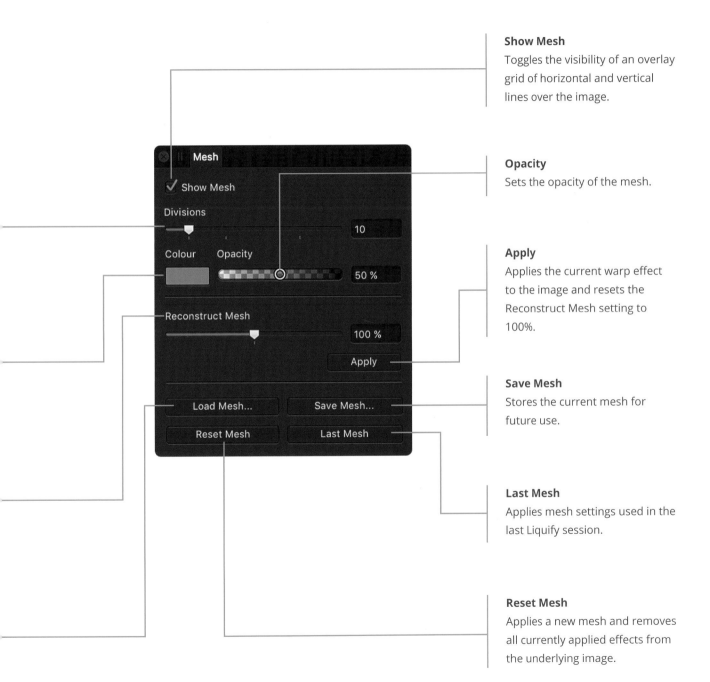

Show Mesh

Toggles the visibility of an overlay grid of horizontal and vertical lines over the image.

Opacity

Sets the opacity of the mesh.

Apply

Applies the current warp effect to the image and resets the Reconstruct Mesh setting to 100%.

Save Mesh

Stores the current mesh for future use.

Last Mesh

Applies mesh settings used in the last Liquify session.

Reset Mesh

Applies a new mesh and removes all currently applied effects from the underlying image.

Brush Panel (Liquify Persona)

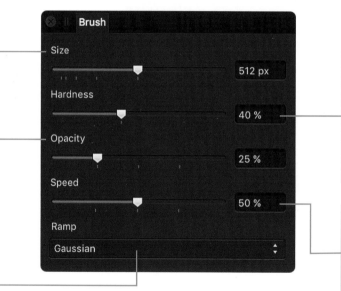

The **Brush Panel** controls the brush settings for the Liquify tools.

Size
Sets the thickness of a brush stroke.

Opacity
Sets the strength of the effect applied with each stroke.

Ramp
Sets the shape at the edge of the brush (and therefore the shape of the mesh after a stroke has been applied).

Hardness
Sets the hardness of the brush edge. Lower percentages giving a softer (more feathered) appearance.

Speed
Sets the speed at which the effect under the brush is applied.

Mask Panel (Liquify Persona)

 The Liquify Freeze Tool applies a mask to the image to protect it from any warping effect, while the Liquify Thaw Tool removes parts of the mask.

Once a mask has been applied, the **Mask Panel** allows you to control and modify it.

Clear Mask
Removes the current mask from the image.

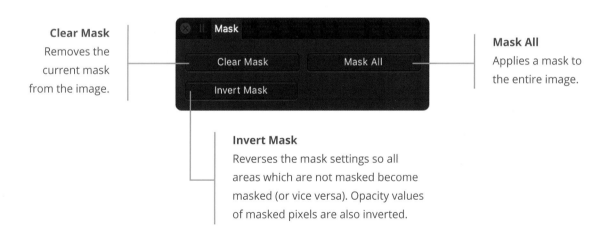

Mask All
Applies a mask to the entire image.

Invert Mask
Reverses the mask settings so all areas which are not masked become masked (or vice versa). Opacity values of masked pixels are also inverted.

Basic Panel (Develop Persona)

As a commonly used panel in Develop Persona, the panel provides standard adjustments which can be applied to your raw image.

Exposure
Adjusts exposure, changes black point and brightness.

Enhance
Adjusts contrast, clarity, saturation and vibrance.

White Balance
Removes undesirable colour casts by adjusting the 'temperature' of the image. The default value is taken from camera settings.

Shadows & Highlights
Applies tonal adjustment to the darkest and/or lightest areas.

Profiles
Sets Output ICC Profile for colour management.

Preset
Adds current
adjustment settings
as a preset or deletes
current preset.
Default will revert
settings to default.

Reset
Sets the adjustment
back to default.

Toggle Adjustment
Uncheck to switch off
the adjustment; check
to switch on again.

Lens Panel (Develop Persona)

The **Lens Panel** provides adjustments which can be used to correct lens distortions and fix lens-related anomalies.

Like the Basic Panel (p. 64), this panel includes preset options as well as a toggle and reset setting for each adjustment.

Lens Correction
Fixes various types of lens distortion by straightening and aligning lines in an image.

Chromatic Aberration Reduction
Fixes chromatic aberration by realigning blue, green, and red planes.

Defringe
Corrects purple fringing (bichrominance) at the edges of high contrast areas.

Remove Lens Vignette
Corrects unwanted vignetting by adjusting the brightness at the edges of an image.

Post Crop Vignette
Removes unwanted lens vignetting after a crop has been applied to an image.

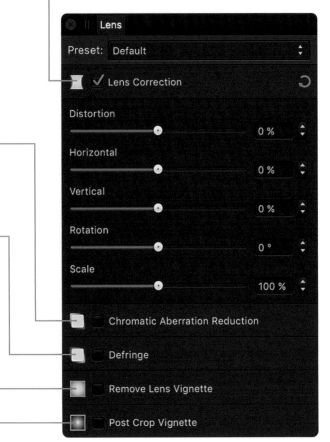

Details Panel (Develop Persona)

The **Details Panel** provides adjustments to refine the edges of images and remove (or add) noise.

This panel also includes preset options as well as a toggle and reset setting for each adjustment.

Detail Refinement
Sharpens edges to add clarity.

Noise Reduction
Reduce and remove random luminance and/or colour noise.

Noise Addition
Adds random pixels to an image to introduce and enhance noise.

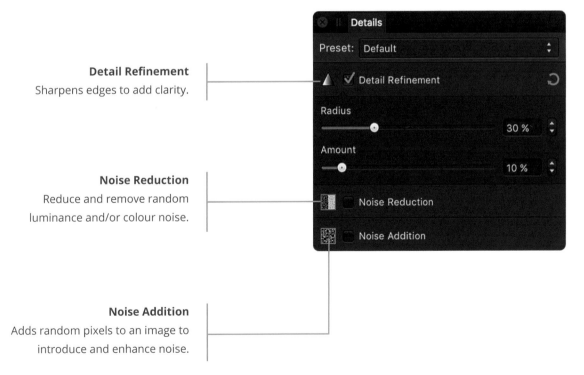

Tones Panel (Develop Persona)

The **Tones Panel** provides adjustments for correcting the tonal values of an image and split toning.

This panel also includes preset options as well as a toggle and reset setting for each adjustment.

Curves
Uses graph manipulation to precisely adjust lightness and contrast.

Black & White
Converts colour to greyscale selectively.

Split Toning
Tints and recolours highlights and shadows.

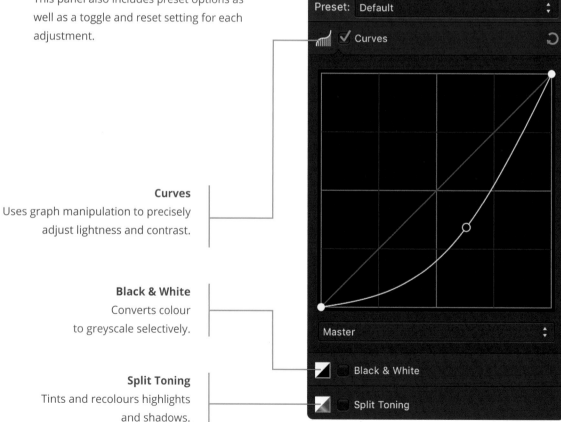

Overlays Panel (Develop Persona)

When used in combination with the Overlay tools on the Tools Panel, the **Overlays Panel** allows you to apply Basic adjustments (p. 64) to painted areas of a raw image.

Opacity
Adjusts the opacity of the selected overlay.

Overlays
Lists the Master overlay along with any added Brush or Gradient overlays.

Add Gradient Overlay
Adds a new overlay which can be modified using the Overlay Gradient Tool.

Add Brush Overlay
Adds a new overlay which can be modified using the Overlay Paint and Overlay Erase tools.

Delete Overlay
Removes the currently selected overlay.

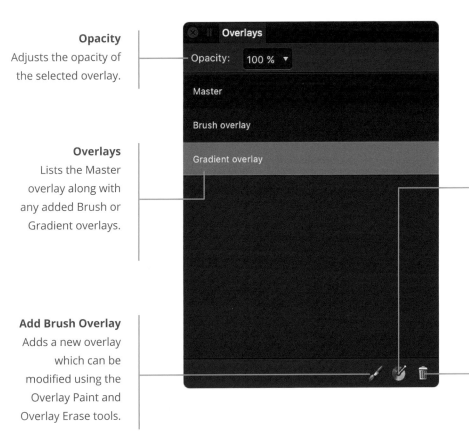

Presets Panel (Tone Mapping Persona)

The **Presets Panel** makes tone mapping a little easier. Use presets to get the look you like and, if needed, use the panel described on the opposite page to fine-tune that final look—especially the **Tone Compression** and **Local Contrast** settings.

Panel Preferences
Create presets from current settings. Categorize and import/export presets.

Category Name

Preset
Click a preset to apply to your image.

Tone Map Panel (Tone Mapping Persona)

The **Tone Map Panel** lets you apply a tone map to your image using a range of tonal settings; both natural or more dramatic results can be achieved.

Tone Compression
Controls how much of the unbounded tonal range to map. Increasing the slider results in more tone compression.

Local Contrast
Adds or removes local contrast. Increasing local contrast helps to boost clarity in the image.

Other settings
The rest of the panel offers the same options as those on the Basic, Details and Tones Panels in Develop Persona. See from p. 64 for details.

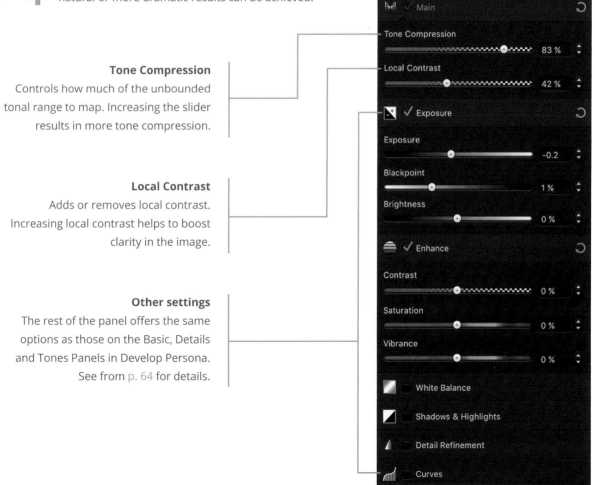

Export Options Panel (Export Persona)

Usually, **File > Export** is adequate for most use cases, where only a whole document export is required. However, Export Persona offers an advanced workspace for selectively and simultaneously exporting your document, layers, and drawn slices to different file formats and sizes.

In the Export Persona, the **Export Options Panel** is used to define default file format settings and those of selected slices. These settings are unique to each file format.

Common export options:

- **Pixel format**—sets the colour mode for the exported image.

- **Resampler**—select which resampling method is used when exporting a file at a different size to the design's original size.

- **Matte**—sets the background colour for the exported image.

- **Quality**—sets the resulting quality of the exported JPEG. Higher quality may result in larger file sizes.

- **ICC Profile**—by default, this is set to the ICC profile of the document. However, the document's ICC profile can be overwritten for the exported file.

- **Embed metadata**—uncheck to strip metadata from the exported image.

Selected PDF export options:

- **Include printer marks**—when selected, the PDF output will show printer marks around the page edge. All printer marks are added by default.

Mode

Define the export options for the currently selected slice or as a default for newly created slices.

Panel Preferences

Create, rename and delete export presets.

Preset

Sets all the options in the panel based on the selected preset.

File format

Choose a file format for the exported file. The panel will then display all the options available for that file format.

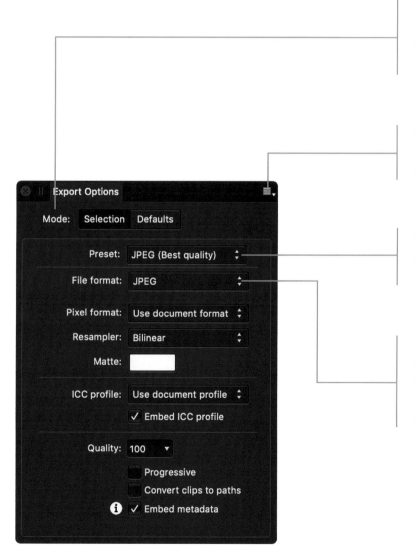

Layers Panel (Export Persona)

 The panel is a version of the Layers Panel in Photo Persona but can additionally define slices from selected layers and control visibility of layers whilst in Export Persona. It works in combination with the Slices Panel.

Export Status
A full, white icon indicates an item will be exported. If no icon appears, the item will not be exported.

Export Visibility

When enabled, the item shows on the page. When disabled, the item will be hidden in Export Persona only.

Visibility

When enabled, the item shows on the page. When disabled, the item will be hidden in both Export and Photo Persona.

Create Slice

Creates a slice from the currently selected layers and groups.

Slices Panel (Export Persona)

The **Slices Panel** gives you precise control over each export area (slice) in your document, defining where it will be exported and to what file format, or multiple formats, and what size(s). The Slices Panel works in combination with the Export Options Panel.

Batch builder
Applies a preset export setup to the selected slice(s), including **Builder** option.

Export preset
Applies a preset export setup to the selected slice(s).

Item
Indicates whether the slice is based on the document, a drawn slice or a layer as well as showing the slice export name and whether there are export issues to resolve.

Export Setup
Specifies the **Path** and **Builder** assigned to the formats to be exported. Allows you to add multiple file formats, each with multiple sizes. Use the plus icon to add a new format or size. Use the cross icon to delete the selected format or size.

Delete Selected Slice

Continuous
Slices are re-exported automatically to the previously 'exported to' folder, if the content within the slice changes.

Panel Preferences
Copies and replaces export setups and formats as well as adding additional formats from copied settings. Create, rename and delete export presets.

From Clipboard Options
Copy the current export format settings, replace the current export format settings, or add the copied export format settings as a new format for a selected slice, respectively.

Select
Uncheck to remove item from **Export Slices (n)** selection; check to add it again.

Export Slice
Exports slice to a specified folder using set format options.

Export Format
Exports specific format for its parent slice.

Export Slices (n)
Exports all currently selected slices to a specified folder. The number of slices selected is shown in parenthesis.

CUSTOMISING YOUR WORKSPACE

Not everyone likes to work in the same way so with this in mind there are options in Affinity Photo that allow you to customise your workspace to your liking.

User Interface Preferences

Tweak the UI to your taste by updating your **Preferences**. Access via **Affinity Photo > Preferences** (Mac) or **Edit > Preferences** (Win) and choose **User Interface** to get the following customisable options:

- **Background Grey Level**—controls the greyscale level of the Document View background.

- **UI Gamma**—adjusts the contrast of the user interface.

- **Font UI Size** (macOS only)—optionally increase the font size of UI text.

- **UI Style**—swaps between a dark or light user interface.

- **Tooltip Delay**—set the length of time before a tooltip appears when hovering over a UI element.

- **Decimal Places for Unit Types**—controls the number of decimal places displayed for each document measurement unit.

- **Automatically lock background layer on import**—locks (or keeps unlocked) an imported image as a background layer.

- **Show Lines in points**—choose whether line width (thickness) displays in points or in the document's measurement units.

- **Show Text in points**—choose whether text is expressed in points or in the document's measurement units.

- **Show brush previews**—choose whether the brush cursor displays a preview of pixels to be placed.

- **Always show brush crosshair**—overlays a crosshair over the brush cursor for better targeting.

- **Monochromatic Iconography**—makes icons display in greyscale.

- **Show Selection in Layers Panel**—reveals selected layer in panel when layer is selected in the document.

- **Auto-commit filters**—choose whether to automatically commit filters while undertaking a new operation with the Apply dialog still open or whether a prompt to Apply or Discard is needed.

- **Auto-scroll to show Selection in Layers Panel**—As you select an object, the panel scrolls to show its layer entry.

- **Enable Touch bar support** – Allows you to utilise the Touch bar on Apple MacBook Pro computers.

Workspace Modes (Mac only)

In the Mac version of Affinity, you can choose from two different workspace modes: **Normal** and **Separated** mode. You can change to either workspace mode from the **Window Menu**.

By default, Affinity Photo will run in **Normal** (single window) mode. This means that all panels and view will be neatly docked together. **Separated mode** has no containing frame, the panels (or panel groups) and toolbars are floating, and each open document has its own view (although you can still create groups).

> When in full screen view, you cannot switch between workspace modes.

Customising your Studio panels

The way your **Studio panels** are set out will depend on what **Persona** you are working in. However, for each Persona you can still customise your workspace to fit your workflow.

If you wish to customise each Persona workspace, you can do so in the following ways:

To hide/show a panel:
- From the **View Menu**, click the panel name on the **Studio** flyout. To show, click the panel name again.

To hide/show all panels:
- From the **View Menu**, click **Toggle UI** (Tab).

To hide/show left/right panel groups (Mac only):
- From the **View > Studio**, click **Show Left Studio** or **Show Right Studio**.

To collapse a panel/panel group:
- Double-click on the active panel label.

To expand a panel/panel group:
- Click on the label of the panel that you want to view.

To move a panel:
- Drag the panel label to its new position, as a free floating panel or as item in an existing panel group.

To resize a panel:
- Drag any corner of a panel.

To dock a panel:
- Drag the panel label to a panel group.
- Drag the panel label to an area of the studio. A highlight indicates where the panel can be docked.

To move a panel group:
- Drag the panel group to a new position, either as a free floating panel or as an item in an existing panel group.

To dock a panel group:
- Drag the panel group to another panel group.
- Drag the panel group to an area of the studio. A highlight indicates where the panel group can be docked.

To reset the Persona's workspace:
- Select the Persona that you want to reset the workspace for and from the **View Menu**, select **Studio > Reset Studio**.

Customising the Tools Panel

The **Tools Panel** can be docked or floating, or shown or hidden, depending on your preference. You can customise the panel to fit your individual way of working by removing tools and adding tools.

To dock/undock the Tools Panel:
- From the **View Menu**, select **Dock Tools**.

To show/hide the Tools Panel:
- From the **View Menu**, select **Show Tools**.

To remove or add a tool:
1. From the **View Menu**, select **Customise Tools**.
2. Drag a tool icon from the **Tools Panel** into the flyout, or vice versa.
3. Click **Close**.

To reset the Tools Panel:
- From the **View Menu**, select **Customise Tools**, then from the flyout, click **Reset**.

Customising the Toolbar

The Toolbar organises some of the most commonly used commands and functions in each Persona to keep them at your fingertips. You can customise your Toolbar in the following ways:

To show/hide tool group labels on the Toolbar:
1. Choose **View > Customise Toolbar**.
2. From the dialog's **Show** pop-up menu, select **Icon Only** or **Icon and Text**.

To hide/show the Toolbar:
- Choose **View > Show Toolbar**.

To customise the Toolbar:
1. Choose **View > Customise Toolbar**.
2. Drag the items from the dialog to the **Toolbar**.
3. Remove items by dragging them off the **Toolbar** and onto your **Document View**.

To reset the Toolbar:
1. Choose **View > Customise Toolbar**.
2. Drag the default set item to the **Toolbar**. This will revert the Toolbar to its original settings.

Your workspace customisation will be remembered between sessions.

KEYBOARD SHORTCUTS

You can quickly access common tools and commands using your keyboard. Many of the shortcuts are the same as those that you use in other apps.

You'll find many of the shortcuts listed next to menu items.

Customising keyboard shortcuts

Learning the keyboard shortcuts in Affinity Photo will speed up your productivity, but you may want to customise shortcuts on an application-wide or on a per-Persona basis. You can also save your customised shortcuts to a file that can be shared with other users or backed up for safe keeping. Go to **Affinity Photo > Preferences** (Mac) or **Edit > Preferences** (Win) and choose **Keyboard Shortcuts** to customise your shortcuts.

> Exported keyboard shortcut files can only be used on the same platform as they were created. A keyboard shortcut file exported from Affinity Photo on a Mac cannot be imported into Affinity Photo for Windows, and vice versa. The extension for the keyboard shortcut file is *.affshortcuts* on a Mac and *.afshort* on Windows.

Available settings are as follows:

- **Persona**—The pop-up menu sets the Persona for shortcut customisation.

- **UI Element**—The pop-up menu displays the menus, commands and operations for the currently selected Persona. A **Miscellaneous** category groups shortcuts for commonly performed operations and lets you switch on/off panels via shortcuts.

- **Apply to all**—If checked, the shortcut applied to a UI element is shared across every Persona. If unchecked, you can uniquely assign a custom shortcut to work just within the currently selected Persona in the initial Persona pop-up menu.

A warning triangle shows if a shortcut has already been assigned to another command. The tooltip will inform you which command.

An arrow symbol indicates that the shortcut is shared between several tools. Hover over the symbol to see the names of the other tools.

To delete a shortcut, click the cross icon at the end of the shortcut entry.

- **Ignore Modifier**—Lets you create shortcuts using a single letter designation instead of using keyboard modifiers.

- **Reset**—All customised shortcuts are reset back to default.

- **Clear All Shortcuts**—All default and customised shortcuts are removed.

- **Load**—Loads a previously saved shortcuts file. This will overwrite your current keyboard shortcut allocations.

- **Save**—Saves the current set of shortcuts to a file for sharing or backup.

RESETTING YOUR WORKSPACE

Now you have a good understanding of the Affinity Photo user interface it's important to ensure your workspace is reset to the default 'factory-supplied' layout before commencing with the projects in this book.

It may be that you've inadvertently customised, repositioned or switched off toolbars or panels previously. By resetting, the project's written instructions will more closely match your own experience.

Reset the Toolbar

On the **View Menu**, select **Customise Toolbar**. Drag the default set of tools at the bottom of the dialog over the Toolbar spanning the top of your workspace and release.

Reset the Tools Panel

On the **View Menu**, select **Customise Tools**. Click **Reset** in the dialog.

Reset Studio Panels

On the **View Menu**, select **Studio > Reset Studio**. This will need to be done for each Persona workspace.

CHAPTER 2

Core Skills

This chapter teaches you the core skills you'll need to get the very best out of the upcoming projects in chapters 3, 4 and 5. Not all projects will use every core skill, but trying out each one in turn will give you a better grounding in Affinity Photo.

You can get all the resources you need for this chapter from **https://affin.co/photocoreskills**

BEFORE YOU GET STARTED

Resources

 You can get all the resources that are referenced in this chapter from:
https://affin.co/photocoreskills

OPENING AND SAVING IMAGES

To open your images in Affinity Photo, you can do one of the following:

- Choose **File > Open** and navigate to an image file.

- From an open window that displays your files, drag and drop an image onto an empty area of Affinity Photo's Document View.

> Once an image is opened in Affinity Photo, it occupies your Document View. The image's dimensions define the document and canvas size.

You can create a blank document using **File > New** for projects which are not based on a single image. We'll look at this later in the workbook.

To save your work, you can choose **File > Save** or **File > Save As** to overwrite the original image or save as an .afphoto project file, respectively.

DEVELOPING RAW IMAGES

Resource

exposure_adjustment.ORF
tonal_adjustments.RW2
advanced_adjustments.RW2

Raw files must be developed first before they can be viewed or edited. When raw files are opened in Affinity Photo, the interface switches to the Develop Persona (p. 17), a dedicated workspace exclusively for this task.

In the Develop Persona, you can apply adjustments and filters to your raw image in a high-precision colour format. When you commit these changes and develop the image, you move to the Photo Persona where you have access to the full set of image-editing tools.

Adjusting image exposure

You can make basic adjustments like **Exposure** to change the brightness and contrast of the image.

1 Use **File > Open** to load exposure_adjustment.ORF.

2 Drag the **Exposure** slider to the right to lighten the image; left to darken it.

3 On the context toolbar, click **Develop** to commit the changes and develop your image.

Tonally adjusting a raw image

You can also apply basic tonal adjustments to your raw images.

1 Use **File > Open** to load tonal_adjustments.RW2.

2 On the **Basic Panel**, check **Shadows & Highlights**.

3 Drag the **Highlights** slider to the left to recover some of the clipped tones.

4 Drag the **Contrast** slider in the **Enhance** section to the right to boost the image's contrast and produce a more vivid tone.

5 Click **Develop** to commit these changes and develop the image.

Making advanced raw adjustments

More advanced popular adjustments to your raw images include altering the shadows, midtones and highlights of your image using a curve graph, as well as sharpening the final image.

1. Use **File > Open** to load advanced_adjustments.RW2.

2. Select the **Tones Panel**.

3. Check **Curves** to display a graph.

4. Click on the lower quarter of the line to add a control node, then drag this node down to produce a "dip" in the graph line. This will deepen the image's tones.

5. Select the **Details Panel**.

6. Check **Detail Refinement**, and drag the **Radius** slider to *30%* and the **Amount** slider to *60%* to add a small amount of fine-detail sharpening.

7. Now click **Develop** to commit these changes and develop the image.

Resource

cropping_composition.jpg
cropping_ratio.jpg
cropping_golden_spiral.jpg

CROPPING

Cropping is commonly used to change or improve an image's composition, or to reframe the image to a particular aspect ratio for print or digital presentation. You can crop freely to any ratio and size, or choose to constrain the crop depending on your delivery requirements.

By default, Affinity Photo performs **non-destructive** cropping, meaning all the image information is retained, even if it is cropped out of the composition. This behaviour proves useful if you decide to change the composition at a later date.

The grid is called a Rule of Thirds grid. It is recognized as a powerful compositional aid amongst the photo editing community.

Cropping an image to improve composition

1 Use **File > Open** to load cropping_composition.jpg.

2 From the **Tools Panel**, select the **Crop Tool** (C).

3 Drag the bottom edge handle upwards until the subject is balanced evenly between the grid lines.

4 Drag the left edge handle to the right until the subject is underneath the intersecting grid lines.

5 From the context toolbar, click **Apply** to commit the crop.

You can uncrop your image later in your session, or in any new session, by using **Document > Unclip Canvas.**

Your compositions always look best when your subject faces into the centre of your image.

Cropping an image to a constrained aspect ratio

Cropping to a particular aspect ratio is useful for both printing and digital delivery.

For print, you can crop to popular size ratios such as 5x7, 4x6 and 8x10, ensuring maximum print coverage—especially if you are using borderless printing.

For digital delivery, you can match monitor aspect ratios like 16x9, 16x10 and 4x3, allowing images to fill the entire screen.

1 Use **File > Open** to load cropping_ratio.jpg.

2 On the **Tools Panel**, select the **Crop Tool**.

3 On the context toolbar, set the **Mode** to *Custom Ratio*.

4 On the toolbar, in the two inputs next to **Mode**, enter *16* and *9*, respectively.

5 On the context toolbar, check **Darken Border** to darken the areas of the image not included in the crop. This helps to visualise the crop.

6 To position the crop area, click once on the grid and drag until you are happy with the composition.

7 Click **Apply** to commit the crop.

Changing the crop overlay

You can experiment with different crop overlays, including **Golden Spiral** (golden ratio, divine proportions), to achieve more interesting compositions that challenge the traditional rule of thirds approach.

1 Use **File > Open** to load cropping_golden_spiral.jpg.

2 From the **Tools Panel**, select the **Crop Tool**.

3 On the context toolbar, set the **Overlay** to *Golden Spiral*.

4 Now drag the crop handles to crop into the image and reposition them until the centre of the spiral is over the female statue's face and the curve flows round to the statue on the right.

5 Click **Apply** to commit the crop.

INPAINTING

Inpainting is Affinity Photo's powerful content removal tool. By sampling image content from surrounding areas, inpainting can remove unwanted elements from images: people, vehicles, dust spots on lenses, hot or stuck pixels, lens flares and so on.

Using the Inpainting Brush

1 Use **File > Open** to load inpainting_people.jpg.

2 From the **Tools Panel**, select the **Inpainting Brush Tool** from the flyout.

3 Drag over the area you want to remove and a red overlay will appear. Continue until you have selected the entire area.

When using the Inpainting brush (and indeed, any brush tool) you can alter the brush width dynamically while painting by using the [and] keys.

4 Release the mouse button and Affinity Photo will perform inpainting. You will find the unwanted area is removed, being intelligently replaced with surrounding image content.

5 Repeat this procedure multiple times to remove all the people from the scene.

Selecting and filling with inpainting

1 Use **File > Open** to load inpainting_landscape.jpg.

2 From the **Tools Panel**, select the **Freehand Selection Tool** (L) from the flyout.

3 Draw a freehand line around the leaves in the top left of the image. Start from the very top corner and drag the cursor under them to the right, then off the page.

Once you release the mouse button, a closed selection will automatically be created. Choose **Edit > Inpaint** and the selected area will be inpainted.

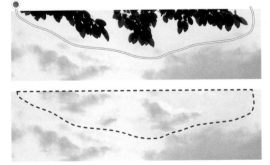

4 From the **Tools Panel**, select the **Rectangular Marquee Tool** from the same flyout as the Freehand Selection Tool and drag over the leaves to the far right.

5 Choose **Edit > Inpaint** to automatically remove leaves in the selected area.

6 Experiment with the **Freehand Selection Tool**, **Rectangular Marquee Tool** and **Elliptical Marquee Tool** to select areas of the image, then use **Edit > Inpaint** to intelligently replace the content. The image contains several small insects, dust spots and birds in the sky that you can practice on!

If you plan to use brush and selection-based inpainting in unison, remember to clear your selection using cmd ⌘ + D (Mac) or ctrl + D (Win) before returning to the Inpainting Tool. Otherwise, you won't be able to use the Tool as edits will be restricted to within the selection area only.

ADJUSTMENTS

Adjustments are the 'bread and butter' of your basic image editing. They typically perform tonal changes, such as altering brightness and contrast and manipulating colour balances. Getting a good grounding on how to use adjustments will help for any image editing scenario.

We'll look at three ways to apply an adjustment—via the Adjustment Panel, Layers Panel and Layer Menu. Brightness / Contrast, HSL and Black & White adjustments illustrate each method.

Changing brightness and contrast

1 Use **File > Open** to load adjustment_brightness_contrast.jpg.

2 On the **Adjustment Panel**, go to the **Brightness / Contrast** category and select the *Lighter* thumbnail to lighten the image.

When applied, the adjustment also displays settings for fine tuning.

3 Drag the **Brightness** slider from *25%* to *10%* to tweak the overall tone.

4 Drag the **Contrast** slider to *100%* for a more punchy look.

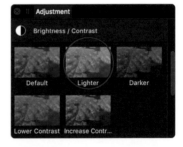

Check your Layers Panel. A non-destructive adjustment layer has been added above your image layer. This means you can modify adjustment settings (by double clicking) at a later time or remove the adjustment—all without destroying the underlying image.

Changing the colour intensity

1 Use **File > Open** to load adjustment_hsl.jpg.

2 On the **Layers Panel**, select **Adjustments** and then *HSL* from the sub-menu.

On the adjustment's settings:

3 Drag the **Hue Shift** Slider to the left or right to significantly alter the hue balance of the image.

4 Drag the **Saturation** slider right to increase colour intensity; left to decrease it.

Levels
White Balance
HSL
Recolour
Black and White
Brightness and Contrast
Posterise
Vibrance
Exposure
Shadows / Highlights
Threshold
Curves
Channel Mixer
Gradient Map
Selective Colour
Colour Balance
Invert
Soft Proof
LUT
Lens Filter
Split Toning
OCIO

HSL

Add Preset | Merge | Delete | Reset

Picker

Hue Shift — -110 °

Saturation Shift — 10 %

Luminosity Shift — 0 %

Opacity: 100 % | Blend Mode: Normal

For a before/after comparison, uncheck the HSL adjustment layer in the Layers Panel temporarily to hide the adjustment.

Making an image black and white

1 Use **File > Open** to load
   adjustment_blackandwhite.jpg.

2 From the **Layer Menu**, choose **New Adjustment Layer > Black & White Adjustment**.

3 Your image will instantly change to black and white, but you can drag each colour slider to influence how the colours are represented.

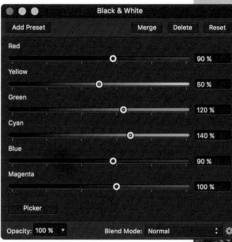

Like the other adjustments, a Black & White Adjustment layer is created in the Layers Panel.

Resource

selection_brush.jpg
flood_select.jpg
refine_selection.jpg

SELECTIONS

Selections are a powerful way of making change to only specific parts of an image. Affinity Photo provides a wide array of selection tools which create selection areas to which adjustments and filters can be applied. They can also be used to restrict brush work to certain areas.

Selection Tools

Affinity Photo has a variety of tools to create accurate selections within your images:

- **Selection Brush Tool**: Arguably the most versatile of the selection tools. It allows you to drag across areas of your image and have the selection boundary snap to edges accurately and intuitively. This makes it easy to select anything from small, detailed areas to larger, more uniform areas like skies and backgrounds.

- **Flood Select Tool**: Creates selections based on similar tones with very little user intervention. You can simply drag on an area of the image to sample it, then drag the mouse forward or back to either increase or reduce the tolerance, respectively, which influences the range of tones to be selected.

- **Marquee Selection Tools**: You can choose from rectangular, elliptical, row and column marquee tools, which quickly create straightforward shape-based selections.

- **Freehand Selection Tool**: Manually creates freehand selections, with a choice of polygonal, magnetic or completely freehand modes. Useful for fine detail selections and selecting tricky edge detail.

- **Refine Selection**: accessible from the context toolbar, this dialog provides additional matting, feathering, smoothing and ramping features to fine tune selections. It's ideal for tackling difficult details like strands of hair on a model.

Creating a selection

1 Use **File > Open** to load selection_brush.jpg.

2 From the **Tools Panel**, select the **Selection Brush Tool**.

3 Starting from the top right, drag to begin creating a selection. The **Selection Brush** is velocity based; moving the cursor more rapidly will increase the snapping tolerance. Move the cursor quickly to the left to select the entire sky.

You can remove areas of the created selection: either by changing the Mode on the context toolbar to Subtract, or pressing the option ⌥ key (Mac) or alt key (Win) whilst dragging.

4 From the **Toolbar**, choose **Invert Selection**. This will now select the building instead of the sky.

5 From the **Toolbar**, choose **Auto Contrast (**or **Filters > Colours > Auto Contrast**). The contrast of the building will be increased; this helps bring out its tone against the flat sky.

6 From the **Filters Menu**, choose **Sharpen > Clarity**.
Use a **Strength** of *50%* then click **Apply**.

7 From the **Toolbar**, choose **Deselect** to remove the
selection and its marquee.

Applying the **Clarity** filter to just the
selection of the building will avoid the
"halo" effect that typically occurs when
using this filter with high contrast edges.

Creating a flood selection

1 Use **File > Open** to load flood_select.jpg.

2 From the **Tools Panel**, select the **Flood Select Tool**.

3 Drag on the clouds to begin creating a flood selection.

4 Move the cursor to the right to increase the selection tolerance until the entire sky is selected.

5 From the **Layer Menu**, choose **New Adjustment Layer > Levels Adjustment**.

Notice the thumbnail for the **Levels Adjustment** in the **Layers Panel** above the Background layer. This adjustment has been 'masked' to the sky region.

(Levels Adjustment) ☑

6 Adjust the **Black Level** to the right (to around *30%*) and adjust the **White Level** slightly to the left (about *90%*) to bring out more detail in the sky.

Another great way to make a selection is to use the **Pen Tool** (**Tools Panel**) to create a closed path consisting of multiple nodes; you can then convert the path into a selection from the context toolbar. This method also allows you to tweak individual nodes using the **Node Tool** for greater accuracy.

Refining a selection

1   Use **File > Open** to load
    refine_selection.jpg.

2   From the **Tools Panel**, select
    the **Selection Brush Tool.**

3   Drag over the background area
    around the model's head to
    select it. Keep moving the brush
    around the background to
    quickly create a selection that
    snaps to the edges of the hair.
    This will create a rough
    selection area.

4   From the **Toolbar** or **Select
    Menu**, choose **Invert Pixel
    Selection**. This will create a
    selection of the model rather
    than the background.

For even better results, you can
intelligently separate hair strands
from the background by refining
the selection.

5 From the context toolbar, choose **Refine**.

6 In the **Refine Selection** dialog, change the **Brush Width** to *300 px* for a larger brush that will cover a wider area.

7 Drag over the areas of the hair then release the mouse button. You will see more areas of the background being added to the selection in-between strands of hair.

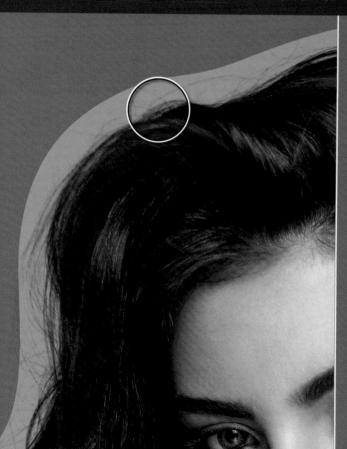

8 Repeat this procedure moving around the image until the overall selection is more detailed.

9 On the **Refine Selection** dialog, change **Preview** to *Transparent*. The background will then become transparent, revealing an alpha matte.

You can use different preview modes available on the Preview pop-up menu to fine-tune your selection. Try Black and White to clearly see the difference between selected and rejected areas.

10 Change the **Output** to *New layer with mask*, then click **Apply**. A new layer with a mask will be created, and the original layer will automatically be hidden.

Output options can help with your preferred workflow. If you intend to work non-destructively, choosing Mask or New layer with mask are good choices as they create non-destructive layer masks.

> Using mask layers is a powerful non-destructive approach to image editing. In combination with selections, they allow you to 'cut out' subjects from their backgrounds without discarding the background information. You can also go back and alter or refine the selection at a later date to improve it.

Resource

masking_addlayermask.afphoto
masking_adjustment.jpg
masking_live_filter.jpg

MASKING

The concept of masking is important to grasp as it lends enormous power to your editing skills, both in regards to compositing and selective editing of your images.

Masks are applied to layers, and they determine which parts of that layer should be shown or hidden. A simple example would be an exposure adjustment limited to just a particular subject rather than the entire image.

Adding a mask layer

1 Use **File > Open** to load masking_addlayermask.afphoto.

You will see an active selection on a stone with a separate background. This is a composite layer from a different image which shows above the main image layer in the **Layers Panel**.

2 As the selection is pre-made, click the panel's **Mask Layer** button to add a mask layer. You'll see the background disappear as it has now been hidden by the mask.

A feature unique to Affinity Photo is that Adjustment and Live Filter layers already have their own masks. This means you can manipulate the mask by simply selecting the adjustment or filter layer rather than having to add mask layers to them.

3 Now that the mask has been added you can see it by expanding the Castlerigg_Stone layer.

4 Finally, click **Deselect** on the top **Toolbar** to remove the marquee and see the final composited result.

Manipulating an adjustment layer mask

1 Use **File > Open** to load masking_adjustment.jpg.

2 From the **Layer Menu**, choose **New Adjustment Layer > HSL Adjustment**.

3 Drag the **Saturation Shift** slider to the right to *50%* to increase the intensity of the image's colours. Also, drag the **Hue Shift** slider a small amount to *7°* to shift the colour hues.

4 Close the dialog. From the **Layer Menu**, choose **Invert**. This will invert the adjustment layer's mask and remove the effect entirely from the image.

5 We're now going to paint the effect back in over certain areas. From the **Tools Panel**, select the **Paint Brush Tool** (B).

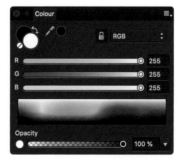

6 On the context toolbar, adjust your brush settings to achieve a moderately large **Width** (*600 px*) and reduce the **Hardness** to *0%*.

7 On the **Colour Panel**, ensure your active colour swatch is set to a pure white. This will ensure the mask layer painting will be at 100% strength.

8 On the left side of the image, paint over the car, traffic lights, bus and reflections in the wet area of the road. This will reinstate the HSL adjustment in these areas and make the colours more intense.

Manipulating a live filter layer mask

The same technique can be applied to live filter layers, used for more creative work: a good example is using a **Diffuse Glow** filter to add a soft 'bloom' effect selectively to an area of an image.

1 Use **File > Open** to load masking_live_filter.jpg.

2 From the **Layer Menu**, choose **New Live Filter Layer > Diffuse Glow Filter**.

3 Drag the **Radius** slider to *100 px*, the **Intensity** slider to *5%*, **Threshold** slider to *15%* and the **Opacity** slider to *100%* to create a warm diffusion effect on the lighter areas of the image.

4 From the **Layers Panel**, expand the **Pixel** layer and select the **Diffuse Glow** layer's thumbnail (highlighting it in blue).

5 From the **Layer Menu**, choose **Invert** to invert the layer's mask and remove the effect on the image.

Width: 600 px ▾　Opacity: 100 % ▾　Flow: 100 % ▾　Hardness: 0 % ▾　More ⊙　Stabiliser ⅄ ⟳　Length: 35 ▾　Symmetry 1 ▾　Mirror　Blend Mode: Normal ▴

6　From the **Tools Panel**, select the **Paint Brush Tool** from the flyout and choose a **Width** of *600 px* and a **Hardness** of *0%*.

7　On the **Colour Panel**, ensure your active colour swatch is set to a pure white. This will ensure the mask layer painting will be at *100%* strength.

8　Now paint over the building, road and traffic lights to reinstate the **Diffuse Glow** effect on these areas.

LAYERS

Layers are incredibly important to a typical image editing workflow—they facilitate advanced editing and, more than any other feature, are the key to unlocking much of Affinity Photo's potential as a non-destructive editor.

Layers adopt a hierarchal stack structure from bottom to top. Layers on top affect layers underneath them. In a typical workflow, you might have an image layer which then has adjustment layers above it. As these adjustment layers are placed above the image layer, they will affect it. Additionally, adjustment layers can influence one another, so experimenting with the order in which they are placed can achieve different results.

Why Use Layers?

Here's a scenario where you might want a non-destructive workflow.

In the image opposite, the sky has been replaced and the poppies in the foreground have been cloned to increase their density. On top of these changes, several adjustment layers have been added to tweak the image tonally. Compare this to the 'before' image to the left.

Images are non-project and for illustration only

Cloned Poppies (Pixel) is a new layer created for the cloned poppies. You can clone content from the lower Background layer onto a new pixel layer—this means you can erase on or modify the 'clone' layer without affecting the base image.

Sky Replacement (Pixel) with several child layers is the replacement sky. It has been copied and pasted into the document and masked to blend seamlessly into the image. It has also had several adjustment layers applied to make it match the image tonally.

The adjustment layers above these (HSL Shift, White Balance, Colour Balance and Curves) are used to give the image its saturated, warm look and final brightness and contrast balance. The HSL Shift adjustment is masked to just the foreground to bring out the vividness of the poppies and grass.

Background (Pixel) is the base image. This remains untouched.

Images are non-project and for illustration only

Layer Types

Let's look at the different layer types possible in a document:

- **Pixel layers**: these are raster layers, and you begin with a pixel layer whenever you open an image or develop one from a raw file. You would also create a pixel layer for raster brush work.

- **Adjustment layers**: these layers provide a wide variety of tonal adjustments and are one of the most common components of a non-destructive workflow—you can re-edit an adjustment layer's settings at any time and control its effect using opacity and blend modes.

- **Live Filter layers**: these layers are similar in principle to adjustment layers. Instead of tonal adjustments however, they achieve blurring, sharpening, distortion and other filter effects non-destructively. Again, as with adjustment layers, you have full control over blending, opacity and masking.

- **Embedded documents**: you can place and embed Affinity documents within other Affinity documents and retain full non-destructive editability. To distinguish them from other layers, they are referred to as embedded documents.

- **Image layers**: you'll see these less frequently. Image layers are regular images that are placed into the document. They can be scaled and transformed non-destructively.

- **Groups**: layers can be grouped together for organisational purposes. When grouped, they are contained in a directory structure that can be expanded and collapsed. Groups can also be used as workflow aids, as they can be masked or have adjustment and filter layers applied to them—thus influencing all layers within the group.

Selecting and moving layers

Tools, filters and other operations are performed on the **currently selected** layer only. A classic example is applying a filter from the **Filters Menu**.

A filter would typically be applied to a pixel layer (usually the base "Background" layer). Attempting to apply it to another type of layer would result in no effect.

> Ensuring you always have the correct layer selected is a fundamental aspect of good photo editing.

Selecting a layer to perform operations

1 Use **File > Open** to load layers_selecting_moving.afphoto.

2 There are currently no layers selected. Click on Background (Pixel) to highlight and select it.

3 On the **Filters Menu**, choose **Noise > Add Noise**.

4 Check **Monochromatic** and drag the **Intensity** slider to *10%*. This adds fine granularity to the image. Click **Apply**.

The effect is then applied to the selected Background (Pixel) layer.

Selecting and moving a layer

1 On the **Layers Panel**, click on the Logo (Image) layer to select it.

2 From the **Tools Panel**, select the **Move Tool** (V).

At the bottom right of your image:

- Drag on the logo to move it around.

- Drag on one of the logo's corner nodes (shown when logo is selected) to scale it.

Manipulating an adjustment or live filter layer

1 From the **Layers Panel**, double-click the (Vignette) layer's thumbnail to display filter settings.

2 Adjust the **Scale** slider to influence the size of the vignette around the image's edges.

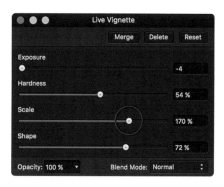

Changing layer ordering

1 From the **Layers Panel**, drag the icon for the (Black & White Adjustment) layer and drag it above the Colour Tone layer. Ensure the blue target highlight spans the entire panel horizontally.

2 Because it is now above the Colour Tone layer, the **Black & White Adjustment** will now affect the tone. This is a prime example of why layer ordering is so important: the adjustment has now entirely overridden the colour toning effect present in the image.

3 Drag the (Black & White Adjustment) layer back underneath the Colour Tone layer to restore the colour toning to the image.

FURTHER MANIPULATING LAYERS

Layer manipulation goes further—layers can be named, locked, hidden, shown and nested (known as 'child layering').

Renaming layers

1 Use **File > Open** to load layers_naming_locking.afphoto.

2 From the **Layers Panel**, select the lower of two layers named (Pixel).

3 Click once on the layer's name and a white input field will appear. Type *Eye colour* and press return.

4 Now select the other (Pixel) layer, and rename this layer *Tone boost*.

Locking/unlocking layers

1 With the newly named Tone boost layer selected, click **Lock/Unlock**.

2 Select the **Move Tool** from the **Tools Panel** and try to drag the layer around. Notice how it cannot be manipulated in any way.

3 To unlock the layer, click the lock icon on the layer entry and try moving it again.

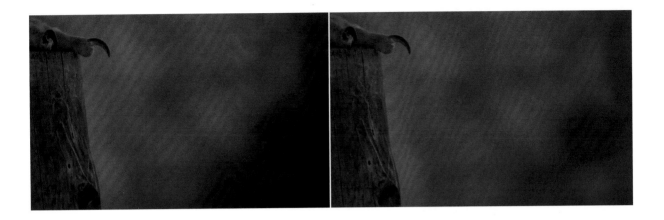

Nesting layers / convert to "child layers"

1 Drag the top (Vignette) filter layer over the Background layer's thumbnail until a vertical blue bar is visible just at the right of the thumbnail.

2 Release the mouse button to nest the Vignette filter into the pixel layer.

3 The Vignette filter will now only affect this pixel layer rather than the layers above the pixel layer. Note how the vignette's appearance changes.

4 Drag the Vignette filter back out into the main layer stack and to the top again, above the (Curves Adjustment) layer.

Showing and hiding layers

1 Click the check box to the right of the (HSL Shift Adjustment) layer to hide its effect. Notice a dramatic tonal difference in the image.

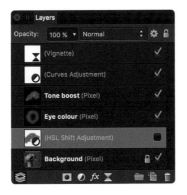

2 Click the layer's check box again to show the effect.

This behaviour applies to any layer—hiding a layer will completely disable any effect it has on the layers underneath it.

Grouping layers

1 Select the Eye colour layer.

2 Press the shift key (⇧) and click the Tone boost layer. Both layers should now be selected.

3 Click **Group Layers**.

4 Single-click this new layer group and rename it to be *Brush work*.

Resource
filter_sharpening.jpg
filter_clarity.jpg
filter_live_unsharp_mask.jpg

SHARPENING

Sharpening is a useful step to include in your workflow as it allows you to boost detail in an image and make it 'pop' visually. There are two distinct types of sharpening: **Global Contrast**, which enhances fine detail, and **Local Contrast**, which gives the appearance of being sharper by enhancing contrast between tones in the image. Sharpening is generally recommended as a final step before exporting or printing your image.

Sharpening fine detail (global contrast)

Sharpening fine detail is useful for enhancing the overall clarity of an image and helps to bring it to life. The amount of sharpening you apply is dependent on personal choice, also taking into consideration the intended delivery.

Imagery intended for web delivery generally needs less sharpening than print, for example. With printed work, small amounts of sharpening may become almost unnoticeable, so don't be afraid to use larger amounts.

1 Use **File > Open** to load filter_sharpening.jpg.

2 From the **Filters Menu**, choose **Sharpen > Unsharp Mask**.

3 To sharpen fine detail, set a small value for the **Radius** slider and boost the **Factor** slider.

4 Click **Apply** to commit the filter.

Adding local contrast enhancement

Increasing local contrast in an image adds to its perceived clarity, and is also a great way of separating tones in busy images.

1 Use **File > Open** to load filter_clarity.jpg.

2 From the **Filters Menu**, choose **Sharpen > Clarity**.

3 Drag the **Strength** slider to the right to increase contrast between tones in the image.

4 Click **Apply** to commit the **Clarity** filter.

Thickening edge detail

1 Use **File > Open** to load
filter_live_unsharp_mask.jpg.

2 From the **Layer Menu**, choose **New Live Filter
Layer > Unsharp Mask Filter**.

3 Drag the **Radius** slider to the extreme right to
100 px.

4 From the **Blend Mode** pop-up menu, choose
Darken.

5 Adjust the **Opacity** option to control the
strength of the effect.

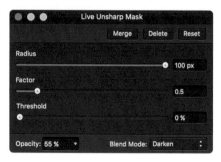

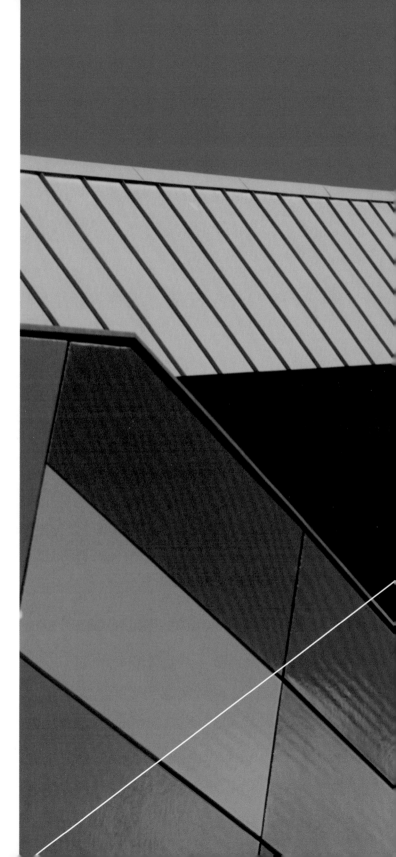

AUTOMATIC ADJUSTMENTS

Resource

adjustment_auto.jpg

There may be occasion where you just want to quickly fix the brightness and contrast, colour distribution or white balance in your images without the manual work of adjustment layers.

For this purpose, Affinity Photo features a small set of "Auto" adjustments.

Using automatic tonal adjustments

1 Use **File > Open** to load adjustment_auto.jpg.

2 From the top **Toolbar**, click either:

- **Auto Levels**. Image tones are spread out over the tonal range.

  or

- **Auto Contrast**. Applies an automatic contrast adjustment based on the current image's contrast.

Using automatic colour adjustments

From the same toolbar, click either:

- **Auto Colours**. Automatically adjusts the intensity of the image's colours for a more even result.

  or

- **Auto White Balance**. Samples white tones in the image and rebalance the colours for a more neutral appearance.

Experiment with your own imagery. Try applying the auto filters in different orders to find the best result.

CHAPTER 3

Enthusiast Projects

In this chapter we'll be covering a range of projects with a focus on photography and photo editing for the amateur photographer or hobbyist alike.

With the help of Serif's in-house photo enthusiast, James Ritson, you'll learn techniques that overcome variable shoot conditions or extend what can be achieved in the field. To complete the chapter, we have a guest contribution from Steven Randolph that looks at focus merging.

1

Peak Country 1: Mam Tor

Lending landscape images some tonal punch by *James Ritson*

An avid landscape and nature photographer, James loves venturing off on days out to capture all kinds of subjects. This project will look at bringing out the tones in a typical landscape image which was shot at Mam Tor in the heart of the Peak District, Derbyshire, England.

Follow James as he aims to maintain a relatively straightforward workflow that incorporates a few popular techniques: adjustment layers, filtering, selections and masking.

BEFORE YOU
GET STARTED

Resources

 You can get all the resources that are referenced in this project from:
https://affin.co/mamtor

Knowledge of Affinity Photo

To get the most from undertaking this project, you will need to:

- Be familiar with the interface of Affinity Photo. You can learn more about the interface in the Interface Tour chapter, starting on p. 13.

- Follow along with example resources by navigating and viewing snapshots that are saved in your project file. Named snapshots are suggested at stages throughout the project. See p. 9.

- Have good core skills. See the skills table below to see which additional aspects of Affinity Photo you need to be confident with to complete this project:

Adjustments	p. 100
Selections	p. 106
Layers	p. 122

SHOOT DETAILS

Having walked up to the top of Mam Tor (not the most demanding trail, I hasten to add), my original plan of capturing a sweeping 360 panorama was dulled somewhat—the top comprises mostly flat ground and spans quite a distance, and would have made for a boring panorama.

Instead, I focused on capturing the views looking out from the edges of Mam Tor to the neighbouring valleys. My general composition plan was to include plenty of foreground detail, and to find unique shapes in the formation of the landscape to use as leading lines.

FILENAMES

mam_tor.tiff

GEAR

TRIPOD:	No
CAMERA:	Panasonic GH4
LENS:	Tokina RMC 17mm f/3.5
LIGHTING:	Natural daylight

SETTINGS

SHOOTING MODE:	Manual
EXPOSURE:	1/1300
APERTURE:	f/5.6
ISO:	200
EXP. BIAS	0
EXP. PROG:	None
METERING:	Pattern
FORMATS:	TIFF

LOCATION

Mam Tor, Peak District, Derbyshire, England

https://affin.co/locmamtor

CONDITIONS

Sunny but cloudy

Resource
mam_tor.afphoto (*Initial image* snapshot)
mam_tor.tiff

POST SHOOT EDITING

For this particular landscape shoot, my plan was to make use of Affinity Photo's layers and non-destructive editing capabilities. Working in this way allows me to open the document at a later date and easily tweak the image. For example, if the delivery requirements change and I need to tailor it for print, I can alter the tones and colours, soft proof the final result, and add additional sharpening if required, all without compromising my original edits to the image.

Affinity Photo was used to dramatically alter the tones and colours in the image and add finishing touches like fine detail sharpening. My intended delivery was for web sharing, so the exporting process will be brief and straightforward.

OPENING YOUR IMAGE

Let's open our image to get started.

- Select **File** > **Open**, then navigate to and select mam_tor.tiff.

Once the image is open, it occupies a locked Background layer.

INITIAL TONE SHAPING

Resource

mam_tor.afphoto (*01. Initial Tone Shaping* snapshot)

The first step is to add a couple of adjustments to begin some initial tonal manipulation.

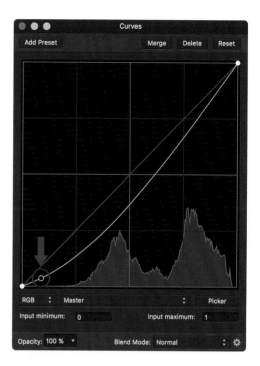

1   On the **Layer Menu**, choose **New Adjustment Layer** > **Curves Adjustment**.

2   From the initial linear graph, drag downwards within the bottom quarter of the graph to create a node. This will darken the shadow tones.

3   To maintain the midtones and highlights, click on the white curve where it meets the Y-axis to create a node, and drag the node upwards to the middle of the graph.

4   Close the Curves adjustment settings.

5   Click on the Background (Pixel) layer to select it.

6   From the **Select Menu**, choose **Tonal Range** > **Select Midtones**.

> I prefer to use Curves because of its flexibility, but if your goal is to simply alter overall brightness and contrast, a Brightness / Contrast adjustment will more than suffice.

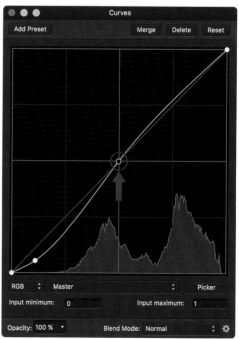

7 With the selection active, from the **Layer Menu**, choose **New Adjustment Layer** > **HSL Adjustment**. The HSL Adjustment has now been 'masked' to just the selected area of the image.

8 From the **Select Menu**, choose **Deselect**. This will remove the marquee and make it easier to see the image.

9 In HSL settings, increase **Saturation Shift** to *20%* and change **Hue Shift** to *6°* to 'redden' the tones. You can see the effect in the fields in the lower right of the image.

BLEND MODE CREATIVITY

Resource

mam_tor.afphoto (*02. Blend Mode Creativity* snapshot)

Now we're going to explore a little trick I like to use to control the separate colour tones whilst achieving a more dramatic look.

1 Click to select the Curves Adjustment layer. This ensures any new layers you add will be at the top of the layer stack.

2 From the **Layer Menu**, choose **New Adjustment Layer** > **Black & White Adjustment**.

3 Change the **Blend Mode** option to *Overlay* and adjust the **Opacity** to *60%*.

4 Drag the **Red** slider all the way to the left (*-200%*). This brings out the earthier tones, especially in the foreground.

5 Drag the **Yellow** slider to the left (*0%*). This takes the edge off the intensity of the foreground and provides a more balanced look.

6 Reduce both the **Cyan** and **Blue** sliders to *50%* just to darken the background and sky slightly. Now close the adjustment settings.

Experimenting with different blend modes on adjustment layers is a great way to find unique tonal manipulations for your images. Try blend modes like Overlay, Glow and Reflect with adjustments like Black & White and Recolour, then control their strength with the layer Opacity.

Black & White

Add Preset   Merge   Delete   Reset

Red   -200 %

Yellow   0 %

Green   100 %

Cyan   50 %

Blue   50 %

Magenta   100 %

Picker

Opacity: 60 %   Blend Mode: Overlay

Resource

mam_tor.afphoto (*03. Creating A Moody Sky* snapshot)

CREATING A MOODY SKY

Having taken care of the foreground tones (for now at least), let's focus on the sky. It's a little too bright and lacking in definition for my liking, so we'll select just the sky and alter it through selective adjustments.

1 On the **Layers Panel**, select the Background (Pixel) layer.

2 From the **Tools Panel**, choose the **Selection Brush Tool** (W).

3 Drag across the sky to select it. The selection will snap to where the background meets the sky.

If your selection accidentally extends downwards over the horizon, hold the option ⌥ key (Mac) or alt key (Win) and paint away the unwanted mountain areas.

4 From the **Layer Menu**, choose **New Live Filter Layer** > **Clarity Filter**.

5 To remove the marquee, from the **Select Menu**, choose **Deselect**.

6 In the filter settings, change the **Strength** to *60%* (maximum). This will accentuate the edges of the clouds in the sky. Close the filter settings.

MORE TONAL TWEAKS

Resource

mam_tor.afphoto (*04. More Tonal Tweaks* snapshot)

At this stage, the image has a summer glow look with warm, saturated colours. However, I want to make a subtle tonal shift in the image using a different approach—a Selective Colour adjustment.

1 Click to select the Black & White Adjustment layer. This ensures any new layers you add will be at the top of the layer stack.

2 From the **Layer Menu**, choose **New Adjustment Layer** > **Selective Colour Adjustment**. With this adjustment, we'll be making use of the different colour options on the **Colour** pop-up menu.

3 With **Reds** selected, drag **Magenta** to *100%*.

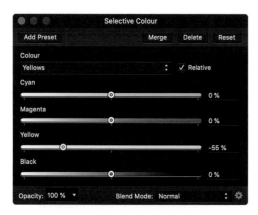

4 From the **Colour** pop-up menu, select **Yellows**. Drag **Yellow** to *-55%*.

5 From the **Colour** pop-up menu, select **Greens**. Drag **Magenta** to *100%* to darken the grass areas slightly.

6 From the **Colour** pop-up menu, select **Blues**. Drag **Cyan** to *100%* to add some subtle blue tone to the sky.

7 Close the dialog.

Resource
mam_tor.afphoto (*05. Finishing Touches* snapshot)

FINISHING TOUCHES

Now that we've got the tone nailed, it's time to add some sharpening to help lift the fine detail in the image.

1 Select the Background (Pixel) layer.

2 From the **Layer Menu**, choose **New Live Filter Layer** > **Unsharp Mask Filter**.

3 In the settings, set **Radius** to *1px* and **Factor** to *3*. This will add some moderate fine detail sharpening and will really help the image 'pop'.

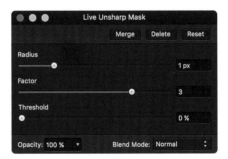

In addition to Unsharp Mask, you can also try a live Clarity filter to add local contrast to your image and increase the "perceived" sharpness.

EXPORTING

With the image complete, all that's left to do is export it for the intended delivery. I want to upload this image to a series of image sharing websites, so I'll opt for a high-quality JPEG export.

1   On the **File Menu**, choose **Export**.

2   From the list of export icons, choose **JPEG**.

3   Ensure the **Quality** is set to *100%*, then click **Export**.

4   Choose a preferred directory to save into, then click **Save**.

Our work here is complete! The exported JPEG file can then be uploaded and shared as required.

2

Peak Country 2: Lumsdale Falls

Bringing an overcast, long exposure image to life by *James Ritson*

Following on from the Mam Tor project, we'll be using manual brushwork in conjunction with adjustment layers and live filter layers to reshape the tones in an image.

A great candidate for this is a long-exposure photograph of a waterfall I took on an overcast day; unedited, it lacks colour and contrast. Although the stream in the middle of the image should be the primary focus, the image is rather washed out as a whole, and so the viewer's eye isn't drawn to one particular area.

BEFORE YOU GET STARTED

Resources

 You can get all the resources that are referenced in this project from:
https://affin.co/lumsdale

Knowledge of Affinity Photo

To get the most from undertaking this project, you will need to:

- Be familiar with the interface of Affinity Photo. You can learn more about the interface in the Interface Tour chapter, starting on p. 13.

- Follow along with example resources by navigating and viewing snapshots that are saved in your project file. Named snapshots are suggested at stages throughout the project. See p. 9.

- Have good core skills. See the skills table below to see which additional aspects of Affinity Photo you need to be confident with to complete this project:

Developing raw images	p. 89
Cropping	p. 92
Inpainting	p. 96
Adjustments	p. 100
Layers	p. 122

SHOOT DETAILS

Exploring Lumsdale Falls, I took some shots of the topmost fall that I thought was most iconic. Although those shots were fine, the overcast day and boring sky meant it wasn't the most inspiring result.

Venturing further down, I discovered several smaller streams that were, at first glance, nothing particularly special. I persisted in getting down to eye level with these streams and was rewarded with a composition of cascading water. The water and rocks filled the frame, revealing some textural detail and depth that made the shot more interesting. Wanting to achieve a motion blur effect on the water but lacking the ND (neutral density) filters to facilitate this, I instead closed the aperture to a small f/16 and used a shutter speed of 1sec. I could only do this and not overexpose the image because of the overcast, drab lighting.

Had it been a bright and sunny day, I wouldn't have come away with that shot. The lesson here is: make the most of your dull days!

FILENAMES

lumsdale_raw.rw2

GEAR

TRIPOD:	Manfrotto PIXI EVO-2
CAMERA:	Panasonic GH4
LENS:	Carl Zeiss Flektogon 35mm f/2.4
LIGHTING:	Natural light

SETTINGS

SHOOTING MODE:	Manual
EXPOSURE:	1 sec
APERTURE:	f/16
ISO:	200
EXP. BIAS	n/a
EXP. PROG:	Manual exposure
METERING:	Pattern
FORMATS:	RAW

LOCATION

Lumsdale Falls, Peak District, Derbyshire, England

https://affin.co/loclumsdale

CONDITIONS

Overcast, middle of Spring

POST SHOOT EDITING

I regularly use Affinity Photo to add some extra depth to images through brushwork and blend modes. It's a similar principle to dodging and burning, except you have more flexibility as you can alter the brush colour and experiment with different blend modes.

With this image, my plan is to rebalance the tones in the image. I want the water to be more prominent, but at the same time I want to bring out the lush greens and reds on the mossy rocks. To finish the image off for printing I'll also add some high pass sharpening and a vignette to darken the edges and narrow the focal point of the image.

DEVELOPING THE RAW IMAGE

We're going to start by opening the raw image in Affinity Photo. This will allow us to maximise the available tonal range by removing the default tone curve and adding our own.

1 Select **File** > **Open**, then navigate to and select Lumsdale_Raw.RW2.

2 On the **Toolbar**, click the **Assistant Options**.

3 Change **Tone Curve** to *Take no action*, then close the dialog.

4 On the **Basic Panel**, check **Shadows & Highlights** and drag **Highlights** to *-100%*.

5 On the **Tones Panel**, check **Curves** and click on the graph line to create a node at the bottom-left of the graph.

6 Click again on the line at the direct centre of the graph, and drag the new node upwards to create a gradual curve.

This combination of removing the tone curve, compressing the highlights and adding a curves adjustment should result in quite a tonally flat image.

7 Click **Develop** to develop the image and move into the **Photo Persona**.

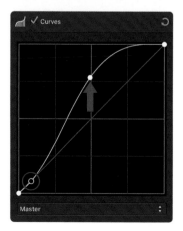

LAYING THE TONAL GROUNDWORK

Resource

lumsdale_falls.afphoto (*01. Tonal groundwork* snapshot)

First, we'll use haze removal to bring back some depth to the image, then begin reshaping the balance of tones in the image using brushwork. By using brushwork, we have finer control over the areas we want to accentuate and draw the viewer's eye to.

Removing haze and tackling low contrast

1 From the **Filters Menu**, choose **Haze Removal**.

2 In Haze Removal settings, increase **Strength** and reduce **Exposure Correction**. Click **Apply**.

Controlling tones with brushwork and blend modes

1 From the **Layers Panel**, select **Add Pixel Layer**.

2 Set the new pixel layer's blend mode to *Overlay* and change layer **Opacity** to *40%*.

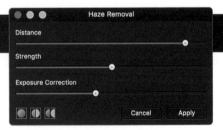

3 From the **Tools Panel**, select the **Paint Brush Tool** (B). On its context toolbar, ensure **Width** is set to *1000 px* and **Hardness** is set to *0%*.

4 On the **Colour Panel**, set the active colour to almost white with a slight blue-yellow tint; this can be achieved by using RGB *255,254,235*.

Further controlling tones

We've begun to see what effect we can have with manual brushwork and blend modes—let's take this further and darken the rocks either side of the water to control where we want the viewer's eye to fall.

5 Now drag and paint over the areas of water. You should gradually see them become brighter and more prominent in the image. You can paint either in one long stroke or multiple strokes; use whichever you find more comfortable.

> For more control over your brushwork, dynamically resize your brush width whilst still painting—use the [and] keys to decrease and increase the width, respectively.

1 From the **Layers Panel**, select **Add Pixel Layer**.

2 Set the *Pixel* layer's **Blend Mode** to *Reflect* and change layer **Opacity** to *40%*.

3 On the **Colour Panel**, set the active colour to a very dark blue; to achieve this, set a colour of RGB *20,20,55*.

4 With the **Paint Brush Tool**, paint over the rocks and background at the top of the image to darken their tones. Use multiple strokes to paint the rocks in the middle of the water.

163

Resource
lumsdale_falls.afphoto (*02. Enhancing image* snapshot)

ENHANCING THE IMAGE

Non-Destructive Inpainting

Now that we've given the image a little bit of life, let's remove some leaves and other little distractions using the Inpainting Brush Tool.

Using this tool on the original Background layer would be destructive, so instead we'll inpaint non-destructively onto a new pixel layer.

1   From the **Layers Panel**, select the Background (Pixel) layer.

2   Select **Add Pixel Layer**. The new layer is then added above the background layer, but under the two brushwork layers: this ensures the brushwork will influence any inpainted content as well.

3   Click the new layer entry and name it *Inpainting*.

4   From the **Tools Panel**, select the **Inpainting Brush Tool** (J). On the context toolbar, set a **Width** of *30 px* and a **Hardness** of *80%*.

5   Finally, on the context toolbar, change from **Current Layer** to **Current Layer & Below**. This inpaints onto the new pixel layer whilst using content from the image layer beneath.

Saturating Tones

With distracting elements in the image removed, we'll move on to accentuating certain colour tones in the image, especially on surrounding plants.

1   On the **Layers Panel**, select the top pixel layer. This ensures any layers we add will appear at the top of the layer stack.

2   From the **Layer Menu**, choose **New Adjustment Layer > HSL Adjustment**.

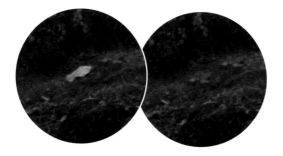

6 Now drag over each distracting leaf on the right-hand rocks to remove them—the area will be highlighted in red until you release the mouse button when the area will be intelligently replaced with surrounding content.

On the **Layers Panel**, you'll see the individual inpainted content on the pixel layer in the layer preview thumbnail. At any point, you can **Hide** this layer and see the original image content underneath, showing that non-destructive inpainting has been achieved.

3 On the HSL Adjustment dialog, change the pop-up menu from **Master** to **Reds** to target the red tones.

4 Drag the **Saturation Shift** slider to *45%*.

5 Change from **Reds** to **Yellows**, then drag the **Saturation** slider to *35%*.

Further brushwork

We're going to push the red and green tones on the rocks even more with some more manual brushwork. Using brushwork with blend modes is a great way of bringing out colour and vibrancy in areas with typically muted tones.

1 From the **Layers Panel**, create a **New Pixel Layer**.

2 Set the layer's blend mode to *Overlay* and change its **Opacity** to *30%*.

3 From the **Tools Panel**, select the **Paint Brush Tool**. On the context toolbar, set the **Width** to *500 px* and ensure the **Hardness** is at *0%*.

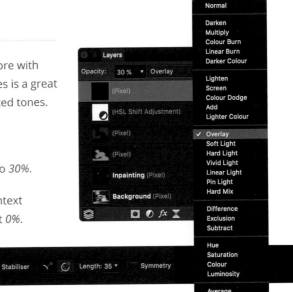

As we're going to enhance existing colours in the image, we'll want to pick a suitable colour from the image itself rather than simply choosing one in the **Colours Panel**.

4 Hold the option ⌥ key (Mac) or alt key (Win) and drag on the image to use the colour picker. Choose a vibrant green from the area of foliage at the very top of the image. Release the mouse button to store the colour.

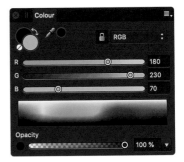

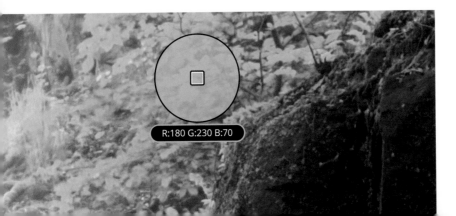

R:180 G:230 B:70

For the purposes of this project, if your colour values can't be replicated by sampling, you can set the values manually in the Colour Panel.

5   Drag over the foliage and mossy areas of the rocks. The painted effect will be a very subtle enhancement of the green tones.

6   On the same pixel layer, we'll also add some brushwork to enhance the red and orange tones in the rocks.

7   Colour pick again, choosing a red/orange tone from the rocks on the right. I picked a colour of RGB *75,45,30*.

8   Using the **Colour Panel**, let's drastically increase the intensity of this colour. Change **R** to *210* and **G** to *130*.

9   Drag to paint selectively over the rock surfaces. Try and target the areas that already have some red tones—inadvertently painting over areas that are greener will result in an odd clash of colours. Again, we're going for a very subtle approach here.

Resource
lumsdale_falls.afphoto (*03. Finishing touches* snapshot)

FINISHING TOUCHES

Now that we've finished all the manual brushwork, we can begin with the final touches. We'll add a vignette, shape the overall tones, add some sharpening and crop to a popular print ratio.

Adding a vignette live filter

Vignetting is a darkening effect introduced at the corners of an image for creative reasons.

1   From the **Select Menu**, choose **Deselect Layers**. This will clear the currently selected layer and allow us to add a live filter to the top of the layer stack without nesting it.

2   From the **Layer Menu**, choose **New Live Filter Layer** > **Vignette Filter**.

3   In the Live Vignette settings, adjust settings so the vignette is perfect for the image's aspect ratio.

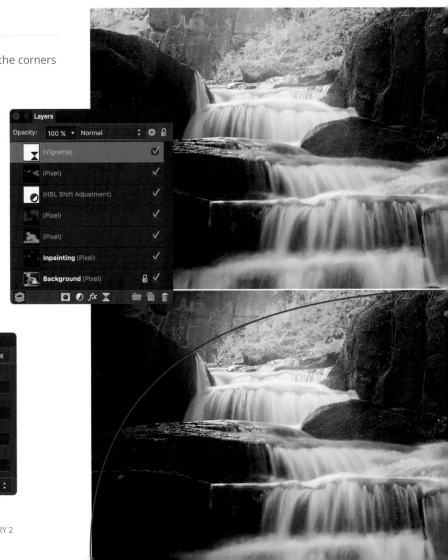

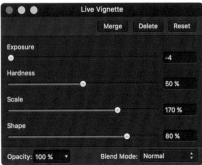

Adding a sharpening high pass live filter

1 From the **Layers Panel**, select the
   Background (Pixel) layer. This ensures the
   next live filter we add will nest as a child layer.

2 From the **Layer Menu**, choose **New Live
   Filter Layer** > **High Pass Filter**. Note the
   layer becomes a child layer of the Background
   (Pixel) layer.

3 In Live High Pass settings, choose a **Radius** of
   1.8 px, check **Monochrome** and set the blend
   mode to *Linear Light*. Setting the correct blend
   mode is important to ensure it functions as a
   sharpening filter.

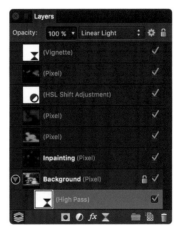

Cropping for print

We're at the final stretch! Now we just need to crop the image to a 6"x4" aspect ratio for printing. This ensures the image will fill the entire paper space (if we're using borderless printing). The aspect ratio we're choosing here means we're going to sacrifice some vertical information in the image, so we need to choose our final crop carefully.

1 From the **Tools Panel**, select the **Crop Tool** (C).

2 On the context toolbar, set **Mode** to *Custom Ratio*. In the two adjacent input fields, enter *6* and *4*. Check **Darken Border** to darken areas outside of the crop boundary, which will aid in deciding the final composition.

3 On the top **Toolbar**, enable **Snapping**. This will ensure the crop boundary snaps to the edges of the image.

4 Move the mouse cursor inside the crop boundary and click once. This will set the crop behaviour to drag mode, as opposed to drawing out a new crop boundary.

5 Drag the crop boundary up near to the top of the image. This focuses the crop composition on the streams of water and will lead the viewer's eye up from the bottom to the top of the waterfall.

6 Click **Apply** to commit the crop.

Affinity Photo performs non-destructive cropping, even when you click Apply. What this means is that parts of the image excluded by the crop's composition are still available, and can be brought back at any time by increasing the crop or resizing the canvas.

Vignette compensation after crop

You'll notice after cropping that the vignette effect has lost some of its prominence. This is because the aspect ratio of the image has changed, therefore the Shape value we chose will need to be adjusted to be narrower. Because the vignette was added as a live filter, this is an easy process.

1 On the **Layers Panel**, double-click the Vignette layer's icon to re-open the **Live Vignette** dialog.

2 Change **Shape** to *55%*. The vignette now better suits the cropped image.

Final tone shaping

We'll add a tonal adjustment to give the image some 'punch' when it's printed.

1 With the Vignette layer selected, on the **Layer Menu**, choose **New Adjustment Layer** > **Curves Adjustment**.

2 In Curves settings, drag the node at the bottom-left of the graph line up slightly to raise the black level of the entire image.

3 Now click on the line a quarter of the way up the graph to add another node. Position it exactly on the first quarter where the quadrants meet. This will crush the shadow tones and slightly reduce the intensity of the midtones and highlights.

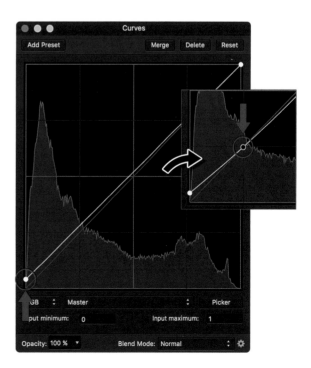

EXPORTING FOR PRINT

With all the work on the image complete, it's time to export a high-quality copy of the image that we can use to print from.

I prefer to export in 16-bit to retain the same precision the image was edited in, but if you're concerned about compatibility you can always export to 8-bit.

1 From the **File Menu**, choose **Export**.

2 From the choice of export formats, choose **TIFF**.

3 Change **Preset** to **TIFF RGB 16-bit**.

4 Click **Export**, choose a suitable destination for your exported image, then click **Save**.

Our work here is complete!

3

Secrets of HDR

High Dynamic Range photo editing by *James Ritson*

Explore the use High Dynamic Range photography to overcome tonal limitations.

BEFORE YOU GET STARTED

Resources

 You can get all the resources that are referenced in this project from:
https://affin.co/hdr

Knowledge of Affinity Photo

To get the most from undertaking this project, you will need to:

- Be familiar with the interface of Affinity Photo. You can learn more about the interface in the Interface Tour chapter, starting on p. 13.

Only source images are supplied with this short project.

INTRODUCTION
TO HDR

Shooting for High Dynamic Range (HDR) is a popular technique that photographers can use to greatly increase the tonal range of an image. A typical digital camera image, when shooting in raw format, may have anything from 10 to 16 stops of dynamic range, which is the amount of tonal range that can be captured.

Sometimes, though, this tonal range isn't enough. You might be trying to photograph scenes with extreme contrast—think of landscapes where the foreground may be in shadow but the sky remains bright, or low-light scenes where you have extreme darkness juxtaposed with the intensity of artificial lighting.

Any situation where you have to make a choice between clipping highlight detail (overexposure) or having noisy shadow detail (underexposure) is hardly ideal.

With HDR, separate images of the same scene are taken at different exposure levels, capturing more detail in the extremes of the image (i.e., in the shadows and highlights).

These images are then merged together to produce a composite image with a much greater tonal range than that of any individual image.

To work with such imagery, HDR images are merged to what's known as **32-bit unbounded**, where tonal information can be stored even if it cannot be displayed.

In this project, we'll explore merging bracketed exposure images and how to tone map the created HDR image for different results tonally and with respect to contrast.

SHOOT DETAILS

The most efficient way to capture images with different exposures is to use **Exposure Bracketing**. Most cameras, both entry level and professional, will have various bracketing features. You may need to consult your camera's manual or guide to find out how to enable bracketing, but here are some steps to shoot bracketed images efficiently:

1 If possible, use a tripod or stabilisation device. If shooting handheld, try and use lens-based or in-body image stabilisation.

2 Enable exposure bracketing on your camera. For the best results, try a wide bracket, e.g. five shots with +3EV/-3EV, or seven shots with +2EV/-2EV.

3 Compose your shot and capture at each exposure (manually or as a burst).

Try setting your quality or format option to RAW+JPEG. This captures in both formats and gives you more options when merging: try the JPEG format for quicker results, and raw format for more detail and precision.

POST SHOOT
EDITING

An important step that follows most HDR merges is tone mapping. The tonal information that an HDR image contains is too great to be displayed properly on most computer screens and devices—they simply can't reproduce the huge range of tones.

To work around this, we employ a technique known as tone mapping—essentially taking a wide range of tones and compressing them into a smaller range that can be reproduced. The two popular methods for achieving this are **tone compression** and **local contrast enhancement**.

Chances are you've seen some HDR imagery, and it has a very distinct look: clear separated tones, lots of detail, somewhat flatter yet simultaneously more intense. You may have also noticed certain issues like 'haloing' or brighter areas around edges that look unrealistic.

These are all traits of tone mapping, particularly when local contrast enhancement is used. It's incredibly easy to 'overcook' or go too far with tone mapping, so exercise some restraint where needed.

HDR MERGING AND TONE MAPPING

Creating an HDR merge

We'll start by merging several bracketed exposure shots into a 32-bit HDR document.

1 From the **File Menu**, choose **New HDR Merge**.

2 Click **Add** and navigate to the downloaded HDR - Window folder, then select P3230573.jpg to P3230577.jpg with the shift key (⇧) pressed, then click **Open**. They will now populate the **Images** list in the displayed dialog.

3 Uncheck **Noise Reduction** as this is predominantly for raw images.

4 Click **OK**.

Affinity Photo will then begin the HDR merge process—it will align the images first, then blend the most detailed pixels from each image to create a much more detailed composite image.

Tone mapping an HDR image

Because **Tone map HDR image** remained checked, the **Tone Mapping Persona** will open, which allows the image's greater tonal range to be mapped into a smaller range.

1 On the **Tone Map Panel**, increase **Local Contrast** to *65%*. This will compress the tones and provide a gritty, detailed look that suits the image.

2 Under the **Enhance** category, reduce the **Saturation** to *-30%* to take some of the orange tones out of the brickwork.

3 Check **Detail Refinement** and drag **Radius** to *100%*, then drag **Amount** to *25%*. This adds an extra layer of detail and 'grit' to the image.

4 Click **Apply** to commit the tone mapping effect.

Using tone mapping presets

The **Tone Mapping Persona** also offers presets to quickly achieve a particular look. Let's try these out with the same image. We're starting in the **Photo Persona** as we've just applied the tone map.

1 From the **Edit Menu**, choose **Undo Tone map**. This will restore the image to its state before the tone mapping was applied.

2 From the **Toolbar**, choose the **Tone Mapping Persona**.

3 From the **Presets Panel** on the left, click the *Detailed* thumbnail from the *Default* category to produce a high-impact high-contrast result. Click on other presets to see the variety of results you can achieve.

4 From the Category pop-up menu, select the **James Ritson Customs** category. Select further presets, offering very different looks and moods. Categories can be created from Panel Preferences at top right.

5 Experiment by tweaking a preset's settings (using the **Tone Map Panel**) to create your own unique look. If you wish to save this as a preset for later use, click **Add Preset**.

6 Once finished, click **Apply** to commit the tone mapping.

Grime and Decay

Bathwater

Grime and Decay works well for urban and architectural photography, producing sharp lines and a balanced tone.

Choose the Bathwater preset for a green-tinged, washed out look.

Miami Bleach

Nighttime B&W

Miami Bleach creates a golden, washed-out tone with increased mid tones.

Nighttime B&W results in a low-key monochrome look that suits low-light photography and images with dull, overcast tones.

REMOVING GHOSTS

'Ghosts' in HDR imagery are areas of the composited image where there was movement between each shot—they show as blurred areas. Affinity Photo has some very efficient automatic ghost removal which can be enabled on the **New HDR Merge** dialog, but removing ghosts manually is also very intuitive and gives you absolute control over your final composition.

- Merge images from the HDR - Beach folder as described previously (p. 180), but disable tone mapping (uncheck **Tone map HDR image**) to remain in **Photo Persona**.

  We'll also be presented with a **Sources Panel**, which we'll use for removing the ghosts. The **Clone Brush Tool** (S) is automatically selected too.

Notice the crashing waves have become blurry and indistinct—the result of merging several images where the waves are moving. We're going to pick the waves from one image and clone them into the final HDR image.

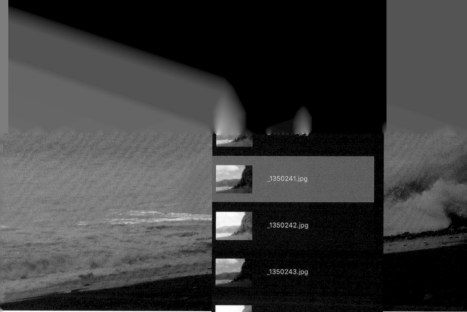

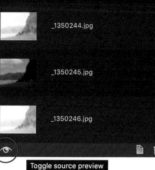

1 On the **Sources Panel**, click **Toggle source preview** and increase the height of the panel (this exposes more source images).

2 Click through the image list on the **Sources Panel**. Each image will preview on the main canvas and you will be able to see the different wave shapes.

3 Pick an image where the waves are sharp and defined, e.g. _1350241.jpg.

4 Now click **Toggle source preview** again to return to the final HDR image.

5 On the context toolbar, set a **Width** of *800 px* and a **Hardness** of *0%*.

6 Move the **Clone Brush** cursor over the waves in the image and drag to clone in the waves from the selected image on the **Sources Panel**.

7 Once you have finished cloning, the image can be tone mapped. Choose the **Tone Mapping Persona** and follow the tone mapping instructions previously (p. 182) to achieve a final tone mapped result (overleaf).

Going Greyscale

Strip out colour for some monochrome punch by *James Ritson*

Removing colour from the mix and shooting in black and white can open up a whole new way of looking at your compositions. You become more keenly aware of shapes, lines and tones, because you now have to work harder to communicate an image based on those aspects.

BEFORE YOU
GET STARTED

Resources

You can get all the resources that are referenced in this project from:
https://affin.co/greyscale

Knowledge of Affinity Photo

To get the most from undertaking this project, you will need to:

- Be familiar with the interface of Affinity Photo. You can learn more about the interface in the Interface Tour chapter, starting on p. 13.

- Have good core skills. For this smaller project, an understanding of adjustments (p. 100) would be beneficial.

SHOOT DETAILS

Shooting in RAW gives you the ultimate flexibility for black and white shooting. It means you can change the camera's picture profile to a monochrome setting, allowing you to shoot and compose to achieve the best black and white result.

The embedded preview images, used during camera review and playback, will be greyscale. The recorded RAW information, however, will include full colour as per usual; this allows you to add your own black and white conversion during editing and take control of the individual colour mixes and tones.

POST SHOOT EDITING

Once the images are taken off the camera, you'll be developing and editing full colour images like normal in Affinity Photo. My raw images were developed in **Develop Persona** (p. 17) using default settings and exported as JPG files.

During editing, a Black and White Adjustment layer will be added to these images, which will give the image a black and white look. Because this adjustment layer is non-destructive, further work can be performed to fine tune the tones in the image.

CONVERTING TO BLACK AND WHITE

Resource

basic_black_and_white_adjustment.afphoto
ilfracombe.jpg

Basic black and white adjustment

We'll start by opening an image and applying a Black & White adjustment layer. Initial results will look unpromising but selectively altering the cyan and blue contributions to the greyscale result makes a dramatic difference.

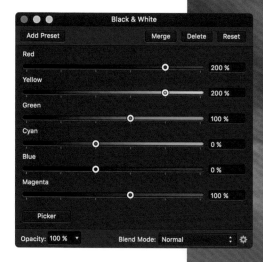

1 From the **File Menu**, select **Open**. Navigate to, select and open ilfracombe.jpg.

2 From the **Layer Menu**, choose **New Adjustment Layer > Black & White Adjustment**.

3 In Black & White settings, tweak the colours to change the tonal balance of the black and white result:

- Drag **Red** to *200%* to increase the intensity of the buildings.

- Drag **Yellow** to *200%* to bring out the foliage and building highlights.

- Drag **Cyan** to *0%* to reveal more sky detail.

- Drag **Blue** to *0%* to further darken the sky.

Additional tonal manipulation

In addition to a basic Black & White adjustment, additional adjustments can be applied to influence the final result.

1   From the **File Menu**, select **Open**. Navigate to, select and open light_painting.jpg.

2   From the **Layer Menu**, choose **New Adjustment Layer > Black & White Adjustment**.

3   In Black & White settings, tweak the colours to change the tonal balance of the black and white result:

- Drag **Yellow** to *200%* to bring out more detail in the ruined structure.

- Drag **Green** to *135%* to increase the intensity of the structure's middle section.

4   On the **Layers Panel**, click the Background (Pixel) layer to select it. Any additional layers will now be added underneath the Black & White Adjustment layer.

5   From the **Layer Menu**, choose **New Adjustment Layer > White Balance Adjustment**. The layer should be in the middle of the layer stack.

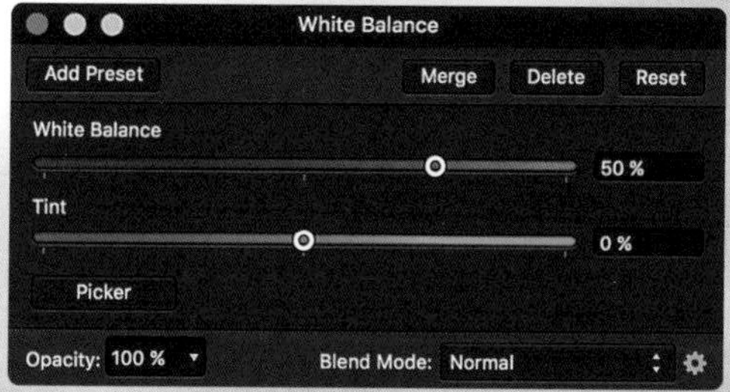

White Balance

Add Preset		Merge	Delete	Reset

White Balance

50 %

Tint

0 %

Picker

Opacity: 100 % ▾   Blend Mode: Normal ⬍   ⚙

6 In the White Balance settings, drag **White Balance** to the right to shift the entire image tonally. Experiment by dragging in either direction and see how the sky and structure tones are affected. I chose a **White Balance** value of *50%* for a more even balance between the structure and sky.

Manual tonal manipulation with brush work

Having looked at influencing the black and white result by using adjustment layers underneath the Black & White Adjustment layer, we'll now take a similar approach using brush work to selectively alter areas of the image.

1 From the **File Menu**, select **Open**. Navigate to, select and open architecture.jpg.

2 From the **Layer Menu**, choose **New Adjustment Layer > Black & White Adjustment**.

3 In Black & White settings, drag **Cyan** to *0%* to bring out the sky detail.

4 On the **Layers Panel**, click the Background (Pixel) layer to select it. Any additional layers will now be added underneath the Black & White Adjustment layer.

5 On the **Layers Panel**, choose **Add Pixel Layer** to create a new, empty pixel layer.

6 Set the new pixel layer's blend mode to **Overlay**, and its **Opacity** to *30%*.

Let's set up a paint brush and start painting.

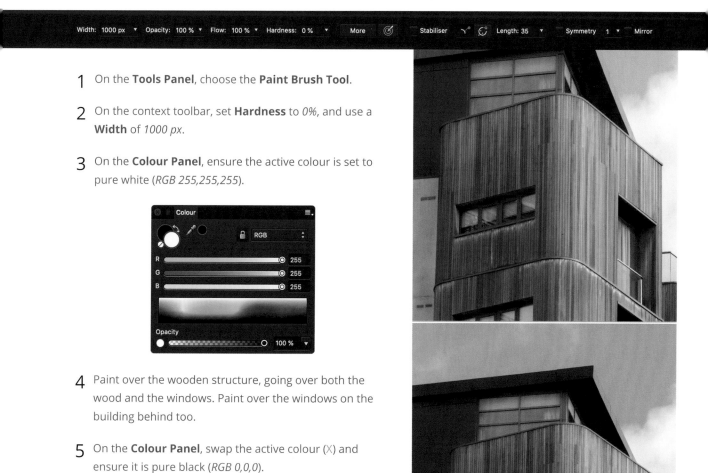

1   On the **Tools Panel**, choose the **Paint Brush Tool**.

2   On the context toolbar, set **Hardness** to *0%*, and use a **Width** of *1000 px*.

3   On the **Colour Panel**, ensure the active colour is set to pure white (*RGB 255,255,255*).

4   Paint over the wooden structure, going over both the wood and the windows. Paint over the windows on the building behind too.

5   On the **Colour Panel**, swap the active colour (X) and ensure it is pure black (*RGB 0,0,0*).

6   Now paint over the sky to darken it.

7 Hide (uncheck) the (Pixel) layer to see how the painting influences the final black and white result. Check it to make the layer visible again.

8 On the **Layers Panel**, select the (Black & White Adjustment) layer. Any new layers will now be added above the black and white adjustment layer.

9 From the **Layer Menu**, choose **New Adjustment Layer > Brightness / Contrast Adjustment**.

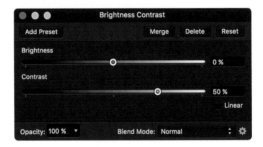

10 Increase **Contrast** to *50%* to finish off the work and produce a punchy monochrome image.

> You can take this approach further by using different colours when painting on the pixel layer, then altering the colour mix within the **Black & White Adjustment**. This way, you can control areas of the image based on the colours you paint with.

5

London Calling 1

Tackling the challenges of urban photography by *James Ritson*

This project and its sister project, London Calling 2 (p. 226), looks at blending correction and creativity in two distinct photographic scenarios: daytime photography and night-time photography, respectively.

BEFORE YOU GET STARTED

Resources

 You can get all the resources that are referenced in this project from:

https://affin.co/london1

Knowledge of Affinity Photo

To get the most from undertaking this project, you will need to:

- Be familiar with the interface of Affinity Photo. You can learn more about the interface in the Interface Tour chapter, starting on p. 13.

- Follow along with example resources by navigating and viewing snapshots that are saved in your project file. Named snapshots are suggested at stages throughout the project. See p. 9.

SHOOT DETAILS

The nature of urban photography can often be very tough on both your equipment and on yourself creatively. Lens distortion, colour fringing, chromatic aberration, high ISO noise, warped perspectives; these are all lens-related or camera-body-related issues that you may struggle with. Getting the right composition can be tricky too. Streets may be too narrow or too wide, filled with obstructions like traffic lights, signs, pedestrians and vehicles; all of which can prevent you from getting that clean, uncluttered shot you might be after.

With limited time in London, my goal was to capture a mixture of iconic and lesser-known areas, primarily focusing on architecture and abstract photography.

Using Affinity Photo, I could push my photography and capture scenes in ways that I otherwise wouldn't attempt. For these daytime shots, I kept mainly to wide-angle and ultra-wide-angle lenses to capture wide scenes of the architecture.

FILENAMES	
shard.tiff, leadenhall_market.tiff, Stacking images	
GEAR	
TRIPOD:	Manfrotto PIXI EVO-2
CAMERA:	Olympus E-M1 mk2
LENS:	Olympus 12-40mm f/2.8
	Olympus 7-14mm f/2.8
	Olympus 40-150mm f/2.8
	Olympus 75mm f/1.8
LIGHTING:	Natural daylight / artificial light
SETTINGS	
SHOOTING MODE:	Manual
EXPOSURE:	Varied
APERTURE:	Varied
ISO:	200-3200
EXP. BIAS	n/a
EXP. PROG:	Manual exposure
METERING:	Pattern
FORMATS:	RAW
LOCATION	
London, UK	
The Shard - https://affin.co/locshard	
Leadenhall Market - https://affin.co/locleadenhall	
St Paul's Cathedral - https://affin.co/locstpauls	
CONDITIONS	
Overcast, Winter	

POST
SHOOT
EDITING

Resource
clean_lines_and_moody_skies.afphoto (*01. Initial image* snapshot) shard.tiff

During editing, we'll employ some techniques to improve the imagery, such as mesh deforming, increasing local contrast, median stacking and haze removal. We'll also make good use of masking, adjustment layers and live filter layers.

Filter layers, being unique to Photo, offer blurring, sharpening and vignetting operations applied as layers, which means they can be tweaked and masked at any time.

CLEAN LINES
AND MOODY
SKIES

We'll start with a fairly straightforward image looking up at the famous London landmark, The Shard, from the ground.

It was a grey, overcast day in London, but hiding behind that white sheet of sky is some promising cloud detail; we just need to tease it out during editing.

Using Haze Removal to bring back the sky

1 Use **File > Open** to load shard.tiff.

2 From the **Filters Menu**, choose **Haze Removal**.

3 Increase the **Strength** slider to reveal more cloud detail, and decrease the **Exposure Correction** slider to darken the image's overall tones. Click **Apply** to commit the effect.

Another great way to bring back sky detail from bright images is to use the **Shadows / Highlights** filter, also found directly on the **Filters Menu**.

Resource

clean_lines_and_moody_skies.afphoto
(*03. Making edge detail pop* snapshot)

Resource

clean_lines_and_moody_skies.afphoto
(*04. Tonal adjustments* snapshot)

Making edge detail pop

We're going to use a technique to 'thicken' line detail in the image and really bring out the building's shape.

1 From the **Layer Menu**, choose **New Live Filter Layer > Unsharp Mask Filter**.

2 Set the **Radius** to its maximum of *100 px*, then change Blend Mode to *Darken*. This applies a huge local contrast boost, but the blend mode prevents the 'halo' effect from appearing where the building meets the sky.

Tonal adjustments and finishing

1 We're now going to give this image a monochrome conversion. From the **Layer Menu**, choose **New Adjustment Layer > Black & White Adjustment**.

2 Increase the **Yellow** colour mix slider to *200%* to make the lower part of the building stand out.

3 We'll introduce a vignette to focus the viewer's eye on the building. Firstly, from the **Select Menu**, choose **Deselect Layers**. We're going to add a live filter layer, and this will stop it from being nested into our currently selected layer.

4 From the **Layer Menu**, choose **New Live Filter Layer > Vignette Filter**.

5 Change the **Exposure** slider to *-4*, **Hardness** to *40%*, **Scale** to *180%* and **Shape** to *80%*.

6 As a final step, we'll give the tones a little more punch. From the **Layer Menu**, choose **New Adjustment Layer > Curves Adjustment**.

7 Drag down on the red line at the bottom left of the graph to add a node—this deepens the shadow tones. Drag near the top of the graph to add a second node, and bring it back up to the red diagonal line.

This provides a nice finishing point for the image.

CORRECTING LENS ISSUES

Resource

correcting_lens_issues.afphoto (*01. Initial image* snapshot)
leadenhall_market.tiff

Wide-angle lenses present their own set of issues like distortion and fringing; ultra-wide-angle lenses exacerbate these issues further.

With this shot of an indoor market area, taken using a 7-14mm wide-angle lens, we not only have a large amount of purple fringing around highlights to contend with, but also mixed lighting (natural light versus artificial) and a slight geometric mismatch between the left and right sides; I tried to stand as centrally as possible when taking the shot, but even so, it could use some correction. We're going to tackle all three of these issues.

Sorting out fringing and contrast

1 Use **File > Open** to load leadenhall_market.tiff.

2 We'll tackle the purple fringing prominent around the windows, where there's an extremely high contrast between the sky and the interior structures.

   Select the **Zoom Tool** (Z) on the **Tools Panel** and drag right to zoom into the roof area to see the problem.

3 From the **Filters Menu**, choose **Colours > Defringe**.

4 Hover the crosshair cursor directly over an area of purple fringing and click to remove all instances of purple fringing.

5 To fine-tune the effect, in the Settings pane, increase **Tolerance** to *90%* and reduce **Edge Brightness Threshold** to *40%*. This will capture more of the purple fringing and remove it.

6 Before we move on, the image looks a little washed out and pale. To quickly correct this, from the **Filters Menu**, choose **Colours > Auto Contrast**.

Correcting the geometry

Looking at the image, we can see an imbalance; the left side is slanted up slightly. From an initial glance, it looks like the image could just be rotated via cropping. However, the architecture isn't perfectly symmetrical from top to bottom, so we're going to fix this now.

1 From the **Filters Menu**, choose **Distort > Deform**.

We need to pick a good reference point for our initial deform node.

2 Zoom in to the top left section of the image and find the point where the top of the pillar meets the curved roof span. Click once to add a node at that corner where they meet:

3 Now pan across to the right and find the equivalent point at the other end of the roof span, then click to add a second node.

4 To help guide our repositioning of these nodes, we'll enable a grid using **View > Show Grid**.

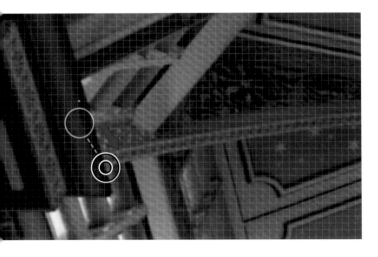
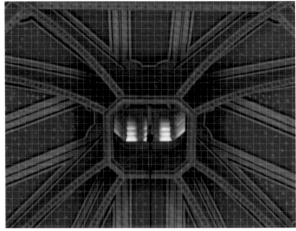

5   Begin dragging the left-hand deform node slightly to the right and down until the central square feature of the ceiling is as symmetrical as possible relative to the grid overlay.

6   This does a good job of lining up the bottom and middle of the image, but we need to reposition the top. Find the middle white beam at the top of the image and click to add a third node:

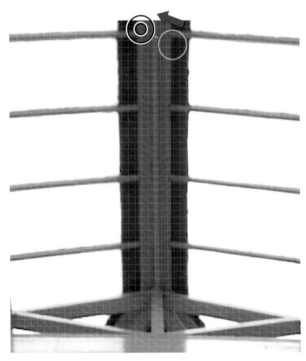

7   When the node is added, the image will shift slightly in position—don't be alarmed by this. The goal now is to line up the middle white beam with the grid line that runs through the ceiling's centre feature.

8 Almost there! The addition and movement of this third deform node will skew the first two nodes slightly, so we'll need to tweak at least one of them— we'll look at the right-hand node.

9 Find the second deform node that was placed between the right-hand pillar and roof span, then bring it up and to the right slightly. Use the grid overlay and centre feature of the ceiling as a guide.

10 Once the result is looking good, click **Apply** in Deform settings.

Achieving perfect symmetry is incredibly difficult. Don't be afraid to experiment with the positioning of the deform nodes, and you can even try adding more nodes to keep certain areas 'rigid' whilst repositioning other areas around them.

As a result of deforming, the sides of the image have been brought inwards to reveal transparent space on the canvas. We'll need to crop into the image slightly to fix this.

1 From the **Tools Panel**, select the **Crop Tool** (C).

2 On the context toolbar, change the **Overlay** to *Diagonals*. This will help us to keep the ceiling's centre feature in the middle of the crop (and subsequently, the final image).

3 Move the crop handles inwards until all the transparent space is cropped out, and align the diagonal overlay with the ceiling centre feature.

4 On the context toolbar, click **Apply**.

Final tonal tweaks

With our image corrected, all that remains is to add some finishing touches.

1 From the **Layer Menu**, choose **New Live Filter Layer > Diffuse Glow Filter**. We'll use this filter to add some visual interest to the flat white areas of the sky through the windows.

2 In the Diffuse Glow settings, adjust values so highlights are softened, mimicking the type of highlight diffusion you get with film.

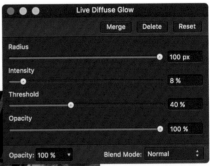

3 Finally, we'll tweak that orange colour cast and bring out some stronger reds in the image. From the **Layer Menu**, choose **New Adjustment Layer > HSL Adjustment**.

4 In the settings, change from *Master* to *Yellows* and set the **Saturation Shift** slider to *-50%*.

5 Change from *Yellows* to *Reds* and set the **Saturation Shift** slider to *25%*. This lends the image quite a distinct, desaturated tone.

This completes our edits on this image!

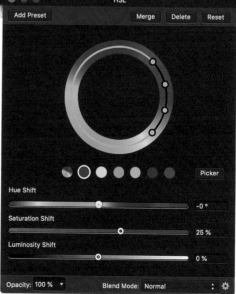

OUT OF MY WAY! PEDESTRIAN AND VEHICLE REMOVAL

In an urban environment it's incredibly tricky to capture iconic shots without including people and traffic. With Affinity Photo and some degree of patience it's possible to achieve this by stacking several images of the same subject and then remove everything but the subject itself.

How this works: you'll want to compose your shot as normal. Over time (anywhere from seconds to minutes), take several images of this same composition, so that any people or traffic move between shots.

The idea is that if one area is obstructed in one image, it will be clear in another. You then stack these images together and average out all that moving content that's different from frame to frame, meaning you end up with a clean, clutter-free result.

Let's get started with this example of St Paul's Cathedral's south portico, where I stood right in front of a busy road in order to get a frontal shot of the building.

You don't have to use a tripod for this; aligning handheld shots with Affinity Photo is easy because stacking auto-aligns your images for you.

Resource

pedestrian_and_object_removal.afphoto (*01. Initial image stack* snapshot)
_1131538.jpg - _1131542.jpg

Stacking the images

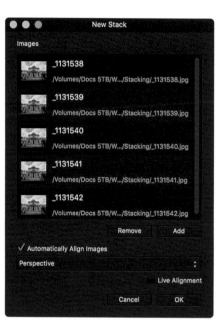

1 Select **File > New Stack**.

2 Choose **Add** and navigate to where you downloaded the resources. Within the Stacking directory, select the five images and choose **Open**.

3 Choose **OK**. The images will be automatically aligned and placed into a stack.

You will then be presented with a clean image with no pedestrians.

On the **Layers Panel**, click the stacking operator on the layer entry for different results. For example, *Minimum* will expose the walking pedestrians.

Fixing the sky

Before further editing, we need to fix the sky. Notice how, as a result of stacking, the sky looks strange as the clouds have slowly moved between shots.

1   On the **Layers Panel**, select the first image in the stack (_1131542.jpg), then from the **Layer Menu**, choose **Duplicate** to create a copy of that layer.

2   Drag this duplicate layer from out of the stack and to the top of the layer list.

3   We now need to mask this duplicate layer as we only want the sky detail from it (the top half of the image). From the **Tools Panel**, choose the **Rectangular Marquee Tool**.

4   Drag from the top of the image down to just below the top of the entrance portico to create a selection.

5 From the **Layers Panel**, click **Mask Layer** to create a mask from the selection; you will see the pedestrians disappear once again, and the sky will now look much better. From the **Select Menu**, choose **Deselect** to dismiss the selection.

Merging and straightening

1 Stacking is computationally expensive and can slow down our editing process, so we'll merge our work so far into a new composite layer to work on. From the **Layer Menu**, choose **Merge Visible**. This will create a composite pixel layer.

2 We need to straighten the resulting image slightly as it's tilted to the right. From the **Tools Panel**, select the **Crop Tool**.

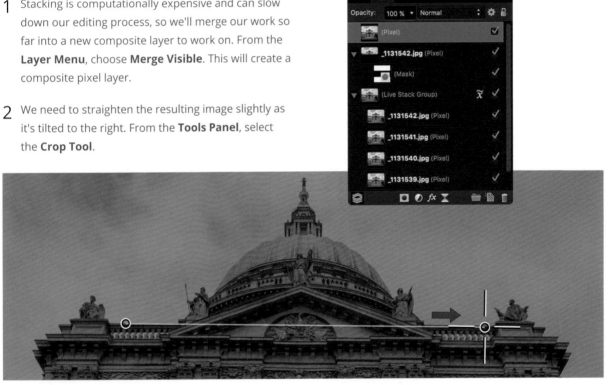

3 Zoom in to the top of the building, then from the context toolbar, choose **Straighten**.

4 Drag across from one side of the building to the other using a suitable guide area. I've chosen the top of the balcony:

5 Once the mouse button is released, the image will be straightened. Zoom out to see the entire image, then move the crop handles in until the newly-created transparent space is cropped out.

6 On the context toolbar, click **Apply** to commit the crop.

Tone mapping

We might want to do some tonal adjustments to try and bring the image to life. A great way to bring out texture with buildings and structures is to use tone mapping.

1 Ensuring the (Pixel) layer is still selected, switch to the **Tone Mapping Persona** on the **Toolbar**.

2 As tone mapping is primarily intended for HDR (High Dynamic Range) imagery, the default settings will be unsuitable. Move the **Tone Compression** slider all the way to *0%*.

3 Increase the **Local Contrast** slider to *30%*; this will start to bring out texture in the building. It will also flatten the tones, which we will compensate for.

4 Under the **Exposure** heading, move the **Blackpoint** slider to *2%* to intensify the image's dark tones. Even such a small adjustment will make a dramatic difference.

As a final adjustment, we'll reduce the colour intensity of the blue sky, as it's distracting the viewer's eye from the real centrepiece of the image, the cathedral itself.

If you feel you have brushed over too much of the building as well as the sky, don't be afraid to select the **Overlay Erase Tool** (E) and erase areas from the overlay.

5 Switch to the **Overlays Panel** and choose **Add Brush Overlay**. Paint across the sky using the brush. It will be a rough selection and will have to include the top section of the building, which is fine.

6 Switch back to the **Tone Map Panel**, then drag the **Saturation** slider to -50%. This will reduce the intensity of the blue in the sky.

7 On the context toolbar, click **Apply** to commit the tone map.

That concludes our edits for this image!

6

London Calling 2

Illuminating the big city
by *James Ritson*

Looking at night-time photography, I'll darken light-polluted
skies, boost colours, and explore night-time HDR shooting.
An interesting approach to noise reduction and classic
perspective correction will be covered too.

BEFORE YOU
GET STARTED

Resources

 You can get all the resources that are referenced in this project from:
https://affin.co/london2

Knowledge of Affinity Photo

To get the most from undertaking this project, you will need to:

- Be familiar with the interface of Affinity Photo. You can learn more about the interface in the Interface Tour chapter, starting on p. 13.

- Follow along with example resources by navigating and viewing snapshots that are saved in your project file. Named snapshots are suggested at stages throughout the project. See p. 9.

- Have good core skills. See the skills table below to see which additional aspects of Affinity Photo you need to be confident with to complete this project:

Adjustments	p. 100
Layers	p. 122

SHOOT
DETAILS

As night fell around London, I changed my techniques slightly to take advantage of the creativity that low-light shooting can offer. I aimed for a mix of long exposure (with low ISO values) and HDR/burst shooting (with high ISO values), allowing me to take advantage of both Photo's HDR Merge and Stacking features.

POST
SHOOT
EDITING

The night-time photography was shot with several editing techniques in mind, including stacking for noise reduction and HDR merging. In addition to this, adjustment layers, perspective correction, brush work and channels manipulation were used for tonal and corrective work.

FILENAMES	
long_exposure.tiff, Stacking directory files	
HDR directory files	
GEAR	
TRIPOD:	Manfrotto PIXI EVO-2
CAMERA:	Olympus E-M1 mk2
LENS:	Olympus 12-40mm f/2.8
	Olympus 7-14mm f/2.8
	Olympus 75mm f/1.8
SETTINGS	
SHOOTING MODE:	Manual
EXPOSURE:	Varied
APERTURE:	Varied
ISO:	200-3200
EXP. BIAS	n/a
EXP. PROG:	Manual exposure
METERING:	Pattern
FORMATS:	RAW
LOCATION	
London, UK	
The London Eye - https://affin.co/loceye	
Big Ben - https://affin.co/locbigben	
Buckingham Palace - https://affin.co/locpalace	
CONDITIONS	
Overcast, Winter, miserable!	

ENHANCING LOW-LIGHT IMAGERY

Resource

enhancing_low_light_imagery.afphoto
(*01. Black & White with a twist* snapshot)
long_exposure.tiff

To begin, we're going to take a long-exposure image and really bring out the colours using brush work. Sometimes enhancing colour is a struggle with low-light imagery, as the extremes between bright artificial lighting and areas in shadow are challenging for any camera. Bright colours are often clipped and are very difficult to tweak in editing.

Black & White with a twist

1   Use **File > Open** to load long_exposure.tiff.

2   From the **Layer Menu**, choose **New Adjustment Layer > Black & White Adjustment**.

3   In Black & White settings, keep values as they are but set the **Blend Mode** to *Multiply*. This will neutralise much of the unpleasant sky tone and lend a slight desaturation to the artificial lighting.

Resource

enhancing_low_light_imagery.afphoto (*02. Bringing out colour* snapshot)

Bringing out the colour

We're now going to bring out the colour in the wheel, background buildings and reflections on the road.

1   On the **Layers Panel**, select the Background (Pixel) layer.

2   On the **Tools Panel**, select the **Sponge Brush Tool**, then adjust using the context toolbar; increase the **Width** to *220 px*, **Hardness** to *0%* and choose the **HSL Saturation** mode.

3   Now carefully paint around the wheel to really bring out the red tones. Additionally, single click on the red lights above the buildings to highlight them too.

We're now going to further bring out the red tones in the image, as well as the reflections on the road.

1   On the **Layers Panel**, choose **Add Pixel Layer** to create a new, blank pixel layer. Set this layer's **Blend Mode** to *Overlay* and its **Opacity** to *30%*.

Width: 300 px ▾   Opacity: 100 % ▾   Flow: 100 % ▾   Hardness: 0 % ▾   More ⌖   Stabiliser ⌐° ⟲   Length: 35 ▾   Symmetry 1 ▾   Mirror   Blend Mode: Normal ▾

2 On the **Tools Panel**, select the **Paint Brush Tool**. Change the **Width** to *300 px* and ensure the **Hardness** is at *0%*.

3 On the **Colour Panel**, set the active colour to *RGB 255,20,0* for a strong red tone.

4 Now paint over most of the red-toned parts of the image; the reflection in the road, the lit buildings in the background and the lights above the buildings. When painting over the wheel again, reduce the **Width** of the brush to around *200 px*; this avoids leaving a glow around the edges.

Resource

enhancing_low_light_imagery.afphoto (*03. Tightening composition* snapshot)

Tightening up the composition

As a final step, we're going to give the image a horizontal crop to remove some of the sky and road in the foreground, which will give a more panoramic feel.

1 From the **Tools Panel**, select the **Crop Tool** (C).

2 On the crop grid, drag the top edge handle down to crop out the sky, and drag the bottom edge handle up to crop out some of the pavement and road. We're aiming for a nicely balanced composition that maintains a good rule-of-thirds balance between the top and bottom of the wheel.

3 Click **Apply** to commit the crop.

That concludes our edits to this image!

STACKING FOR POWERFUL NOISE REDUCTION

Stacking for noise reduction is popular with astrophotographers, but is explored to a lesser degree for other types of photography. The idea is to shoot a burst of images for a composition; these images are then stacked and averaged to remove or reduce elements (i.e., sensor noise) that differ between images. It means you can shoot a series of handheld images at a high ISO (e.g., 3200), then gain a significant reduction in noise without compromising the detail.

1 Select **File > New Stack**.

2 In the dialog, choose **Add** and navigate to where you downloaded the resources. Within the Stacking folder, select the ten images (beginning with _1120541.jpg) and choose **Open**.

3 Click **OK**. A new document will open with all the images placed into a live layer stack.

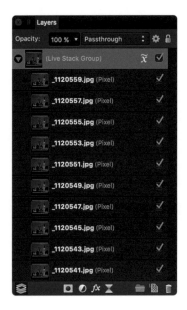

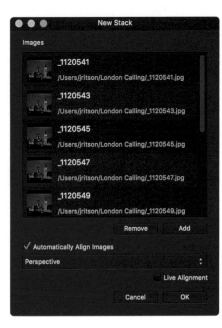

Resource

stacking_for_noise_reduction.afphoto (*01. Stacking the images* snapshot)
Stacking folder (_1120541.jpg - _1120559.jpg)

You can preview a single image by expanding the stack on the **Layers Panel** and 'isolating' it; click the image thumbnail with the option ⌥ key (Mac) or alt key (Win) pressed. This reveals the extent of noise removed by stacking.

4 Now we'll create a merged composite layer that we can work on further. From the **Layer Menu**, choose **Merge Visible**. A new pixel layer will be created. For improved editing performance, hide the Live Stack Group by unchecking it in the **Layers Panel**.

Before

After

Heavy tonal work

It's time to heavily alter the tones in this image. The combination of light pollution in the sky and mixed artificial lighting has resulted in an unpleasant orange colour cast.

1 From the **Filters Menu**, choose **Apply Image**.

2 In the dialog, click **Use Current Layer As Source**, then check **Equations**.

The goal here is to use a simple channel-based equation to shift the image's tonal balance.

3 Change the **Equation Colour Space** from *RGB* to *LAB*.

4 Under the **DB** entry, replace the initial Sb entry with *lerp(Sa,Sb,0.2)*. Lerp stands for linear interpolation, and we're essentially mapping the 'b' channel to a mix of both the 'a' and 'b' channels. Click **Apply**.

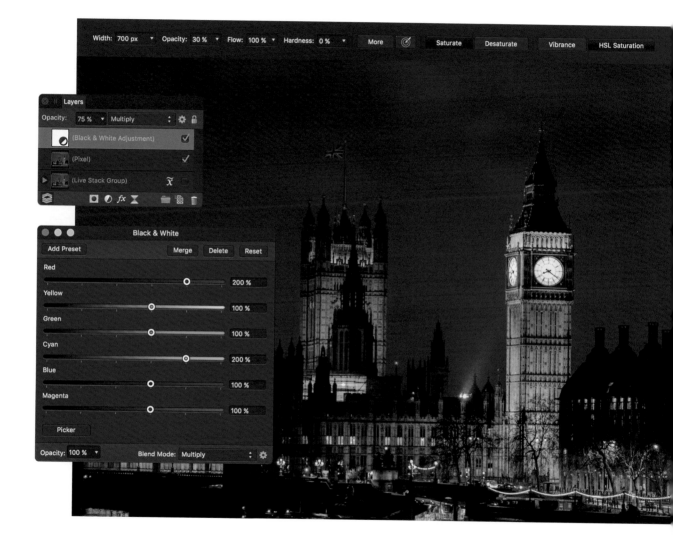

Additionally, we're going to employ the same technique used for the London Eye image previously (p. 230), i.e. Apply a Black and White adjustment (with Multiply blend mode) and saturate selectively with the **Sponge Brush Tool**; use adjustment settings shown above.

Target those red and blue tones to make them pop! Go over the same area several times to build up layers of saturation.

237

Resource

stacking_for_noise_reduction.afphoto (*03. Finishing touches* snapshot)

Finishing touches

It's time to finalise this image by adding some diffusion and tweaking the tones.

1 From the **Select Menu**, choose **Deselect Layers**, then from the **Layer Menu**, choose **New Live Filter Layer > Diffuse Glow Filter**.

2 In the Live Diffuse Glow settings, adjust values as shown. This produces a diffusion effect on most of the foreground, adding a soft glow without being too overpowering.

3 From the **Layer Menu**, choose **New Adjustment Layer > HSL Adjustment**.

4 For *Master*, *Reds*, *Yellows* and *Cyans*, change the **Saturation Shift** in each to *-30%*, *30%*, *-40%* and *30%*, respectively. This takes more colour out of the sky whilst keeping the buildings and artificial lights vibrant.

We're now finished with this image!

HDR AT NIGHT

One great way of enhancing detail and tackling the challenging dynamic range conditions that night-time imposes is by shooting a bracketed series of exposures and HDR merging them. HDR merging blends the most detailed pixels from the images and can improve the overall 'precision' and quality of the image—even with high ISO imagery.

HDR Merging

We'll merge our three exposures and tone map the results in the **Tone Mapping Persona**.

1 Select **File > New HDR Merge**.

2 In the dialog, choose **Add** and navigate to where you downloaded the resources. Within the HDR folder, select the three images (beginning with _1131808.tif) and choose **Open**.

3 In the New HDR Merge dialog, check **Automatically remove ghosts**. Uncheck **Noise Reduction**, as we don't need to use it, then choose **OK**. The images will then be aligned and merged to a 32-bit HDR document.

4 From the **Presets Panel** (*Default* category), choose *High contrast black and white* to produce a monochrome look.

High contrast black and white

5 On the **Tone Map Panel**, reduce **Tone Compression** to *0%* and increase **Local Contrast** to *60%*. Click **Apply** at top left to commit the tone map.

Perspective correction

We're now going to correct the unwanted 'trapezoid' effect the building exhibits.

1 With the (Pixel) layer selected, select the **Perspective Tool** from the **Tools Panel**.

2 In Perspective settings, set **Mode** to *Source* and reposition the top corner handles of the grid over the building top corners.

To help when aligning the handles to horizontal, try turning **Snapping** on via the **Toolbar**.

3 Reposition both bottom corner handles to the bottom of the metal fencing so the slant matches that of the building.

4 Once the perspective grid is lined up, switch **Mode** to *Destination*.

5 Drag the two top handles outwards to line them up vertically to the two bottom handles. Snapping makes this process easier.

6 Once you're happy that the building's verticals are straight, click **Apply**.

The perspective correction has created some unwanted alpha transparency which we can remove.

1 From the **Tools Panel**, select the **Crop Tool**.

2 Drag the bottom edge handle upwards to crop out most of the transparency; also drag the right edge handle slightly to the left to centre the building.

3 Click **Apply**.

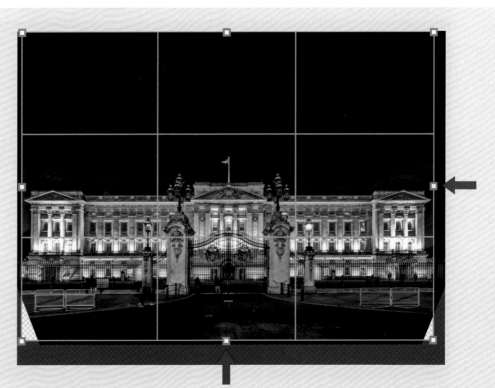

Resource

HDR_at_night.afphoto (*03. Filling in the blanks* snapshot)

Filling in the blanks

We're now going to fill in the remaining transparent areas by inpainting them.

1 With the (Pixel) layer selected, on the **Layer Menu**, choose **Rasterise**.

2 From the **Tools Panel**, select the **Inpainting Brush Tool**.

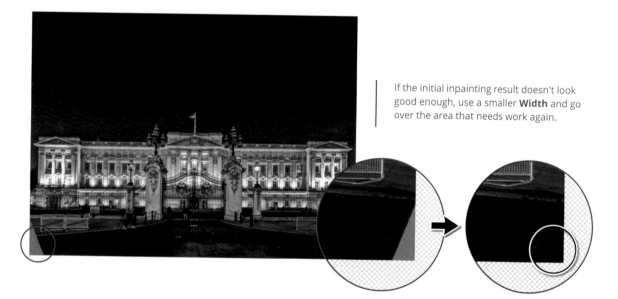

If the initial inpainting result doesn't look good enough, use a smaller **Width** and go over the area that needs work again.

3 On the context toolbar, set a larger **Width**; a value of *120 px* will suffice. Zoom in to each corner and brush over the transparent area.

Resource

HDR_at_night.afphoto (*04. Finishing touches* snapshot)

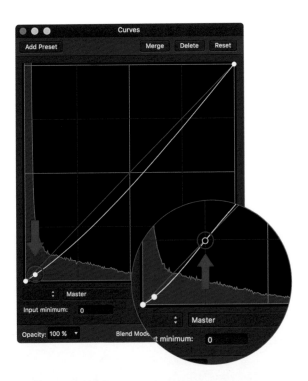

Finishing touches

1 From the **Layer Menu**, choose **New Adjustment Layer > Curves Adjustment**.

2 In Curves settings, click on the white graph line near the bottom left of the graph to create a node, and drag it vertically downwards.

3 Click on the curve on the first quarter line to create a second node, and drag it upwards to meet the red diagonal line.

This will deepen the shadow tones slightly whilst giving the midtones and highlights a slight raise. Finally, we'll crop the image again to tighten the focus on the building.

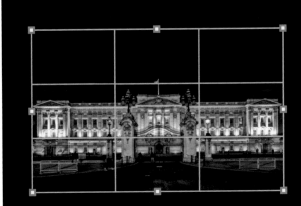

1 From the **Tools Panel**, select the **Crop Tool**.

2 Drag the top edge handle down until the top horizontal thirds line sits just under the flag.

3 Click **Apply**.

We're now finished with the editing of this image! However, because we began by merging images to an HDR document, we're working in a 32-bit unbounded colour format. This is nothing to worry about as Affinity Photo is smart enough to convert the colour format and colour profile when exporting to an 8-bit format (such as JPEG) or 16-bit format (such as TIFF).

7

Mother of Millions

Expanding depth of field with Focus Merging
by *Steven Randolph*

Focus merging brings together many images of differing focus points. With some additional retouch work the results are truly stunning.

BEFORE YOU GET STARTED

Resources

 You can get all the resources that are referenced in this project from:

https://affin.co/motherofmillions

Knowledge of Affinity Photo

To get the most from undertaking this project, you will need to:

- Be familiar with the interface of Affinity Photo. You can learn more about the interface in the Interface Tour chapter, starting on p. 13.

- Follow along with example resources by navigating and viewing snapshots that are saved in your project file. Named snapshots are suggested at stages throughout the project. See p. 9.

- Have good core skills. See the skills table below to see which additional aspects of Affinity Photo you need to be confident with to complete this project:

Adjustments	p. 100
Masking	p. 116
Layers	p. 122
Sharpening	p. 132

INTRODUCTION

Macro photography can reveal amazing worlds that are unseen in everyday life. Even ordinary objects can reveal staggering detail when viewed up close.

Unfortunately, the laws of physics conspire against us. As we get closer to the photographic subject our depth of field shrinks. We can use smaller and smaller apertures to try and compensate, but then we are left with a new challenge. As the size of our aperture gets smaller, the optical resolution of our image also shrinks, leaving us with a 'soft' image.

The advent of modern computers gives us a solution to our problems. We can use a large aperture to preserve all the detail we want, then take a series of images with different focus points and merge the in-focus areas together. This expands the depth of field, and maintains our image sharpness and resolution!

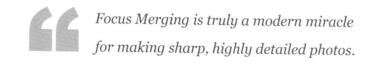

Focus Merging is truly a modern miracle for making sharp, highly detailed photos.

SHOOT DETAILS

> *It was a warm and dreary Florida winter at Weedon Island. My initial plan to capture some interesting plant species was being thwarted by overcast sun and a 20mph sea breeze.*

Focus Merging requires a series of images with relatively little movement between them, and I was not going to get that here. My plan changed from struggling with poor lighting conditions, to taking the photos under more controlled conditions. On my way home, I spotted a tall plant stalk just starting to bloom. It was an invasive succulent from Madagascar called Mother of Millions (*Bryophyllum delagoense*), named for the hundreds of plantlets that bud at the ends of its leaves. I trimmed a stalk, leaving about 15cm (6in) of stem with the flower and set it in a small container with some water.

Once back at the studio I filled a small bottle with water, then wedged the stalk into the bottle with paper towel so it was secure.

For this project, I would be taking images of a slightly larger subject than I usually do with a lens that can autofocus and a diopter (close-up filter) attached. As a result, I decided to use the lens's focus ring instead of a more complex automated setup, turning the ring carefully between each photo to get a good set of images.

Getting started with shooting images for focus merging needn't be daunting; you can still achieve good results with just a tripod and a lens that can be manually focused, adjusting focus slightly between each shot.

FILENAMES	
motherOfMillions-1.jpg - motherOfMillions-41.jpg	

GEAR	
TRIPOD:	Yes
CAMERA:	Canon 80d
LENS:	Canon EF 50mm f1.8
	Raynox DCR-150 Diopter
LIGHTING:	Flash

SETTINGS	
SHOOTING MODE:	Manual
EXPOSURE:	1/200
APERTURE:	4.0
ISO:	100
EXP. BIAS	0
EXP. PROG:	None
METERING:	Evaluative
FORMATS:	JPG

LOCATION	
Studio	
https://affin.co/locmom	

CONDITIONS	
Cool and well lit	

A dedicated macro lens is a good investment if you're keen about macro photography. However, you can also 'reverse' your normal lenses for greater magnification (look up 'lens reversing rings' on the Internet) or use macro extension tubes.

Some cameras also offer focus bracketing; you determine the number of shots to take and the focus differential, then upon pressing the shutter the camera will automate the process, adjusting focus between each shot.

POST SHOOT EDITING

Resource

mother_of_millions.afphoto (*01. Focus Merging* snapshot)
MotherOfMillions-1.jpg - MotherOfMillions-41.jpg

With the photos 'in hand', it was time to assemble everything. My first step was to use Affinity Photo's **Focus Merge** function to do all of the 'heavy lifting' for us. Because the Focus Merge algorithm cannot tell what is desirable detail and what is not, I expected to retouch a few artefacts that arose from merging.

After that, some reconstructive surgery was needed on areas where details were washed out by overlapping objects—I used a combination of cloning and healing tools. With retouching done, it was time to correct some lighting issues related to the background. Finally, I wanted to sharpen and adjust the colour and contrast.

FOCUS MERGING

The initial stage begins with Focus Merging the image sequence.

1 Select **File > New Focus Merge**.

2 In the Focus Merge dialog, click **Add**, then navigate to and select MotherOfMillions-1.jpg and then MotherOfMillions-41.jpg with the shift key (⇧) pressed. All 41 images should be selected.

   It's really useful to add images in Date Taken order. This helps to navigate through source images 'front to back' during retouching later.

3 Click **Open**, and then click **OK**.

   Depending on your computer's specification, the focus merging operation may take some time to process.

Once Focus Merging starts, it will proceed through three steps: image alignment, depth map creation, and finally merging all the images together. When the operation completes we will be left with our focus merged image on the (Pixel) layer and an automatically opened **Sources Panel**.

Resource

mother_of_millions.afphoto (*02. Removing Halos* snapshot)

REMOVING HALOS

When an edge defocuses between images, it creates a contrast gradient that can sometimes confuse the Focus Merging algorithm into treating it as desirable detail. This causes halos and contrast artefacts around edges.

Affinity Photo allows us to selectively retouch from our Sources Panel's input images using both cloning and healing.

1 On the **Tools Panel**, select the **Clone Brush Tool** (S).

2 On the tool's context toolbar, ensure Source is set to *Global*.

3 Select **Layer > New Layer** to retouch onto and name it *Halo Correction Global Cloning*.

In order to preserve sharp edges and fix the halos near the edges, we want to retouch only from source images that are in focus near the areas we want to edit.

4 At the bottom left of the **Sources Panel**, click the eye icon to preview source images. Click through the images to preview the one that is in focus near the area you will work on (images numbered 27 to 30 worked for the area below). Click the eye icon again to untoggle source image visibility.

5 With a large-width **Clone Brush** and **Hardness** set to *0%*, paint away the halo so it blends into the background.

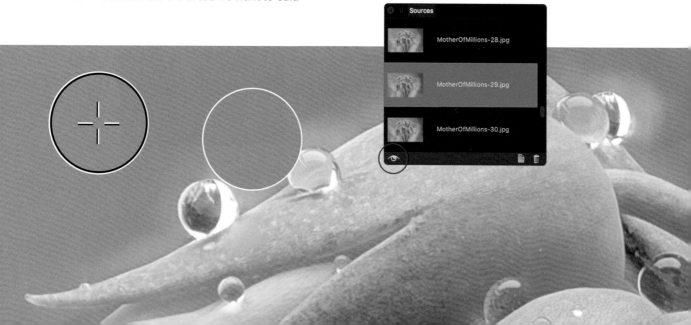

6   Move along the outside of the flower looking for more halos, while previewing, selecting and cloning-in new in-focus source images as you go. Remember that you need to constantly swap to the source image that is most in focus for that area.

After looking through a few source images you should get a feel for the depth of the image and retouching speed up as you settle in to the flow.

> By default, the Sources Panel will appear undocked but will be of a fixed height. To reveal more source images, increase the panel's height by dragging from the bottom of the panel.

Local cloning

To finish off correcting halos, I created an additional layer called *Halo Correction Local Cloning* and changed the context toolbar's Source from *Global* to be *Layers Beneath*. In doing so, I was able to correct small areas by cloning from the merged document's lower (Pixel) layer. Before cloning, I used the option ⌥ key (Mac) or alt key (Win) to set the clone source directly from the canvas.

Resource
mother_of_millions.afphoto (*03. Retouching* snapshot)

RETOUCHING LOST DETAIL

While focus merging we often have one object in front of another. When the rear object comes into focus, the front object blurs to be larger than its original size. The area between the front object when it is in and out of focus creates a space where the front object's blur obscures the background object as it comes into focus. This leads to a loss of detail at the transition where the two objects intersect.

This is detail that we can never retrieve. But that doesn't stop us from faking it. The combination of the Clone and Healing brushes together makes for fast and seamless retouching.

Cloning to lay out patches of detail

1   Create a new layer to clone onto, naming it *Retouch Cloning*.

2   Select the **Clone Brush Tool** and set the Source on the context toolbar to *Layers Beneath* and set the **Hardness** to *0%*.

3   Press the option ⌥ key (Mac) or alt key (Win) while clicking the area of the image you want the tool to sample from.

4   Brush in the soft areas with details from nearby areas. Don't worry about the painted-in detail being blotchy and poorly blended in for the moment.

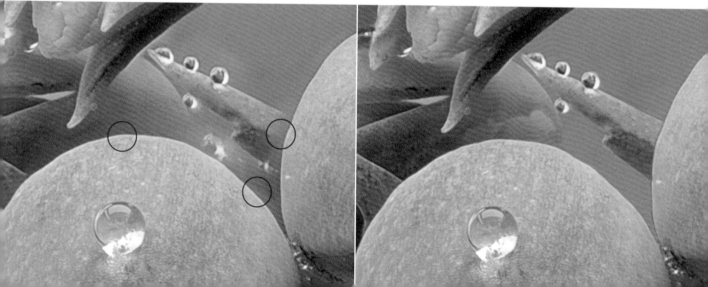

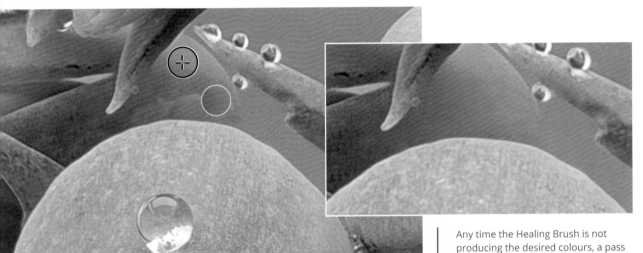

Any time the Healing Brush is not producing the desired colours, a pass with the Clone Tool first will help set the colour.

Healing to blend in tones and colour

1 Create a new layer, naming it *Retouch Healing*.

2 From the **Tools Panel**, select the **Healing Brush Tool** (J), then set the Source to *Current Layer & Below* and set the brush **Hardness** to *0%*.

3 Just as with cloning, hold the option ⌥ key (Mac) or alt key (Win) and click an area you wish to sample from.

4 Paint over any splotchy areas that you cloned. The healing brush samples details from the point you select, but samples colours and tones from around the brush. We first went over the area with the clone brush to set the colours and tones of the area we want to fix, and now we use the healing brush to blend the colours in smoothly.

GLOBAL ADJUSTMENTS

Now the hard work is done, all that's left is to adjust the colour and sharpen our image.

- From the **Layer Menu**, select **New Live Filter Layer > Unsharp Mask Filter**. Since the image is already pretty sharp, it's best to exercise moderation. Set the **Radius** to *0.9 px* and the **Factor** to *0.616*.

From **Layer > New Adjustment Layer**, apply several adjustments one by one:

- Select **White Balance Adjustment** and set **White Balance** to *-3%* to remove a little bit of the yellow cast in the image.

- Select **Vibrance Adjustment**, and set **Vibrance** to *-18%*.

- Select **HSL Adjustment** and move the **Saturation Shift** to *22%* to give more intense colours.

- To darken the shadow a little, select **Curves Adjustment**. To prevent the highlights and midtones from being affected, click on the graph line at the upper right of the graph to introduce a node (**1**), then click to add another node (**2**) in the bottom quarter of the graph; dragging the node downwards to darken the shadows.

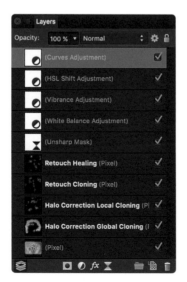

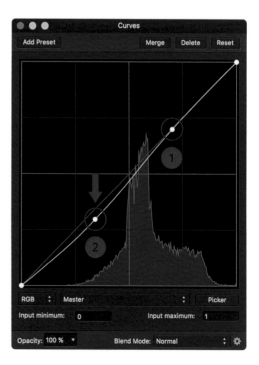

BACKGROUND DITHERING

Resource

mother_of_millions.afphoto
(*05. Background Dither* snapshot)
(*06. Background Correction* snapshot)

When halos were removed with the clone brush, small colour gradients between our cloned area and the original background layer were created, shown as visible seams. To fix this, I zoomed the image out to see the problem areas better and used the healing brush on a new *Background Dither* layer (placed above Retouch Healing layer) while sampling from the background to brush away the seams. The healing brush blends or dithers between the two slightly different colour gradients and adds some noise it samples.

BACKGROUND CORRECTION

With our retouching done we can zoom out a bit and get a feel for the image. I found the darker right side of the background a little distracting. To fix this, I'll shift the hue and lightness using an adjustment layer and masking.

1 Above the Background Dither layer, create a new HSL adjustment by going to the **Layer Menu** and select **New Adjustment Layer > HSL Adjustment**. Name the layer to *Background Gradient Fix* and move the Unsharp Mask layer to top of the layer stack.

2 With the HSL Adjustment layer selected, add a mask using **Layer > New Mask Layer**, then invert the mask by selecting **Invert** from the same menu.

> To reveal your mask temporarily, press the option ⌥ key (Mac) or alt key (Win) while clicking the adjustment layer's mask thumbnail.

3 Select the **Paint Brush Tool** (B) and set its **Hardness** to *0%*, **Radius** to *4000 px* and its colour to white.

4 On the **Layers Panel**, with the mask thumbnail selected, paint in the area you want to be affected. In this case the darker right side of the image.

5 Select the Background Gradient Fix layer and adjust its HSL settings (below) so it blends in with the rest of the image.

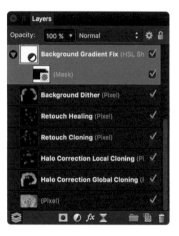

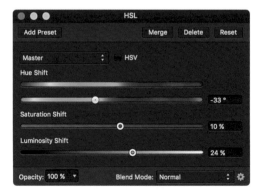

To finish the background, create a Corner Saturation HSL adjustment layer with a **Saturation Shift** of *54%*. Use masking to affect just the very bottom-right corner of the image, where more saturation is needed.

We're done! With all the Focus Merge artefacts removed, you wouldn't even know the photo was composed of 41 images.

When you do things right, people won't be sure you've done anything at all.

CHAPTER 4

Commercial

Leaving the Enthusiasts chapter behind, this chapter focuses on how Affinity Photo can be used in commercial environments.

We'll explore fashion retouching, landscape panoramics, print design and food retouching.

Elegance

Keeping portrait retouching real by *Mark Ivkovic*

Follow Mark as he takes a subtle and sympathetic approach to great product retouching, using a mix of classic and contemporary techniques.

BEFORE YOU
GET STARTED

Resources

 You can get all the resources that are referenced in this project from:
https://affin.co/elegance

Knowledge of Affinity Photo

To get the most from undertaking this project, you will need to:

- Be familiar with the interface of Affinity Photo. You can learn more about the interface in the Interface Tour chapter, starting on p. 13.

- Follow along with example resources by navigating and viewing snapshots that are saved in your project file. Named snapshots are suggested at stages throughout the project. See p. 9.

- Have good core skills. See the skills table below to see which additional aspects of Affinity Photo you need to be confident with to complete this project:

Developing raw images	p. 89
Adjustments	p. 100
Masking	p. 116
Sharpening	p. 132

SHOOT DETAILS

FILENAMES	
elegance.dng	

GEAR	
TRIPOD:	No
CAMERA:	Leica M9
LENS:	Leica 50mm f/2 Summicron
LIGHTING:	Natural window light

SETTINGS	
SHOOTING MODE:	Manual
EXPOSURE:	1/160
APERTURE:	f/2
ISO:	320
EXP. BIAS	0
EXP. PROG:	Manual
METERING:	External light meter (Sekonic)
FORMATS:	RAW

LOCATION
Bates Mill Studio, Huddersfield, England UK
https://affin.co/locelegance

CONDITIONS
Indoor but overcast day

POST SHOOT EDITING

With this photograph my main aim for post production was to enhance the feel of the image sympathetically whilst retaining the honest beauty of the subject. Portrait retouching can be seen as a dark art with many different approaches. I'll take you through my process and the reasons behind doing what I do, providing you with ideas and techniques to bring to your own portrait work.

Going from the original Leica DNG raw image to finished file ready for output, I'll explain how I deal with variations in skin tone, fix blemishes, enhance make-up, all while retaining a true representation of my subject. I'll give insights into my use of frequency separation, layer blend modes, dodge & burn, local colour enhancement and careful use of 'liquify' warping effects.

RAW DEVELOPMENT

Upon opening the raw image in **Develop Persona** the first task is to take off the automatic tone curve that is being applied to the image. I like to do this as I have the freedom to make my own decisions about tone.

1   From the **File Menu**, select **Open**, and then navigate to, select and open elegance.dng. The raw image is loaded in Develop Persona.

2   On the **Toolbar**, select **Assistant Options**.

3   Change the **Tone curve** setting to *Take no action*.

I then need to tweak some basic adjustments to prepare the image to be retouched.

- At the top-right of the **Toolbar**, enable **Show Clipped Highlights**.

This will show areas of 'blown' highlights (i.e., lost detail) as a red overlay. In this case, an area of the background and the subject's left cheek has been clipped in the highlight so I'll 'pull back' the 'lost' detail.

4   In the **Basic Panel**, lower the **Exposure** slider until the red clipped overlay disappears (*-0.6* is about right).

5   I also noticed a general lack of shadow areas in the image so I opted to deepen the blacks by adjusting **Blackpoint** to *6%*. This can be a trial-and-error procedure— adjust the sliders until you find your own happy medium. My point of reference was the shadow areas of the Iris and the hair.

6   **Clarity** is adjusted to remove a little of the softness caused by the strong backlight, while reducing **Vibrancy** makes the skin tones less strong.

7   To finish raw development, click **Develop**. This creates our initial developed image in the Photo Persona as a single Background layer.

 As I know I'm going to be retouching the image anyway, I treat raw development as a base stage and then jump to Photo Persona to work on the developed file there.

IMAGE REVIEW

When retouching photographs, once I have the base image I'll make a plan (or some notes) of what to do to before I begin. This will keep things under control for later.

My main aim is to emphasise my subject rather than make any larger changes. As a result, the retouching will be subtle and soft, working on skin texture and colour to make it more uniform. I'll emphasise the make-up and give the eyes a little enhancement just to amplify the effect of my subject's gaze. The left-hand cheek of my subject has lost a lot of colour detail so I'll also show you a little trick to bring back highlights that have been lost.

> *I'd advise making changes a little at a time and to constantly check back to your original base image to make sure you're not getting carried away!*

RETOUCHING SKIN: FREQUENCY SEPARATION

Resource

elegance.afphoto (*01. Frequency separation (Low)* snapshot)

This method of retouching up until a few years ago was a fairly laborious task. However, Affinity Photo now provides a direct filter to enable frequency separation, which is pretty handy. It essentially separates the image's details from its colours, leaving you with two layers to work on independently.

How is this of use? Well you can alter tone without altering texture. For example, you can even out skin tone and blotchy areas by brushing over with tones sampled from 'good' areas while the original detail and texture in that area remains untouched.

- **High frequency** layer: holds the **detail** information such as **texture** and **edges**.

- **Low frequency** layer: holds all the **tone** information (hue).

Enabling frequency separation

1 On the **Filters Menu**, select **Frequency Separation**.

2 Drag the High Frequency/Low Frequency Split screen slider to reveal more or less of your 'detail' and 'tone' layers, respectively.

3 Adjust the **Radius** setting in the Settings pane. A setting of *1.5 px* is perfect as it pulls enough skin texture into the High Frequency Layer (detail) without pulling through too much of the tonal imperfections.

4 Click **Apply**.

5 On the **Layers Panel**, click on each layer name and rename them. Change High Frequency to be named *Detail* and Low Frequency to *Tones*.

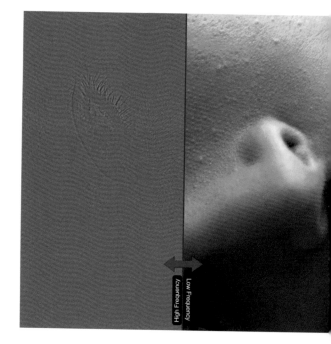

An increasing Radius value increases detail in the High Frequency layer while at the same time increasing blurring in the Low Frequency layer (and vice versa). The key is getting a balance. As a useful tip, try zooming into an area of high detail and adjust the Radius setting for that.

LOW FREQUENCY: TONES

Bump retouching

1   Select the Tones layer.

2   On the **Tools Panel**, select the **Healing Brush Tool**.

3   On the context toolbar, set a small soft-edged brush (**Width** *15 px*, **Hardness** *0%*). Check **Aligned** so the sampling cursor will move in relation to the brush cursor.

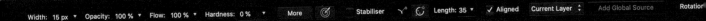

Width: 15 px ▾   Opacity: 100 % ▾   Flow: 100 % ▾   Hardness: 0 % ▾   More   ⊘   Stabiliser   ⅄° ↻   Length: 35 ▾   ✓ Aligned   Current Layer ⇕   Add Global Source   Rotation

4   Press the option ⌥ key (Mac) or alt key (Win), while selecting a 'source' area under the cross-hair cursor from which to sample from. Choose an area that looks similar to the target area to be corrected.

5   Drag (don't click) over the target area with the white circular cursor to soften the bump's appearance.

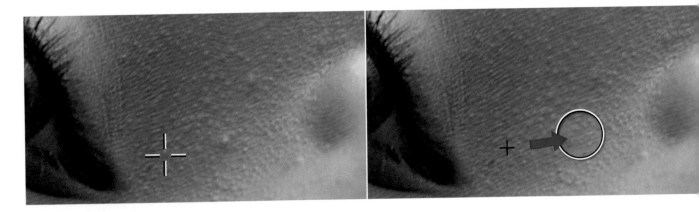

I'll often keep selecting new sample areas by further clicking with the option ⌥ key (Mac) or alt key (Win) as I move around the skin, always trying to sample a source close to where you are working on to retain the correct overall tones. Once set, it's just a matter of working around the face, painting over the areas and small blemishes.

> *Paint rather than click, as I find I get better results with a small brush painting over the area of a bump rather than setting the brush to bigger and just clicking once per bump.*

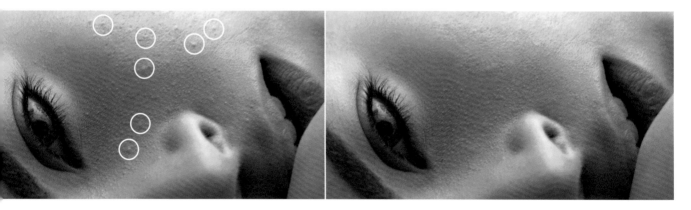

This can be a long process so keep clicking back to your original to see your progress, ensuring that you're not removing too much of anything. The idea is to retain the feel of the skin but to lessen the imperfections.

Blemish retouching

Larger areas of imperfection can also be treated with the Blemish Removal Tool.

1 With the Tones layer still selected, select the **Blemish Removal Tool** from the same flyout as the Healing Brush Tool.

2 Set the brush **Width** so the white circular cursor just encompasses the size of the blemish area that needs work and simply click to fix.

Improve your productivity by using the [or] keys to increase or decrease the brush width as you paint!

Remember to keep scrolling back through your **History Panel** to see how you're progressing with skin retouching, make sure you're not 'going too far' and make sure the texture is still there. It's very easy to get carried away and become obsessed by every slight bump, so remember to keep it believable. Good retouching should essentially go unnoticed in the final output.

Adjusting skin tone

Many times in portrait work the subject may have differing skin tones from face to body. This can be due to the light, make-up or skin issues. At this point, I want to alter the tone of the skin throughout the image to unify it somewhat.

1 Select the Tones layer, then click **Add Pixel Layer**. Name the layer *SkinColouring*. This enables me to alter the tone without having to worry about the texture and detail.

2 Set the layer's blend mode to *Colour*. With this mode, whatever colour I choose can be painted on to the layer and applied non-destructively to the layers below. This lets me apply more localised make-up tweaks.

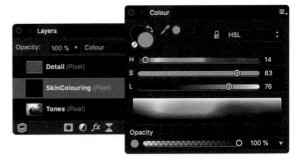

3 Let's sample a good skin tone. Use the **Colour Picker Tool** (I) to look for the tone you feel is a best natural fit. My picked colour (*RGB 245,167,143; HSL 14,83,76*) was sampled from the subject's left cheek.

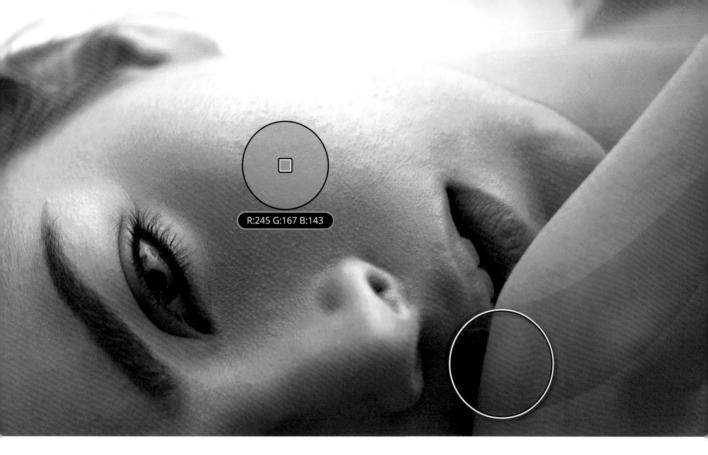

R:245 G:167 B:143

4 On the **Tools Panel**, select the **Paint Brush Tool** (B), and a soft-edged brush (**Hardness** *0%*) on the context toolbar.

5 Paint over the entire skin. You'll see the image looking a little strange, but don't worry we'll be lessening the effect next.

6 On the **Filters Menu**, select **Blur > Gaussian Blur** and set a **Radius** of *3 px*. The idea here is to soften your brush work and edges.

7 Lower the layer **Opacity** so until you find your happy medium for the effect. Remember you're looking for a natural averaging of the tones, not to strongly alter them. I chose *16%* but anywhere between *10* to *25%* is acceptable.

Recovering skin highlights

Here's a little trick if your exposure has lost highlight detail in skin areas (seen on shiny skin and with strong light sources). Using a similar method as before, you can paint back some colour into the cheek.

1 Add a new pixel layer directly above the SkinColouring layer, named *HighRecover*.

2 Using an average soft brush with *10%* **Opacity**, *0%* **Hardness** and our previous sampled skin colour (*HSL 14,83,76*), paint back in some colour into the cheek and the tip of the nose. I'm not looking to have a perfect strong skin tone here but just to add some colour back to my highlights.

Dodge & Burn Sculpting

Next up I'll be enhancing the shape of my subject by amplifying the way the light is sculpting around her. I'll be looking at where the light is falling and where the shadows have formed, I'll then emphasis the effect by dodging (brightening) the highlights and burning (darkening) the shadows.

For highlights, I'll primarily work on the areas on the left of, and under the nose.

1 Create a new layer directly above the HighRecover layer. Name it *Dodge&Burn(Sculpt)*.

2 Apply a *50%* Greyscale fill. From the **Swatches Panel**, select the *Black 50%* swatch.

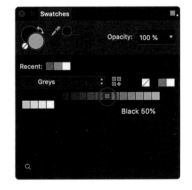

3 Select **Edit > Fill**, choosing the *Primary Colour* option.

4 Set the layer's blend mode to *Overlay*.

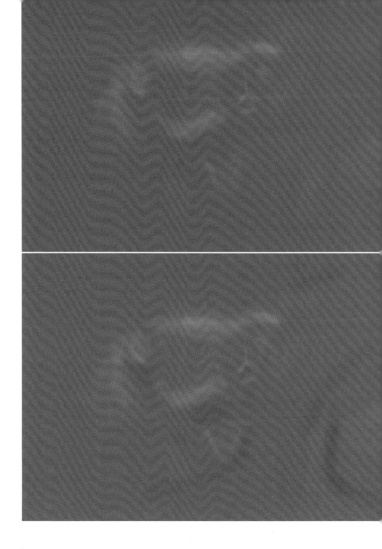

This will have no effect on our image as yet but by painting with dodge and burn tools you'll affect the lighting.

5 Select the **Dodge Brush Tool** and use a subtle soft brush of *10%* **Opacity**. Looking at the highlights and starting with a large brush, paint highlights to lighten, then slowly add to the image and reduce the brush size as you go.

6 Select the **Burn Brush Tool** with less **Opacity** (*5%*). Start with a larger brush width and work down (reducing width) as you paint over shadows. Look at how the light is falling and if you wish to enhance bone structure.

7 Lower the layer **Opacity** (to about *50%*) to get the effect you want.

To see the greyscale layer in isolation at any time, click on the layer's thumbnail with the option ⌥ key (Mac) or alt key (Win) pressed.

As with any skin effect, be careful of not going too strong with it as the appearance can quickly become 'too much'. Layer Opacity is your friend!

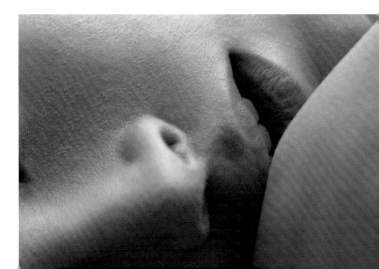

Resource

elegance.afphoto (*02. Frequency separation (High)* snapshot)

HIGH FREQUENCY: DETAILS

Now for the high frequency layer. I want to give the texture and edges a little 'pop' by sharpening up the details—this isn't a 'finishing' sharpen but just keeps things looking good.

1 Select the Detail layer.

2 On the **Layer Menu**, select **Duplicate**.

3 Drop the new layer's **Opacity** down to *25%*, keeping the layer's Blend Mode set to *Linear Light*.

Skin Texture

I now want to improve skin texture by introducing noise—this gives the appearance of soft delicate and natural skin.

1 Create a new 50% Greyscale layer above the duplicated layer as before, naming it *SkinTexture* and setting the blend mode to *Vivid Light*. The greyscale appearance will disappear.

2 On the **Filters Menu**, select **Noise > Add Noise** and adjust settings so a small amount of graininess is introduced.

3 Change the layer **Opacity** to *50%*.

To make the noise visible only over the skin, let's introduce a 'hide all' mask and then slowly reveal noise.

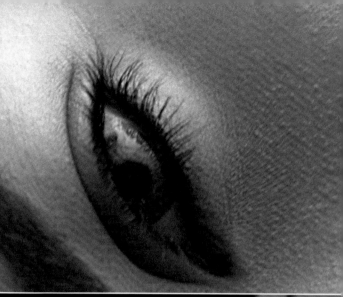

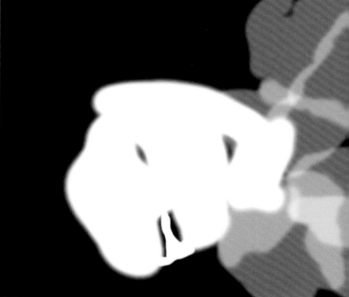

4 On the **Layer Menu**, select **New Empty Mask Layer**.

5 With the **Paint Brush Tool**, paint in the noise using a white brush on the selected mask layer. Apply brush strokes (*100% Opacity* and **Flow**; *50%* **Hardness**) slowly over the skin of the face, taking care to not go over the eyes and open area of the mouth.

6 Drop the **Opacity** to *75%*, then *50%* for the rest of the skin of the body, so noise is less visible in out of focus areas.

Use the number keys on your keyboard to quickly change the stroke opacity (e.g., 4 = 40% opacity, 4 and 3 = 43% opacity).

The final mask (in isolation) should show painted areas of varying opacity (white reveals more noise). To finish off, I'll group all these layers together into a Skin group for ease when coming back to them later.

Resource
Elegance.afphoto (*03. Retouching make-up* snapshot)

RETOUCHING MAKE-UP

The next step is to enhance the make-up on our subject. I'll give the lips a little more colour saturation, along with adding a little colour to the eye shadow. Plus, I'll shape the eyebrows and lastly give the eye a little bit more 'pop'.

For each area, I use a separate 'Colour blend or Hue Blend layer' much like previously with the skin tone layer—I'll sample the colour I wish to use and paint over the area I want to effect. I tend to interchange between hue and colour blend, colour has a stronger effect so is useful for stronger colours, hue is much softer and subtle so good for that kind of area.

Lips

1 Above the Skin group, create a new pixel layer with a *Colour* blend mode and name it *Lips*.

2 With the **Colour Picker Tool**, sample some colour from the subject's lip, then slightly increase the **S** (saturation), e.g. from *36* to *40*.

3 Paint the whole lip area, this time being careful around the edges. Give this layer a subtle **Gaussian Blur** (*3 px*) from the **Filters Menu** and lower the **Opacity** to around *30%*.

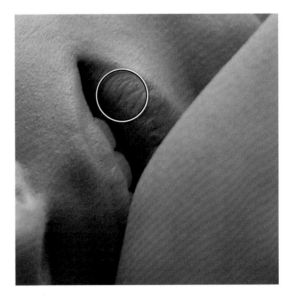

> *I prefer to have good make-up in place before taking photographs, but these techniques are handy if you later notice areas that aren't quite right.*

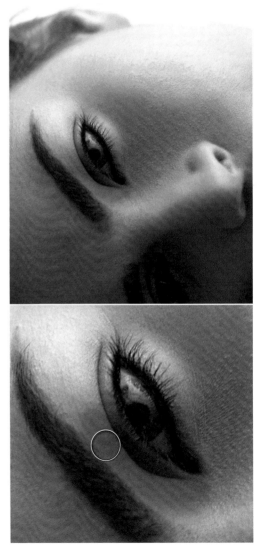

Eye make-up

1   Create a new layer called *Eye Make up* with a *Hue* blend mode. Paint using a darker colour (*HSL 11,48,28*) than the lips, and a softer brush with **Opacity** of *50%*, then *75%*.

2   Paint the area above the eye but below the brow to apply eye shadow.

3   Lower the layer **Opacity** to around *75%*.

Now the Lips and Eye Make Up layers are finished, group them into a *Make Up* group using **Arrange > Group**.

Eyebrow shaping

The eyebrows need darkening a little and have their shape added to using a similar method to that used for eye shadow make-up.

1 With the Make up group selected, choose **Insert inside the selection** on the **Toolbar**.

2 Create a new pixel layer named *Brows* with an *Overlay* blend mode. This will be nested inside the group.

3 With a soft brush, sample a dark hair colour from the image and then just paint over the area of the eyebrows, adding extra to any part you wish to extend. Reduce the **Opacity** to lessen the effect as needed.

To shape the eyebrows a little more, I draw hairs back into areas I wish to fill. Create a new *Brow Shape* layer (*Normal* blend mode), and with a *1 px* brush, use the very dark colour we just sampled and draw the eyebrow hairs, following the natural direction of the hairs as you paint.

I tend to cross the hairs I paint too, to create a more 'matted' look.

To finish the eyebrows, apply a **Gaussian Blur** (*0.2 px*) and drop **Opacity** to a level where you can't see the brush strokes anymore (about 70% is fine).

This technique can also be used to add eyelashes around the subject's eye.

Enhancing eyes

The eyes are always an important final part to retouching—they are what we tend to look at first and they draw us into the portrait, so by giving them a little 'pop' we can make the subject even more appealing.

Using similar methods to those already we'll amplify the highlights and boost the shadows of the eye and iris.

1 On a new Pixel layer called *Eye Enhance*, set an *Overlay* blend mode.

2 Pick a small, soft brush and sample the highlight/catch light area in the eye. With the **Paint Brush Tool**, paint the sclera (white of the eye) along with the highlight on the iris.

3 Sample the pupil area for a deep colour and now paint the deep shadows of the pupil, around the edge of the iris and around the eyeliner area.

4 Apply a gentle **Gaussian Blur** (*4 px*) and lessen the effect by lowering the opacity until you're happy with the appearance.

Play with the blend modes to get the look just right.
I finally opted for a *Hard Light* blend mode with a layer **Opacity** of *19%*.

LIQUIFY

Liquify Persona offers some useful warping tools to affect the image. Instead of performing a Liquify operation early in the project, I decided to flatten all layers together, warping from that single layer.

Enlarging the eyes

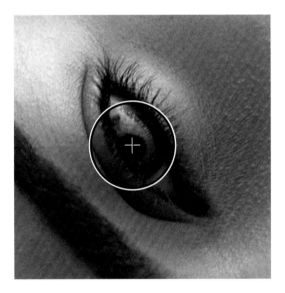

For this image, I'm just going to give the eyes a small increase in size.

1 On the **Layer Menu**, select **Merge Visible**. This creates a flattened new layer from only visible layers which can be named *Merged*.

2 Select **Liquify Persona** from the **Toolbar**.

3 Using the **Liquify Pinch Tool** (U), set the brush **Size** with the [and] keys to be slightly larger than the eyeball (around *300 px* on the **Brush Panel**).

4 Press the left mouse button until the eye grows to your preferred size.

Resource
elegance.afphoto (*05. Sharpening* snapshot)

SHARPENING

To finish, I tend to apply a quick sharpen. This step isn't for output and I'll often sharpen again depending upon how the image will be used.

Taking care not to affect noise previously added, I chose a Clarity filter.

- On the **Filters Menu**, select **Sharpen > Clarity**. Set the **Radius** to around *0.7 px*.

That finishes this retouching project!

You can use some or all of these procedures to enhance your own portrait work, always keeping in mind that a light touch will keep the overall effect real and believable.

For a more fantasy-like look, you could boost layer opacity or saturate your colours further—the power of Affinity Photo gives you complete flexibility to experiment. You're limited only by your own imagination!

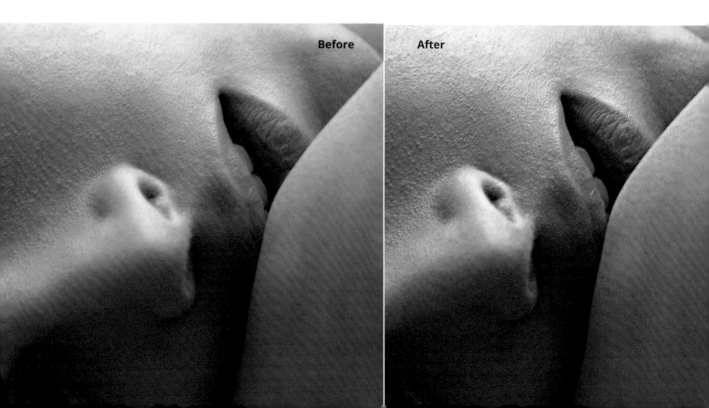

Before   **After**

2

Torres Del Paine

Creating stunning panoramics by *Timothy Poulton*

With Affinity Photo's automatic stitching engine and processing tools, you have everything you need to create award-winning panoramic works of art.

BEFORE YOU GET STARTED

Resources

 You can get all the resources that are referenced in this project from:

https://affin.co/torres (RAW/TIFFs/JPGs/Project file; 1.9GB)

https://affin.co/torresjpg (JPGs/ Project file; 1GB)

Knowledge of Affinity Photo

To get the most from undertaking this project, you will need to:

- Be familiar with the interface of Affinity Photo. You can learn more about the interface in the Interface Tour chapter, starting on p. 13.

- Follow along with example resources by navigating and viewing snapshots that are saved in your project file. Named snapshots are suggested at stages throughout the project. See p. 9.

- Have good core skills. See the skills table below to see which additional aspects of Affinity Photo you need to be confident with to complete this project:

Developing raw images	p. 89
Cropping	p. 92
Adjustments	p. 100

SHOOT DETAILS

Sunrise at Lake Pehoé in Chile Patagonia is one of the most popular locations I take my customers to on tour. Staying at the campsite right on the shore of the lake makes for a stunning setting for landscape photography. With all my tours, timing is everything: during Autumn, the sunrise across the mountains makes a perfect side-light effect, my favourite style of shooting.

To capture the Torres Del Paine scene, pre-sunrise (during nautical twilight) when the clouds catch the first light illuminating the mountains, I opted for a 25-s exposure which has the effect of creating movement in the clouds and smoothing out the choppy waves on the lake.

Timing is everything in this scene and preparation is the key—to shoot multiple frames you need to have everything setup, all your gear needs to be level with settings in manual mode, ready to go once the magic happens.

Image selection is the first step. It's important to ensure that all the frames have at least a 25% overlap and are exposed correctly using the same on-camera White Balance, Exposure, ISO and Aperture value.

FILENAMES	
_DSC6480.NEF to _DSC6488.NEF	
GEAR	
TRIPOD:	Sirui W2204
CAMERA:	Nikon D810
LENS:	Schneider 28mm Tilt Shift
LIGHTING:	Natural
SETTINGS	
SHOOTING MODE:	Manual
EXPOSURE:	25/1
APERTURE:	f/22
ISO:	160
EXP. BIAS	0
EXP. PROG:	Manual
METERING:	Spot
FORMATS:	RAW
LOCATION	
Torres de Paine	
Región de Magallanes y de la Antártica Chilena, Chile	
https://affin.co/loctorres	
CONDITIONS	
Perfect	

PRE-PROCESSING THE IMAGES

Resource

_DSC6480.NEF to _DSC6488.NEF

If you wish to skip this section, I've already processed the nine raw images into TIFF files for you. Go to p. 297 to continue.

Image adjustments

In Affinity Photo, we're going to develop each raw file in turn and export each as a high-quality image file; we'll then stitch these exported image files together to make the panorama.

1 Use **File > Open** to load one of the .NEF raw files (e.g., _DSC6480.NEF).

2 On the **Basic Panel**, set **Exposure** to *1*.

Set **Clarity** to *10%*. This will help 'open up' shadows and boost the contrast.

> When using Clarity, make sure you check for nasty halos in the final result. Like everything in life, it's all about moderation and extracting the most detail without pushing too hard.

I underexpose my images due to the dynamic range of the Nikon D810 and Affinity Photo's incredible ability to bring out detail in the shadows. With a slight adjustment, I have the correct exposure for my style of imagery, I prefer to embrace my 'dark side' in photography and believe it creates a fantastic mood.

Sharpening and Noise Reduction (Optional)

Increasing Clarity enhances the perceptual sharpness of the image. We don't have to, but we can also add some fine detail sharpening too. On the **Details Panel**, set the following options:

- Check **Detail Refinement**, and set **Radius** to *10%* and **Amount** to *60%* for a crisper image.

- Under **Noise Reduction**, set **Luminance** to *5%*. This softens the grain-like noise slightly.

Developing and Exporting

- After adjusting the raw development settings, develop the image by choosing **Develop**.

Now that the image has been developed, we've moved into the **Photo Persona**. From here, we'll export the image into a folder ready for panoramic stitching.

1 Choose **File > Export**.

2 On the format options, choose **TIFF**.

3 From the **Preset** pop-up menu, ensure *TIFF RGB 8-bit* is selected, then choose **Export**.

4 Navigate to a suitable folder, and click **Save**.

5 Repeat the above procedures for the remaining eight raw images, until you have a set of nine TIFF images in the folder ready for stitching.

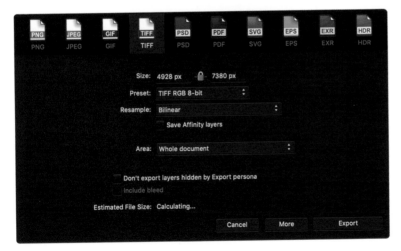

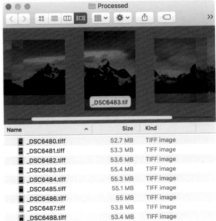

STITCHING & EDITING THE PANORAMA

Resource

torres_del_paine.afphoto (*01. Initial panorama stitch* snapshot)
_DSC6480.TIF to _DSC6488.TIF or _DSC6480.JPG to _DSC6488.JPG*

Creating the panorama

It's time to stitch the exported TIF images and create the panorama.

1 From the **File Menu**, choose
   New Panorama.

2 Choose **Add** and navigate to
   where you exported the
   images. Select them all and click
   Open.

3 Click **Stitch Panorama** to stitch
   images together. Once
   processed, a preview image of
   the stitched panorama will be
   created in the Panoramas
   window.

4 Click **OK**.

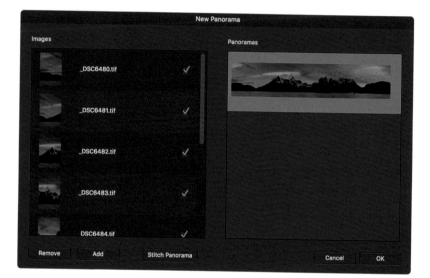

* For a reduced download time,
use the resources downloaded via
https://affin.co/torresjpg which
contain only the project file and
JPGs (not raw or TIFF files).

*What I love about Affinity Photo's stitching
engine is its ability to calculate a final
panorama with limited stitching or parallax errors,
even with moving objects like clouds and water.*

Resource
torres_del_paine.afphoto (*02. Cleaning up* snapshot)

You'll see that post-stitching, the top image edges show transparency tapering out. This is due to the difficulty of keeping the camera truly level over such a wide panoramic scene. It's a minor issue that can be easily fixed by cropping.

5   On the **Tools Panel**, select the **Crop Tool** (C).

6   On the context toolbar, click **Crop to opaque**, then choose **Apply** to commit the panorama.

7   In Photo Persona, rename the Panorama layer to be *Background* in the **Layers Panel** and lock it using the lock symbol.

Cleaning up

Although the stitching engine is very accurate, with long-exposure shooting you might still have to clean up a few sections of an image that have been affected by light change and movement.

First, we'll draw a selection area that restricts clean up to the sky only, while protecting the mountain from change. The sections (a) and (b) need fixing.

1   On the **Tools Panel**, choose the **Flood Select Tool**.

2   Drag right across the sky above to the problem area (a) until the **Tolerance** reaches around *15%*. The skyline will be selected precisely.

If the marquee selection is making it difficult to see the stitching errors, you can turn it off by toggling **View > Show Pixel Selection**. Don't forget to turn it back on for future use though!

3 On the **Tools Panel**, select the **Clone Brush Tool** (S).

4 On the context toolbar, increase the **Width** to *200 px* and reduce the **Hardness** to *0%*.

5 Zoom in to the problem area (a), and at a nearby point, click with the option ⌥ key (Mac) or alt key (Win) pressed to set it as the clone source.

6 Drag over the problem area to retouch and correct it.

7 Repeat this step for the other problem area (b).

8 Once the retouching is complete, from the **Select Menu**, choose **Deselect**.

Continue fixing any more stitching alignment errors, e.g. along the waterline, using the same cloning technique.

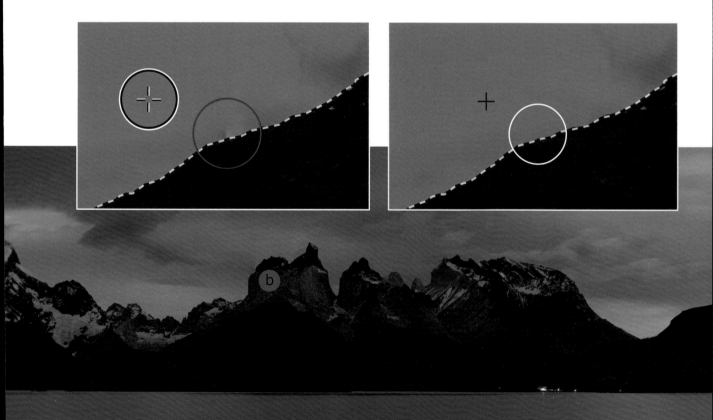

Blocking

A technique I have developed over the years when stitching panoramas is **Blocking**; selecting sections of the scene and squeezing and stretching to balance the overall composition. My aim here is to stretch the mountains to correct compression with the lens and to give the scene more power. I also need to add more water; we'll achieve both objectives using this technique.

1   On the **Tools Panel**, select the **Crop Tool** (C).

2   Drag the top handle up and the bottom handle down to extend the crop region beyond the document's boundaries. Extend the bottom area of the crop more than the top.

3 On the context toolbar, choose **Apply** to commit the crop and extend the document's canvas.

4 On the **Tools Panel**, select the **Rectangular Marquee Tool**. Drag and create a selection roughly 1/3 up the mountains towards the top of the image. You can drag from outside the canvas to ensure the selection encompasses the canvas edge.

5 From the **Layer Menu**, choose **Duplicate**. This will duplicate the selected content.

6 On the **Tools Panel**, select the **Move Tool** (V). Now drag the top edge handle up until the new layer stretches to fill the empty canvas.

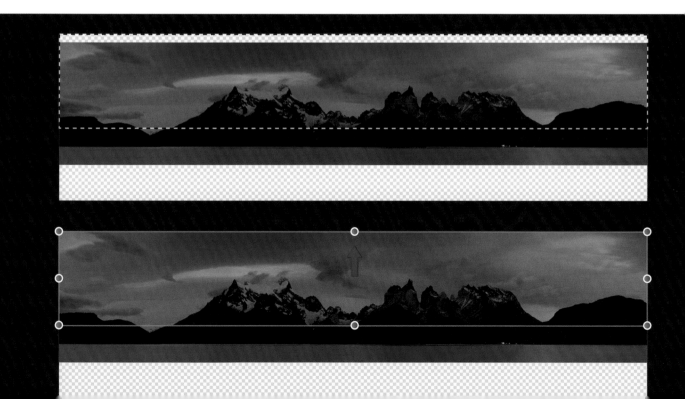

7 Now we'll take the same approach to extend the water. From the **Select Menu**, choose **Deselect**, then on the **Layers Panel**, select the original Background (Pixel) layer.

8 As before, from the **Tools Panel**, select the **Rectangular Marquee Tool**. Drag and create a selection over the water, starting from off canvas.

9 From the **Layer Menu**, choose **Duplicate**. Once again, from the **Tools Panel**, select the **Move Tool**. Now drag the bottom edge handle down until the water stretches to fill the empty canvas.

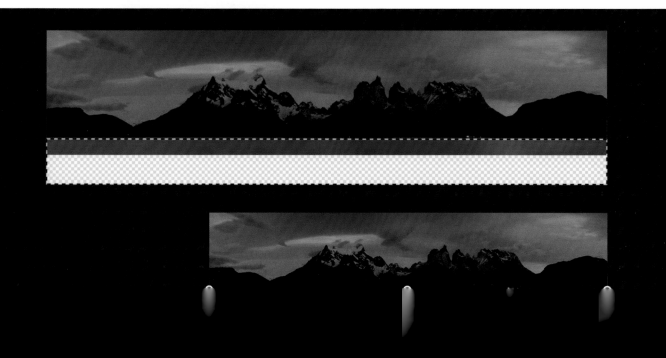

10 On the **Tools Panel**, choose the **Perspective Tool**, then ensure **Show grid** is unchecked in Perspective settings.

11 Drag the bottom-left and bottom-right corner handles outwards to skew the water and change the angle of the reflections.

12 Click **Apply** to commit the perspective filter.

13 To clear the selection, from the **Select Menu**, choose **Deselect**.

Cropping

Cropping is a crucial part of processing, balancing the composition and overall dynamics of the scene.

1 From the **Tools Panel**, select the **Crop Tool**.

2 Drag the left and right edge handles in to crop off some horizontal space—the brightly lit highest mountain peak should fall within the top-left intersection on the rule-of-thirds grid.

3 On the context toolbar, choose **Apply** to commit the crop.

4 Before continuing, we'll flatten the document to simplify the layer structure and make further retouching work easier. From the **Document Menu**, choose **Flatten**. A single pixel layer will be created in the **Layers Panel**.

TONAL ADJUSTMENTS & FINISHING

Resource

torres_del_paine.afphoto (*05. Dodging & Burning* snapshot)

Dodging & Burning

We'll now bring the image to life using dodging and burning to highlight 'hero' parts of the scene and to darken the mood at the top and bottom of the image, respectively.

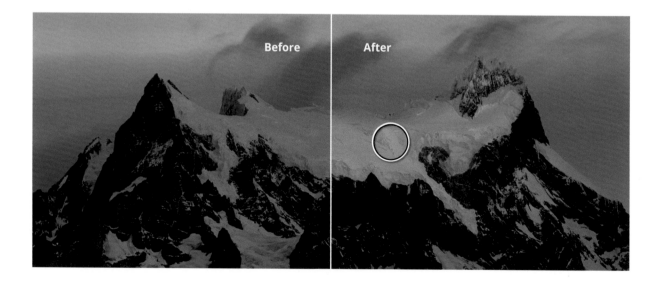

To dodge, so highlights are boosted:

1 From the **Tools Panel**, select the **Dodge Brush Tool**. On the context toolbar, set the **Width** to *350 px*, **Opacity** to *15%* and change **Tonal Range** to *Highlights*.

2 Now brush over key areas of the image to intensify their highlights; where the light hits the peak snow covering (below), already lit mountain faces and the brighter areas of the water (overleaf).

Remember to resize brush width as you paint using your [and] keys—this makes it quicker and easier to tackle smaller areas.

The **Dodge Brush** and **Burn Brush** tools are applied at *15% Opacity*. This means you can build up 'layers' of tonal work by going over the same areas several times.

The next step is to burn, so areas of the sky and water are darkened, bringing out mood in the scene (like a vignette effect).

1   On the **Tools Panel**, select the **Burn Brush Tool**. On the context toolbar, set the **Width** to *2000 px* and change **Tonal Range** to *Shadows*.

2   Brush along the top of the image onto the sky; don't be afraid to go over it several times to build up layers of brush work.

3   Now brush along the bottom of the image onto the water using the same approach.

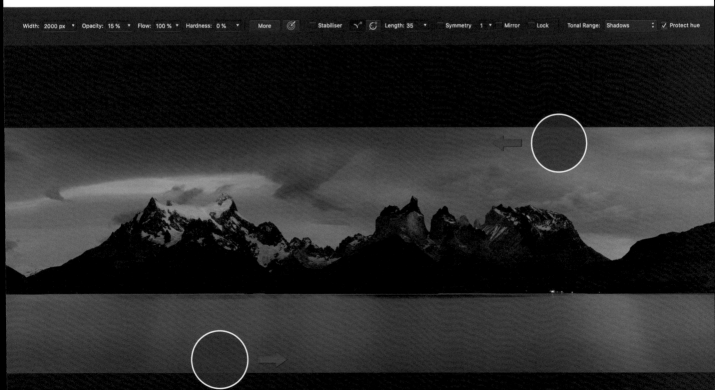

Resource
torres_del_paine.afphoto (*06. Adjustments* snapshot)

Adjustment Layers

At this stage I start adding non-destructive Adjustment Layers.

1 From the **Layer Menu**, choose **New Adjustment Layer > Vibrance Adjustment**.

2 On the dialog, drag the **Vibrance** slider to *20%*. This allows me to saturate all the right sections of the scene without introducing any clipping.

3 From the **Layer Menu**, choose **New Adjustment Layer > Exposure**. We're going to mask this adjustment to give the water more depth.

4 On the dialog, set the **Exposure** slider to *-2*, **Opacity** to *40%* and change the **Blend Mode** to *Hard Light*.

5 Ensuring the (Exposure Adjustment) layer is still selected, from the **Layer Menu**, choose **Invert**. This will invert the adjustment's mask.

6 From the **Tools Panel**, select the **Paint Brush Tool**. On the context toolbar, choose a **Width** of *2000 px*. **Opacity** should be set to *100%* and **Hardness** to *0%*.

7 On the **Colour Panel**, ensure the active colour is set to a pure white (RGB *255,255,255*). Now brush across the water and it will darken; this is because we're adding this area of the image back into the adjustment mask.

8 From the **Layer Menu**, choose **New Adjustment Layer > Levels Adjustment**.

9 In settings, set **White Level** to *73%*. This adds a glowing feel to the scene.

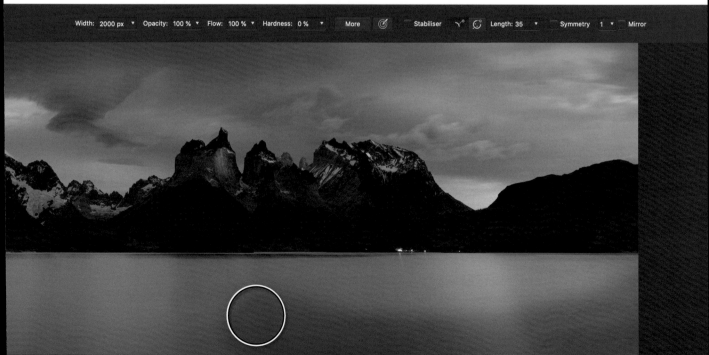

Resource

torres_del_paine.afphoto (*07. Live filters* snapshot)

Live Filters

Live Filters are a great way to create and make non-destructive adjustments on the fly with loads of refinement.

1   On the **Layers Panel**, select the flattened (Pixel) layer.

2   From the **Layer Menu**, choose **New Live Filter Layer > Clarity Filter**.

3   In settings, set **Strength** to *35%*. This gives the mountain range a pin-sharp look.

Now we'll add some Gaussian Blur with blending options to give the image a mystical glow.

4   Once again, on the **Layers Panel**, select the flattened (Pixel) layer.

5   From the **Layer Menu**, choose **New Live Filter Layer > Gaussian Blur Filter**.

6   In settings, set **Radius** to *0.7 px* and change the **Blend Mode** to *Overlay*.

7   With the (Gaussian Blur) layer selected, click **Blend Ranges**.

8 On the **Source Layer Ranges** spline graph, uncheck **Linear** and drag the left node down to the bottom of the graph. Drag in the middle of the graph to create a new node, and drag it downwards and slightly to the right. This blends the Gaussian blur filter strongly into the highlights, but tapers the effect off towards the shadows.

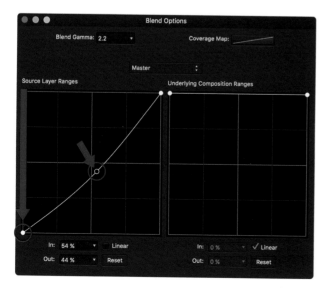

Finishing touches

Finally, we'll add some finishing touches with some freestyle dodge brushing to further bring out the tones in the image.

1 With (Pixel) layer selected, choose the **Dodge Brush Tool** again.

2 Using the previous brush settings, dodge over various parts of the mountain range, water and sky to intensify the tones and round off the image.

Our editing on the image is complete.

> *Affinity Photo suits my freestyle and painterly style of creative processing, with a plethora of tools at hand.*

3

Search the Woods

Book covers for print and e-books by *Bodo Bertuleit*

In this project, I'll show you how to design a professional book cover, with emphasis on applying artistic text, using textures and experimenting with blend modes. As a final touch, the book cover design will be exported for both hi-res printing and as e-book covers of differing sizes.

BEFORE YOU
GET STARTED

Resources

You can get all the resources that are referenced in this project from:
https://affin.co/searchthewoods

Knowledge of Affinity Photo

To get the most from undertaking this project, you will need to:

- Be familiar with the interface of Affinity Photo. You can learn more about the interface in the Interface Tour chapter, starting on p. 13.

- Follow along with example resources by navigating and viewing snapshots that are saved in your project file. Named snapshots are suggested at stages throughout the project. See p. 9.

PROJECT DETAILS

My work focuses mainly on the creation of book cover designs, classical graphic design and web assets. In the last couple of years, I've been working with both Affinity Designer and Affinity Photo apps, with both being perfect for my needs.

For this project, I use Affinity Photo to create a book cover design based on a set print size. In reality, book covers can be wildly different sizes depending on geography, standards and publisher, so you may need to adjust your settings to suit.

The principle of book design remains the same though—choosing the right page size, CMYK document setup and print profile will produce great results!

> Your page size and colour management settings should be obtained from either the client or your print company.

DOCUMENT SETUP

Let's set up our document for professional printing so that a paperback cover, of front cover size 5.25" x 8.0" (**W/H**), is being created.

1 Select **File > New**.

2 Choose a document **Type** of *Print (Press-Ready)* to set up a CMYK document. Set **Document Units** to *Inches*, then uncheck **Portrait** as we want a single landscape spread incorporating back cover, spine and front cover. Adjust the remaining settings as shown.

The page dimensions are not 5.25" by 8" for two reasons: firstly, the **Page Height** includes the margin settings for top and bottom (2 x 0.12") and the **Page Width** is also greater to take account of the front and back cover plus **Left Margin** and **Right Margin** settings (2 x 0.12" again). Secondly, to account for the spine, I've added 0.77" to the **Page Width**.

> We've simulated bleed here, as the margins act as non-printing bleed guides and the extended page dimensions allow images to run over the margins to allow your printers to trim the covers.

New Document

Type: Print (Press Ready)
Page Preset: <Custom>
Document Units: Inches

Colour:
Colour Format: CMYK/8
Colour Profile: Coated FOGRA39 (ISO 12647-2:2004)
Transparent background

Dimensions:
Page Width: 11.51 in   Portrait
Page Height: 8.24 in
DPI: 300

✓ Include Margins
Left Margin: 0.12 in   Right Margin: 0.12 in
Top Margin: 0.12 in   Bottom Margin: 0.12 in
Retrieve Margin from Printer

Cancel   OK

Metric
Page Width: 292.4 mm (incl. spine width 19.56 mm)
Page Height: 209.3 mm
All 'bleed' margins: 3 mm

Setting up guides

The use of non-printing guides can help a lot, in our case to visualise the spine area.

1   On the **View Menu**, select **Guides Manager**.

2   Add two vertical guides for the spine position at *5.37 in* and *6.14 in*.

I initially created a cover template within the project file as a Cover Template (Size) layer, which I've kept switched off in the project file. You can switch it on to refer to at this point, then hide it when finished with.

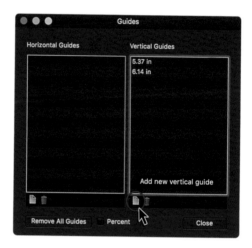

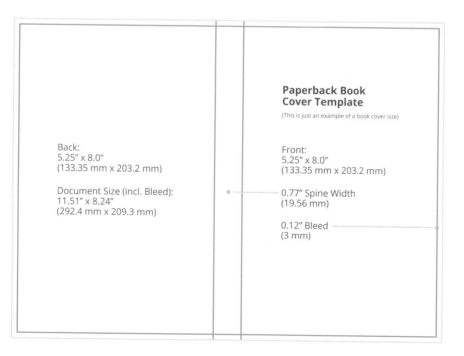

**Paperback Book
Cover Template**

(This is just an example of a book cover size)

Back:
5.25" x 8.0"
(133.35 mm x 203.2 mm)

Document Size (incl. Bleed):
11.51" x 8.24"
(292.4 mm x 209.3 mm)

Front:
5.25" x 8.0"
(133.35 mm x 203.2 mm)

0.77" Spine Width
(19.56 mm)

0.12" Bleed
(3 mm)

USING
ROYALTY FREE
IMAGES AND FONTS

It's not always practical to source your own images whether you're running a business or not. Fortunately, collections of royalty-free images are available on the Internet for you to use.

Downloading royalty-free images

Websites such as Unsplash, 123RF, Fotolia, Getty Images, and Pixabay (to name but a few) are free to use. For this project, I sourced images from http://unsplash.com

Use the first two resource links above to source the image files.

Downloading fonts

In the same way as I can use royalty-free imagery, I use royalty-free Internet-sourced fonts equally. Here, we'll be using a lovely advertising font called Antonio which is suited to large title text.

The last resource link above will download the Antonio font family from FontSquirrel as found here https://affin.co/FSantonio

Installing fonts

1 Open the downloaded zip file and open and read the licence file.

2 For *Mac*: Double-click the downloaded font files and select **Install Font**.

   or:

   For *Windows*: Right-click the downloaded font files and select **Install**.

Antonio

Download Font ⊕

Glyph

Aa

Characters

ABCDEFGHIJKLMNOPQRSTUVWXYZ
abcdefghijklmnopqrstuvwxyz
1234567890
¬!"£$%^&*()_+{}:@~|<>?

Styles

**The Quick Brown Fox
jumps over the lazy dog**

Resource
search_the_woods.afphoto (*01. Background* snapshot)
Your downloaded forest image (jpg)

BACKGROUND

The first step is to insert the background image.

1 Open the forest image in Affinity Photo with **File > Open**.

2 Copy and paste the image into your project, dragging it upwards to reveal more undergrowth, then scale the image down slightly, so you've left the clearing in the forest in the centre of the front cover.

3 Rename the layer to be *Background Image (Forest)*.

I'll add a linear gradient to make the sky appear darker.

1 On the **Layers Panel**, select **Add Pixel Layer**.

2 On the **Tools Panel**, select the **Gradient Tool** then drag a gradient down from centre-top to centre-bottom of the page.

3 On the context toolbar, click the gradient swatch and assign the selectable circular nodes in the gradient spectrum to be black (left node) and *0%* **Opacity** (right node); drag the **Mid Point** marker from *50%* to *70%*.

4 Back on the **Layers Panel**, set the Blend Mode of this layer to *Darken* and name it *Gradient-Black-Transparent*.

> If you want the gradient to remain editable for future adjustment, use a fill layer (**Layer > New Fill Layer**) instead of a pixel layer.

Resource
search_the_woods.afphoto (*02. Person* snapshot)
person.png

PERSON

The downloaded image needed some work, so I cropped down and cut out the image from the original photo, exporting it as a transparent PNG file named person.png. Now, we can add the person and let him 'glow' a little.

1 Open, then copy and paste the person.png image as a new layer, naming it *Person*.

2 Position the person centrally on the right side of the spread. The **Transform Panel** shows my settings.

3 From the **Effects Panel**, check **Outer Glow**, choose white as the **Colour** and adjust other settings.

Resource

search_the_woods.afphoto (*03. Fog* snapshot)

FOG

Let's try a little painting and erasing to introduce some fog to the scene.

1 Select the Person layer, then on the **Layers Panel**, select **Add Pixel Layer**.

2 On the **Tools Panel**, select the **Paint Brush Tool** and paint with a soft white brush over the lower part of the forest so that uneven and 'layered' fog clouds are formed. Make sure that the lower part of the person (below the knee) is covered by fog.

3 Finish off by naming the layer *Fog*.

If necessary, erase on this layer with the **Erase Brush Tool** in some places (brush settings as before, but with **Opacity** at *10%* and **Hardness** at *0%*).

> I used 27 separate brush strokes here to give a sense of depth to the fog—otherwise, continuously painting a single stroke lessens the effect.

A LITTLE MOOD

I want to 'cool down' the scene and create the right mood. The forest needs to suggest a cold frosty evening or maybe the break of dawn.

1 On the **Layers Panel**, select **Add Pixel Layer**.

2 On the **Colour Panel**, choose a blue tone (*CMYK 70,27,0,0*), then with the **Flood Fill Tool** (G) enabled, click on the new layer.

3 Set the layer's Blend Mode to *Colour*, and name the layer *Mood*.

Access CMYK Colours from the Colour Panel's pop-up menu—simply change RGB to CMYK.

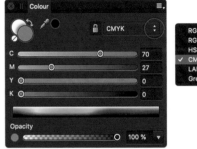

Resource
search_the_woods.afphoto (*05. Flashlight beam* snapshot)

FLASHLIGHT BEAM

The flashlight beam is one of the most important components of the book cover and adds greatly to the atmosphere. We'll introduce some basic vector curve drawing and editing to form the beam.

1   On the **Layers Panel**, select **Add Pixel Layer**.

2   On the **Tools Panel**, select the **Pen Tool** and draw the shape of a light cone.

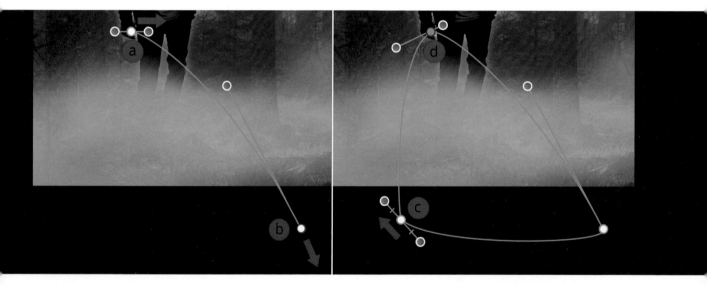

- Drag the cursor at the person's hand by a short distance (**a**) and release.

- Off the page, drag the cursor downwards (**b**) and release.

- Still off the page, move cursor left and drag upwards a short distance (**c**) and release.

- Click on the initial node (**d**) to close the curve, forming a shape.

If needed, reshape the curve by pressing the cmd ⌘ key (Mac) or ctrl key (Win) and drag white nodes and/or blue handles into final position.

3 From the context toolbar, convert the vector shape to a selection using **Selection**. Fill this selection with white, then deselect with **Select > Deselect**.

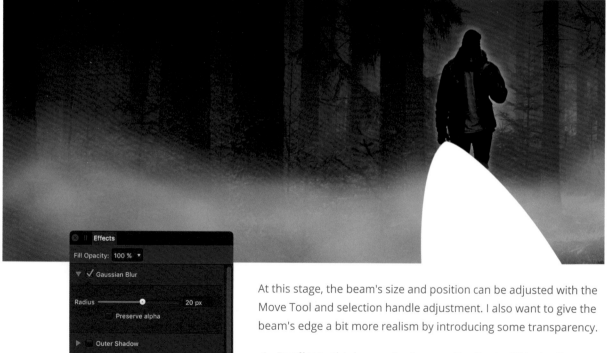

At this stage, the beam's size and position can be adjusted with the Move Tool and selection handle adjustment. I also want to give the beam's edge a bit more realism by introducing some transparency.

4 **Duplicate** this layer using **Layer > Duplicate**. Hide the first flashlight layer and apply a **Gaussian Blur** (*20 px*) using the **Effects Panel** on the duplicated layer.

5 Make visible the underlying layer (with the sharp edges) and use the **Erase Brush Tool** on this layer to paint over the edges with low opacity on the eraser.

6 Rotate this layer anti-clockwise by around *4°* (drag the top-right corner handle upwards) so there is an offset between sharp and blurred edges. This gives a bit more realism to the beam.

7 Select both flashlight layers then choose **Arrange > Group**.

I'll now introduce some masking to paint away some of the beam.

8 With the group selected, click **Mask Layer** on the **Layers Panel**.

9 Using the **Erase Brush Tool** (same brush settings as before), paint on the selected (Mask) layer to mask out the lower area of the beam. The glow of the flashlight should now fade out in the lower part in the fog.

10 Rename the group and pixel layers to be *Flashlight-Rays*.

Finishing off, let's add the illuminated flashlight itself.

11 Create a new pixel layer called *Flashlight*, then draw a circular selection over the person's hand with **Elliptical Marquee Tool**, keeping the shift key (⇧) pressed.

12 Use the **Flood Fill Tool** to fill the selection with white and give it a **Gaussian Blur** of about *6 px*.

Resource
search_the_woods.afphoto (*06. Text* snapshot)
Texture.jpg

TEXT

Text in your project can take two forms: **Artistic text** or **Frame text**. The former always scales as it is resized, while the latter flows within its text frame container. This makes these text types great for use in titling and paragraph 'body' copy, respectively, as we'll see now.

Book Title

First, we'll create the title of the book.

1 Choose the **Artistic Text Tool** and type *SEARCH THE WOODS* on the front page. Add a line break after the first word.

2 On the context toolbar, use the settings to format the selected text. The **Fill** colour is *CMYK 0,89,78,0*.

3 For good inter-line spacing, click **Character** on the toolbar to adjust **Leading Override** to *80 pt*.

The Character Panel exposes more advanced typographic settings.

Adding a texture

Using combinations of raster textures and blend modes gives you a variety of effects, especially effective on title text. We'll introduce a wood effect on the title.

1 On the **File Menu**, select **Place**. Navigate to, select and open Texture.jpg. Drag the cursor over the title text and release.

2 On the **Layers Panel**, drag this Texture layer directly under the title text layer and set its Blend Mode to *Multiply*.

3 With the Title layer selected, click **Layer Effects** on the bottom of the panel. Enable **Inner Shadow** and **Outer Glow** and adjust settings. Set **Colour** to *white* and *CMYK 100,81,51,69*, respectively.

Instead of Texture.jpg, you can experiment with 15 other royalty-free natural textures by downloading them from https://affin.co/phototextures.

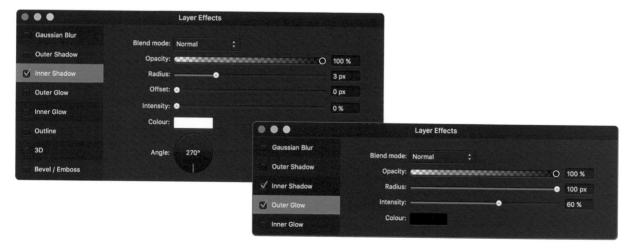

Adding more text

For the author:

Choose the **Artistic Text Tool** and enter the author name *JUSTIN B. LAKER* (**Font** *Antonio, 34 pt, Bold*, colour *white*).

For back cover text:

1 For the heading, type *IT'S LATE NOVEMBER...* (**Font** *Antonio, 22 pt, Bold*, colour *CMYK 16,90,84,5*).

2 Enter book summary text below the heading using the **Frame Text Tool** (**Font** *Antonio, 12 pt, Regular*, colour *white, Justified Left*).

For spine text:

1 Choose the **Artistic Text Tool**, insert the title of the book and the author name using the same colours as the front cover text.

2 Set the text size to *30 pt* and rotate the text anti-clockwise by the top-right handle by 90°. Use the shift key (⇧) to snap to vertical. Rotate clockwise for UK/US.

Aligning your text

Up to now, all your text may not have been perfectly centred—this may have been quite tricky as you've had nothing to align to. We can fix this by using **snapping** and the temporary use of a drawn rectangle.

1   On the top **Toolbar**, switch on **Snapping**.

2   With the **Rectangle Tool** on the **Tools Panel**, draw a rectangle (no fill or stroke) stretching from guide to margin, snapping to each.

3   When you reposition your text you'll find that a green vertical line appears indicating that the text is perfectly centre-aligned to the rectangle (and therefore the page).

4   Continue using this method to align the rest of the text on the cover.

You can delete the rectangle now.

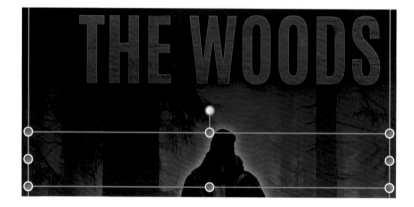

FINISHING TOUCHES

Resource

search_the_woods.afphoto (*07. Finishing touches* snapshot)
publishers-logo.png

Let's optimize a few things before the project is completed. First, we'll highlight the person's outline slightly.

1 On the **Layers Panel**, select the Person layer.

2 From the **Toolbar**, select **Insert behind the selection**.

3 Back on the panel, select **Add Pixel Layer** to place the layer below the Person layer.

4 With **Paint Brush Tool** enabled, paint around the person's head with a soft white brush. Not too much, as the light must not compete with that of the flashlight beam.

It's also the right time to resize or reposition the person into his final position. Finishing off, I added a vignette—I thought this was a nice touch to draw the eye to the centre of the page.

5 Select the Background Image (Forest) layer and select **Filters > Colours > Vignette** and drop the **Exposure** to *-1.25*.

I could have used a non-destructive approach for the vignette by using **Layer** > **New Live Filter Layer** > **Vignette Filter**.

Width: 1050 px ▾ Opacity: 40 % ▾ Flow: 25 % ▾ Hardness: 0 % ▾ More ⊘ Stabiliser ⌄° ⟳ Length: 35 ▾ Blend Mode: Normal ▾

Finally, let's insert the logo of the publisher. This was a supplied transparent PNG file that I obtained from my publisher.

1 Choose **Select > Deselect Layers**.

2 On the **File Menu**, select **Place**. Navigate to, select, and open publishers-logo.png.

3 Scale the logo down, placing it at bottom centre.

EXPORT

Let's produce some deliverables from this project. First, ask your client or print company exactly what export settings are required for the print and for the e-book cover.

Soft-proofing check

At export, or at any time, you can get a visual 'heads-up' of how your print will appear using a chosen 'proofing' colour profile to define the colour space.

1 Choose **Select > Deselect Layers**.

2 On the **Layers Panel**, select **Adjustments**, then *Soft Proof* from the pop-up menu.

3 In the dialog, choose your profile and preview your output.

> Remember to hide the Soft Proof adjustment layer once you've finished, as its effect will be included in the output otherwise.

Exporting for print

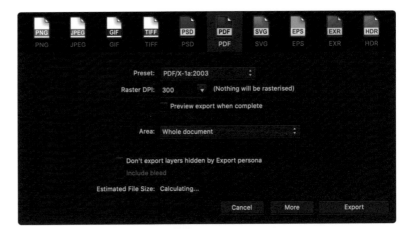

1 On the **File Menu**, select **Export**.

2 Select the PDF thumbnail, and then a **Preset** of *PDF/X-1a*.

3 Click **Export**.

> Remember to let your printer know your intended page size and that you've increased it to account for margins as bleed.

Export as e-book cover

A nice feature of Affinity Photo is that I can create e-book cover graphics from directly within the app. At any time, I can export multiple sizes of my graphic simultaneously without affecting my project.

For this project, I'm planning on creating e-book covers of widths *657 px*, *1400 px* and *1536 px*. These are all popular dimensions used in e-book publishing.

1 On the **Toolbar**, switch to **Export Persona**.

2 With the **Slice Tool** (S), drag a rectangular slice on the front cover so it fits perfectly within the guide line and the page margins.

3 On the **Slices Panel**, choose an **Export preset** of *Single JPEG (High Quality)*.

4 On the **Export Options Panel**, change the **Pixel format** to be *RGB 8-bit*.

5 Name your slice entry to be *ebookcover* and then expand the slice entry.

6 To set the exported slice's width and associated file naming:

- Enter the width (in pixels) on the slice item, e.g. *657w*.

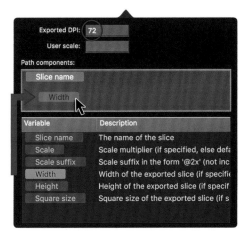

- Click the adjacent file name (ebookcover.jpg) to set the **Exported DPI** to *72* and edit the path components: Delete **Scale Suffix** and replace it with **Width** by dragging up from the **Variable** list to the **Path Components** box.

7 Click the **+** button directly under the JPEG icon, and repeat for the other sizes.

8 To export all slice sizes, click the export button on the parent slice.

That completes the Search the Woods project! I hope you enjoyed it.

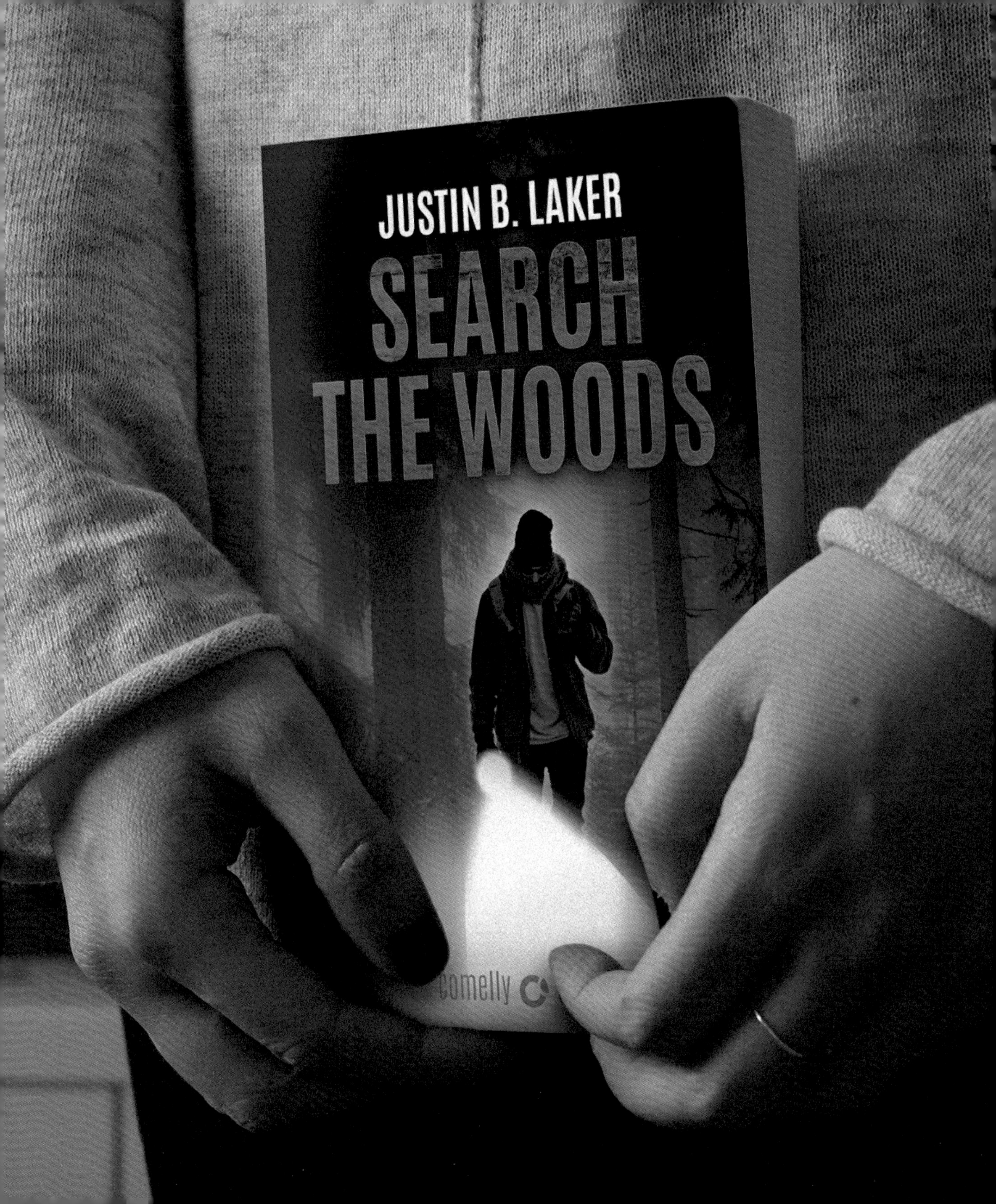
JUSTIN B. LAKER
SEARCH THE WOODS
comelly

Grilled Cheese Pull

A craveable creation
by *Jordan Gaunce*

Help Jordan prepare his 'to-die-for' cheesy lunch while learning how compositing and mesh warping can play a part in food retouching.

BEFORE YOU
GET STARTED

Resources

You can get all the resources that are referenced in this project from:

https://affin.co/cheese

Knowledge of Affinity Photo

To get the most from undertaking this project, you will need to:

- Be familiar with the interface of Affinity Photo. You can learn more about the interface in the Interface Tour chapter, starting on p. 13.

- Have good core skills. See the skills table opposite to see which additional aspects of Affinity Photo you need to be confident with to complete this project.

Inpainting	p. 96
Adjustments	p. 100
Selections	p. 106
Masking	p. 116

SHOOT DETAILS

Food photography is everywhere; in magazine ads, product packaging, fast-food menus, and even on our friend's Instagram pages.

Our food is going to stand out, and that means making it look natural, gooey and most of all creating a desire to eat that grilled cheese right now. We are creating 'craveability'.

We'll accomplish this by performing colour adjustments and using mesh warping to create a creamy texture with the cheese.

I would like to thank Brandon Voges for his artistic eye and the use of his photos for this project. Brandon and I work together on projects just like this one at Bruton Stroube Studios in St. Louis, Missouri, USA.

FILENAMES

Cheese-01.jpg - Cheese-07.jpg

GEAR

TRIPOD:	Yes
CAMERA:	Canon 5DS
LENS:	Canon 50mm f/1.2 USM
LIGHTING:	Studio light

SETTINGS

SHOOTING MODE:	Manual
EXPOSURE:	1/160
APERTURE:	f/5.6
ISO:	100
EXP. BIAS	0
EXP. PROG:	Nil
METERING:	Spot
FORMATS:	RAW (supplied as JPGs)

LOCATION

Bruton Stroube Studios

https://affin.co/locbrutonstroube

CONDITIONS

Perfect

POST SHOOT EDITING

PASTING AND MASKING THE IMAGES

The main draw for me using Affinity Photo for this project is the Mesh Warp Tool. It's so easy to use and maintains the integrity of the pixels.

No smearing of pixels helps in the workflow so you don't have to retouch messy surfaces caused by distortion. By using multiple images for the cheese layers, we're going to build up a yummy cheese pull that has depth and pop.

To get started, we'll composite three images together: the background plate, then two shots of the hand model holding the grilled cheese.

1 Drag Background.jpg into Affinity Photo or use **File > Open** to select the file.

2 Do the same procedure for Right-Hand.jpg. Use **File > Open** to select it and click **Open** on the dialog. The image will open in a new window.

3 Choose **Edit > Copy**, then move across to the Background.jpg window. From here, choose **Edit > Paste** to paste the image as a new layer.

4 The image will be pasted in with the same name: Background. To keep our layers organised, we'll rename this. On the **Layers Panel**, click once on the layer text. You can type a new name and hit return. We'll name it *Right-Hand*.

5 Now we need to repeat this opening, copying and pasting process for the second image, Left-Hand.jpg. Rename this layer to be *Left-Hand*.

Masking the bread

With our layers created, we'll begin masking parts from each to use in our composite.

1 From the **Tools Panel**, choose the **Selection Brush Tool**.

2 On the **Layers Panel**, select the Left-Hand layer, then drag over and around the left hand and the half of the sandwich it is holding.

3 This will create a selection of the area we want to use. Choose **Refine** from the context toolbar.

4 The selection will be matted and become softer. Drag over specific areas to matte them further, e.g. the outline of the bread near the thumb, and the model's sleeve where the fabric is detailed.

5 Click **Apply** to commit the selection.

6 From the **Layers Panel**, click **Mask Layer** to add a mask layer based on the selection. You'll now see a 'double' sandwich—this will disappear once we mask the right-hand image. Remove the active selection marquee by choosing **Select > Deselect**.

7 On the **Layers Panel**, select the Right-Hand layer.

8 Drag to create a selection around the right hand and grilled cheese sandwich. Use **Refine** on the context toolbar to open the **Selection Refinement** dialog.

9 Just matting the selection should be accurate enough. Click **Apply** to refine the selection, then from the **Layers Panel,** choose to add a **Mask Layer**.

10 To remove the selection marquee, choose **Select > Deselect**.

Once the hands are masked, you can also experiment and reposition them with the **Move Tool** (V). For example, you could move the left hand in slightly to close the gap between the hands.

RETOUCHING THE COMPOSITE

Before we move on, we need to tidy up the images, as we have some wayward crumbs on the hands. We also have some areas on the Background layer which need cleaning up, so we'll tackle that too.

1 On the **Layers Panel**, click the check boxes next to the Left-Hand and Right-Hand layers to hide them temporarily, then select the Background layer.

2 On the **Tools Panel**, select the **Inpainting Brush Tool**.

3 Paint over the stick until it is completely highlighted, then release the mouse button to remove it. You may need to increase the brush width slightly using the **Width** option on the context toolbar.

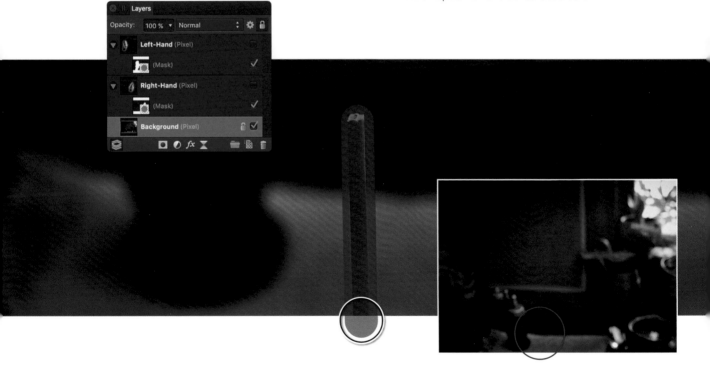

4 On the **Layers Panel**, click the Right-Hand layer's check box to show the layer again, and also make sure it's selected.

5 With the **Inpainting Brush Tool** selected and a suitable width (between *45 px* and *70 px*), and paint over the crumbs and release the mouse button to inpaint them out.

6 On the **Layers Panel**, switch on and select the Left-Hand layer.

7 Use the **Inpainting Brush Tool** with a suitable width (around *7 px*) to paint over and inpaint the small black marks on the thumbnail.

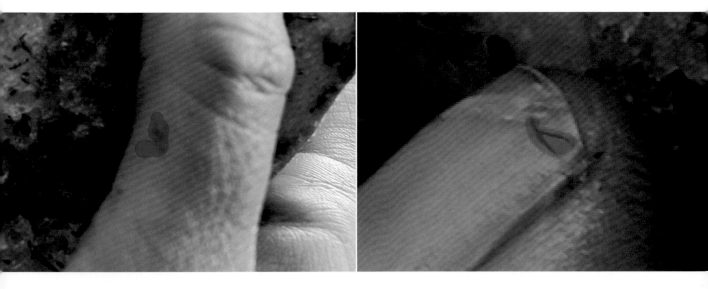

Cloning the cheese marks

Tackling the cheese marks on the nail is a little more complicated—we'll use cloning to replace these areas on the nail.

1 From the **Tools Panel**, select the **Clone Brush Tool** (S).

2 On the context toolbar, set **Width** to *35 px* and **Hardness** to *0%*. The goal here is to set a suitable source area from further down the nail, then drag to clone over the top of the nail where the cheese is.

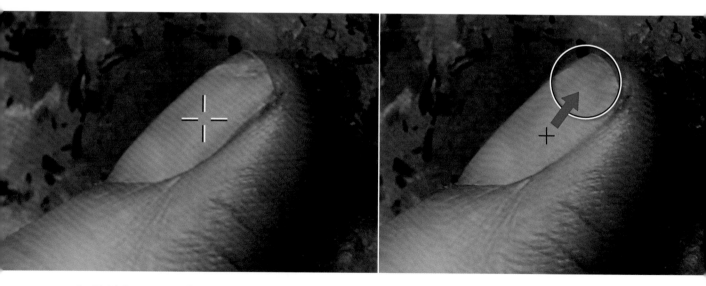

3 Hold the option ⌥ key (Mac) or alt key (Win) and click further down the nail to set the source area. As you hover over the top of the nail, you will see a preview of the cloning you are about to perform.

4 Drag over the top of the nail and go over the areas you want to replace gradually. You may need to perform two or more passes, resetting the source area as you go.

PLACING
THE CHEESE

Resource

Cheese-02.jpg
Cheese-05.jpg
Cheese-06.jpg

Now we come to the fun part: adding in some extra gooey cheese and using the **Mesh Warp Tool** to give it that melted look. We can composite as many images as we need for this process, and we have a bank of seven to work from.

Importing & masking

1 Use **File > Open**, then locate and select Cheese-06.jpg. Select it and click **Open** to open it as a new document.

2 Choose **Edit > Copy** to copy the image, then move back across to your composite document.
Use **Edit > Paste** to paste the image in as a new layer. The layer should be added above the topmost layer which was previously selected. If not, drag the new layer to the top of the layer stack.

3 For organisation, we'll rename this new layer to be *Cheese-06*.

4 Repeat the procedure for Cheese-02.jpg and Cheese-05.jpg.

5 We'll group the layers to organise them. Cheese-05 is already selected, so hold the cmd ⌘ key (Mac) or ctrl key (Win) and select Cheese-02 and Cheese-06. Choose **Arrange > Group** to move the layers into a new group. We can rename this group to *Cheese*. Hide this group by clicking its check box.

Creating the hero mask

To help with compositing, we'll create a mask from the main 'hero' bread (the two main bread halves).

1 From the **Tools Panel**, choose the **Selection Brush Tool**, then select the Left-Hand layer. Drag over the left hand bread, making sure to only select the top slice.

2 Do the same for the other hand: select the Right-Hand layer, then create a selection of just the top slice.

3 Invert the selection by choosing **Select > Invert Pixel Selection**.

4 Select the Cheese group again and show it by clicking its check box. Add a **Mask Layer** to this group, then choose **Select > Deselect**.

Extracting the cheese

The hero mask will make the composition look messy to begin with—we need to hide some of the cheese layers and work on just one at a time.

1 Hide the Cheese-05 and Cheese-02 layers, then select Cheese-06.

2 From the **Tools Panel**, choose the **Selection Brush Tool**. Drag around just the areas of cheese that you want to use from this layer, e.g. just the bottom part. Don't worry if you select too much of the bread, as this will be hidden by the hero bread mask.

> Working with multiple layers and masks can become visually busy: a great tip is to click on the Cheese-06 layer with option ⌥ key (Mac) or alt key (Win) pressed to isolate the layer or mask.

3 To make things easier for mesh warping, choose **Layer > Duplicate**. This will create a duplicate of just the selected area from the cheese layer. Remove the selection marquee using **Select > Deselect**, then delete the original Cheese-06 layer by selecting it and pressing **Delete**.

4 We'll transform the cheese layer before warping it. From the **Tools Panel**, select the **Move Tool** (V).

5 Feel free to experiment, but as an example, move the cheese down and to the right slightly by dragging it, then rotate it slightly to the left.

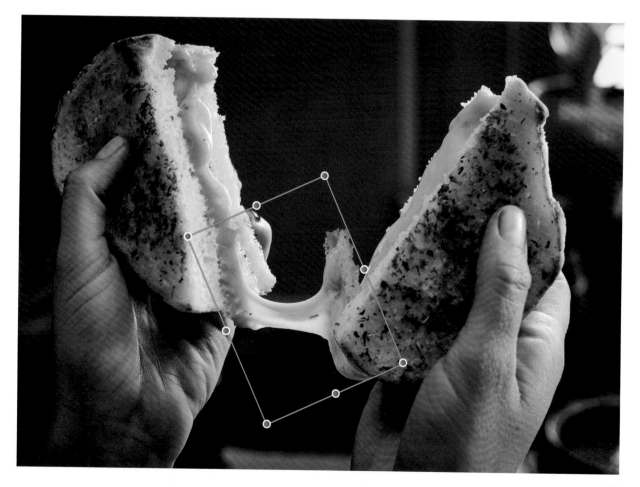

MELTING THE CHEESE

Now we'll get to warp the cheese around and make it match up with the bread edges.

1 From the **Tools Panel**, select the **Mesh Warp Tool**.

2 Drag the four corner nodes to move the cheese around. Double-clicking anywhere within the mesh box adds a node and pins that area in place. You can drag these nodes around to warp the mesh.

3 You can add many nodes to get the cheese positioned correctly. Don't worry about it looking unfinished, as we will refine the blending with layer masking. Click **Apply** on the context toolbar to commit the mesh warping.

You can select multiple nodes and move them at the same time: drag anywhere within the box (not on a node) to create a selection marquee, then drag over the nodes you wish to select.

You can also drag the lines in-between the nodes to alter the curvature of the mesh warping. This may prove handy for producing a more natural-looking cheese.

Tidying up the cheese

Now we'll tidy the cheese layer up and fine-tune its appearance by using masking to hide some of the unfinished areas.

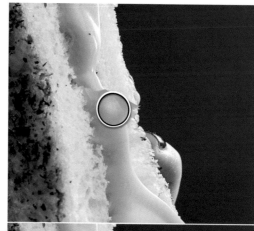

1. To the Cheese-06 layer, add a **Mask Layer**, expand the parent layer and select the newly created (Mask) layer by clicking its thumbnail.

2. Select the **Paint Brush Tool** from the **Tools Panel**.

3. Set a suitable **Width** (between *100 px* and *200 px*), decrease **Hardness** to *0%* for a soft edge, and set the active colour to pure black on the **Colour Panel**.

4. Paint onto areas of the cheese you want to hide. Where you mask will depend on the result of the mesh warp, so evaluate by eye and judge what looks best.

Now we've completed one cheese layer, we can repeat the above procedures for other cheese layers to build up a full composite—experiment until you find a result that makes you salivate!

For each layer, you will need to cut out the cheese, mesh warp it, then clean the result up with a mask layer.

> You can also experiment with the layer order, which changes how the cheese layers blend with one another. I placed the Cheese-02 layer above Cheese-05 layer as my preference.

Finishing off the cheese

You may notice the highlights in the cheese are too bright and distracting. We'll add an adjustment to correct this, and also flatten our cheese layers into one pixel layer to make further work easier.

1 Select the topmost layer in the Cheese group, then choose **Layer > New Adjustment Layer > Selective Colour Adjustment**. This ensures the layer is clipped to the group and will only affect the cheese.

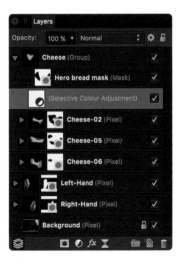

2 On the adjustment dialog, set **Colour** to *Whites*, then drag **Magenta** to *5%* and **Yellow** to *15%*.

3 Select the composite cheese layers, with the shift key (⇧) pressed, then choose **Arrange > Group**, then **Layer > Rasterise**. This will flatten the cheese composite into a new pixel layer, which we'll rename to *Flattened Cheese*.

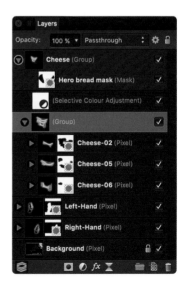

You may want to duplicate the whole Cheese group first before grouping and rasterising the cheese layers. This preserves a backup (here named Cheese old) in case you want to go back and tweak the composite.

4 We can now perform further mesh warping and masking to our flattened cheese layer—feel free to experiment and tweak the shape to your liking.

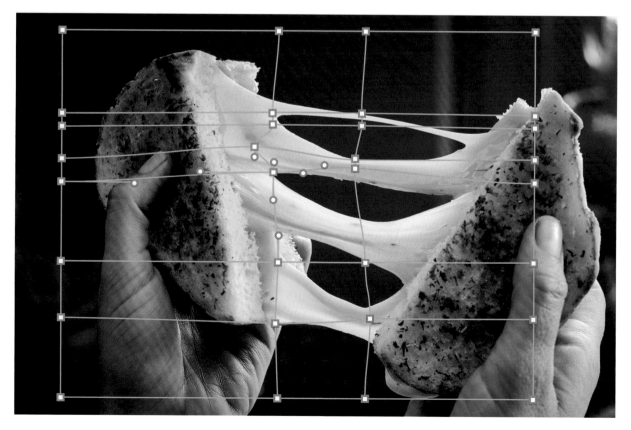

MODIFYING THE TONES

Next, we'll perform selective adjustments on both the cheese and the bread, and we'll also modify the overall tone of the image and add a little glow to the window area.

1 Select the Flattened Cheese layer.

2 Choose **Layer > New Adjustment Layer > Curves Adjustment**. It will clip into the Cheese group.

3 On the Curves spline graph, click-drag in the middle to add a node and drag it downwards. This will darken the midtones in the cheese layer. You can also rename this adjustment (*Cheese Tone* for example)

> We can be more selective about how adjustments are applied by choosing **Layer > Invert**. This will invert the layer's mask, and you can then paint into the areas you want to bring back using the **Paint Brush Tool** with a white colour.

Toning the bread

1 Select the Left-Hand layer, then choose **Layer > New Adjustment Layer > Curves Adjustment**. We'll name this *Bread Tone*.

2 Create two nodes on this graph to produce a curve that gets steeper towards the highlights. Switch from *Master* to *Green* and pull the green line down slightly using a node in the middle.

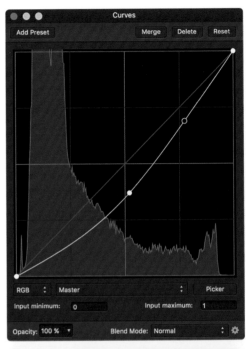

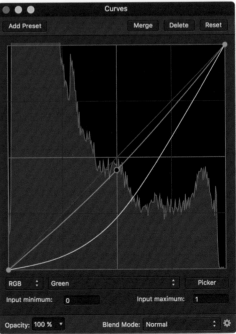

Width: 357.6 px ▾   Opacity: 50 % ▾   Flow: 100 % ▾   Hardness: 0 % ▾   More ⊚   Stabiliser ⌄° ↻   Length: 35 ▾   Blend Mode: Normal ▴

3 Now choose **Layer > Invert**. This will invert the adjustment's mask, removing the effect it has on the image.

4 With the **Paint Brush Tool**, paint over the white areas and the top of the bread slice to bring the adjustment's effect back in. Use a white brush with a low **Opacity** setting on the context toolbar and build up 'layers' for a more realistic effect.

FINISHING TOUCHES

Our final steps will be adding a hazy glow to the top right of the image, final tonal adjustments using Curves and Levels and cropping the composition to tighten it up.

1 On the **Layers Panel**, select the Cheese group. Choose **Add Pixel Layer** to create a new empty pixel layer. Rename it to *Soft Glow* and set its blend mode to *Screen*.

2 Select the **Paint Brush Tool** from the **Tools Panel**, choose a soft white brush from the **Brushes Panel**, then set the context toolbar to **Width** *900 px*, **Opacity** *5%* and **Hardness** *0%*.

3 Setting a low opacity builds up gradual layers of 'haze' and produces a graduated effect. Paint over the top right of the image where the window is and move towards the bread.

4 Paint over the window area multiple times to build up more of an effect.

5 The result wants to be a very subtle enhancement. If you feel the effect is too overdone, don't forget to tweak the **Opacity** of the Soft Glow layer too.

Levels & Curves

1 Choose **Layer > New Adjustment Layer >
Levels Adjustment**.

2 On the adjustment dialog, change from *Master* to *Blue*
on the pop-up menu, then drag the **White Level**
slider to *94%*. This lends the image a slightly cooler
tone and removes the yellow colour cast.

3 Choose **Layer > New Adjustment Layer >
Curves Adjustment**.

4 Drag the bottom left node in to the right, which
crushes the black tones and make the image look
punchier. Create a node just before the middle of the
graph and drag it upwards slightly, which adds a
slight boost to the mid-tones and highlights.

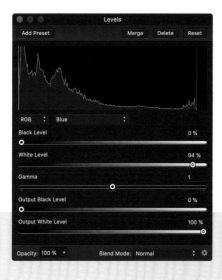

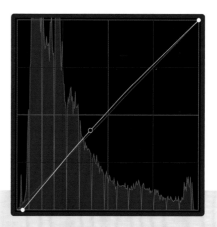

Final cropping

As a last step, we'll crop the image to remove some space
from the composition and make the cheese pull more
prominent.

1 From the **Tools Panel**, select the **Crop Tool** (C).

2 Drag the left, top and bottom nodes on the cropping
box to bring them in slightly, cropping slightly more at
the bottom, then choose **Apply** to commit the crop.

That wraps up the edits to our image. Who fancies a
cheese sandwich?

CHAPTER 5

Creative Effects & Techniques

In this chapter we've brought together some creative effects that are proving popular in the digital art community. The eye-catching results are achievable by all experience levels.

We'll also explore some great creative techniques such as realistic compositing and brush design/retouch.

1

The Snow Queen

A double-exposure portrait
by *Emi Haze*

Join Emi as he creates the popular double exposure effect in
Affinity Photo using a combination of blend modes, masking
and selections.

BEFORE YOU GET STARTED

Resources

 You can get most of the resources that are referenced in this project from:
https://affin.co/snowqueen

Knowledge of Affinity Photo

To get the most from undertaking this project, you will need to:

- Be familiar with the interface of Affinity Photo. You can learn more about the interface in the Interface Tour chapter, starting on p. 13.

- Follow along with example resources by navigating and viewing snapshots that are saved in your project file. Named snapshots are suggested at stages throughout the project. See p. 9.

- Have good core skills. See the skills table below to see which additional aspects of Affinity Photo you need to be confident with to complete this project:

Adjustments	p. 100
Selections	p. 106
Masking	p. 116

PROJECT DETAILS

About double exposure

Double exposure is a photographic compositing technique that combines two images into a single image. Traditionally, it is a technique in which the camera shutter is opened more than once to expose the camera film multiple times, usually to different images.

Bringing photos together creates a coherent image that can be beautiful, nostalgic or unsettling, depending on photo choice and how you combine them. With double exposure, you can create a surreal and fantastic world that stretches the imagination.

Following this project, you'll have learned the fundamental steps to creating this very attractive and powerful effect.

OPENING
IMAGE

Resource

snow_queen.afphoto (*01. Background* snapshot)
https://affin.co/girlportrait

The initial step is to download the girl's portrait, available as a royalty-free image, and add it to Affinity Photo.

1   Download the image from the web address in the above Resource box.
    (1276x1920px without site sign-up; 2000x3008px with site sign-up)

2   Open the image (portrait-1754894.png) in Affinity Photo using **File > Open**.

The image is added as a locked background layer.

Resource

snow_queen.afphoto (*02. Selectionrefine* snapshot)

SELECTION
AND REFINE

The next step is to cut out the girl from the background.

1   From the **Tools Panel**, select the **Selection Brush Tool** and set the context toolbar's brush **Width** to about *150 px*.

To paint away unwanted areas from the selection, press the option ⌥ key (Mac) or alt key (Win) and drag over the area.

2   Drag the cursor over the girl to 'paint' the selection area. The selection will snap to where the background meets the girl's outline.

Refining the selection

1. From the context toolbar, select **Refine**.

2. Drag along the selection edge with the Adjustment brush set to *25 px*, but reduce or increase the brush size at your convenience using the [or] key, respectively.

3. In the dialog, set **Smooth** to *9 px* to make the selection edge softer (especially on the top of the nose).

4. From the dialog's **Output** pop-up menu, select *Mask*.

5. Click **Apply**.

6. Rename this layer from *Background* to *Girl*.

> The main purpose of refinement was to get a very clean outline. I wanted to retain some, but not all, hair above the necklace as well as soften the outline of the nose and lips.

PLACING IMAGES

Now we're going to place the snow mountain image over the girl image and create a new background. The mountain image is carefully overlaid using my eye as judgement—I found that the top tree line offered an interesting alternative to the girl's hair.

1. Download the image from the web address in the above Resource box.

2. From the **File Menu**, choose **Place**.

3. From your Downloads folder, select the image (austin-smart-70353.jpg) and choose **Open**.

4. Drag from the top-left corner of the page downwards to the bottom right to size the image roughly equivalent to the girl image. On fine-tuning, my final preferred position and image sizing were as shown in the **Transform Panel**.

5. Rename this layer from austin-smart-70353 to *Snow Mountain 01*.

> For better visibility, you could drop the mountain layer's opacity temporarily while positioning.

Creating a background

1. From the **Layer Menu**, choose **New Layer**.

2. Drag the Pixel layer to the bottom of the panel's layer stack.

3. From the **Tools Panel**, choose the **Colour Picker Tool** (I) and click the cursor on the light blue sky of the Snow Mountain layer to pick the background colour.

4. Select **Edit > Fill**, then from the fill dialog, choose **Primary Colour** and then **Apply**.

5. Rename this layer to be *Background*.

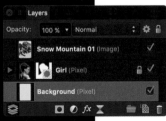

An alternative to this is to create a Fill Layer (**Layer > New Fill Layer**) from the already sampled colour.

BLEND MODES

This stage is really important because we're going to mix the two images with the use of blend modes and layer masks.

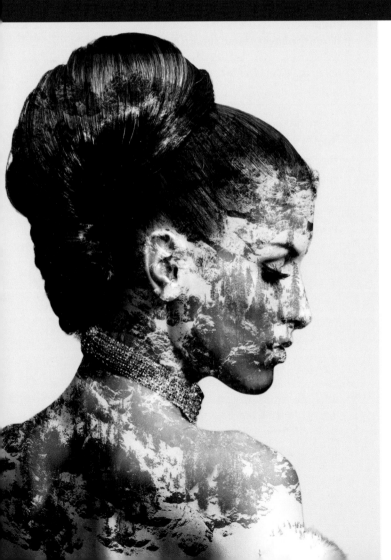

1 On the **Layers Panel**, select the Snow Mountain 01 (Pixel) layer.

2 Change the **Blend Mode** option to *Overlay*.

3 To create a selection from the girl's outline, click on the Girl layer's mask thumbnail with the cmd ⌘ key (Mac) or ctrl key (Win) pressed.

4 From the **Layer Menu**, select **New Mask Layer**.

5 From the **Select Menu**, choose **Deselect**. This will remove the selection and make it easier to see the image.

Blending allows us to combine different elements, colours and images in a single work and in the best way, creating incredible shape and colour compositions.

6 From the **Tools Panel**, choose the **Paint Brush Tool**.

7 On the **Brushes Panel**, select the 128 px Round Soft Brush from the Basic category; adjust context toolbar settings (as shown above) then paint away (in black) the mountain image from some of the girl's face.

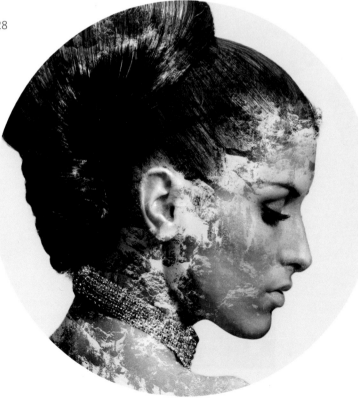

8 Select the Snow Mountain 01 (Image) layer (not its mask). From the **Layer Menu**, choose **Duplicate**.

9 Change the new layer's **Blend Mode** to *Lighten*.

10 Click the layer's mask thumbnail to select the layer mask, and paint around the girl's eye with the same brush as before (adjust **Opacity** to *100%* not *60%*). This unmask process brings out the eye detail more.

11 Rename this layer *Snow Mountain 02*. Each layer should be masked now.

RETOUCHING

Retouch 01: Cloning out unwanted hair/head outlines

It is time for the first phase of retouching. What we'll do is delete the residual portion of the girl's head outline.

1 With all layers deselected, select **Layer > New Layer**.

2 From the **Tools Panel**, select the **Clone Brush Tool**.

3 On the **Brushes Panel**, select the 128 px Round Soft Brush from the Basic category, and, on the context toolbar, adjust the **Width** to *120 px*.

4 From the context toolbar, select *Current Layer & Below* on the **Source** pop-up menu, so the source can be picked up from lower layers.

5 Let's pick up the clone source. Press the option ⌥ key (Mac) or alt key (Win) and click the crosshair cursor anywhere on the light blue sky to sample it.

6 Paint out the girl's hair and the head outline.

7 Rename the layer *Retouch 01*.

Resource

snow_queen.afphoto (*06. Retouch2* snapshot)

Retouch 02: Cloning trees

In this second phase, we're going to clone at the top of the girl's head to two separate locations nearby to give the surface more detail and variety.

For the first location, repeat the steps in Retouch 01 (p. 377), with the following changes:

- Use the same brush as before but use a **Width** of *350 px*.

- Clone source: pick up the trees at the front of the girl's head (a) using the crosshair cursor.

- Name the new layer *Clone Trees 01*.

For the second location, repeat the previous steps using the same clone source but:

- From the **Tools Panel**, select the **Move Tool** to reposition the cloned trees. Use the bounding box to resize them.

- To flip the selection, press the ctrl key and click (Mac) or right-click (Win) and choose **Transform > Flip Horizontal**.

- Rename this layer *Clone Trees 02*.

Instead of resizing the cloned selection manually, you could use **Scale** on the tool's context toolbar—this would have enlarged the area automatically while cloning.

Retouching 03: Finishing off

In this last phase of retouching we're going to achieve two objectives—fixing small details in the image, and hiding the right arm and shoulder of the girl.

For the former, use a similar cloning technique as before, but:

- Use a Round Soft Brush, but use a varying **Width** (*10-100 px*) from context toolbar.

- Name the new layer *Retouch 02*.

Using retouching, I was able to clean up the girl's forehead, back of the head and blurring in the trees at the top of the head.

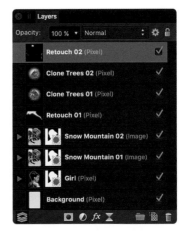

To clone out the right shoulder:

- Use a Round Soft Brush, but use a varying **Width** (*150-350 px*) and **Opacity** (*60-100%*) from context toolbar.

- Name the layer *Retouch 03*.

Resource

snow_queen.afphoto (*08. Livefilters* snapshot)

LIVE FILTERS

Now that we've finished with retouching, for better manageability and performance we'll merge all the layers in preparation for applying live filters and colour adjustments.

1 Select the Retouch 03 (Pixel) layer.

2 From the **Layer Menu**, choose **Merge Visible**. All visible layers are flattened to a new layer.

3 Name this new layer *The Snow Queen*.

4 With this layer selected, from the **Layer Menu**, select **New Live Filter Layer > Clarity Filter**.

Before

After

5 In the Live Clarity settings, change the **Strength** to *60%* to accentuate the general clarity of the image.

6 With The Snow Queen layer selected, from the **Tools Panel**, select the **Sharpen Brush Tool** and paint with a soft round brush (set **Width** to *100 px*; **Opacity** to *60%*).

Use the tool on areas around the girl's head where you want to add local contrast and increase the picture sharpness.

> Live filter layers are totally non-destructive—they can be changed or deleted at any point.

FINAL ADJUSTMENTS

To finish the look, we're going to add some adjustment layers to emphasize the white of the snow over the mountains and the overall cold tones. A subtle crop will also be carried out.

1   From the **Layer Menu**, choose **New Adjustment Layer > Selective Colour Adjustment**.

2   In the Selective Colour settings, from the **Colour** pop-up menu, select *Whites*.

3   Drag **Black** to *-100%*.

4   Apply a mask to this selected layer using **Layer > New Mask Layer** then paint on the mask with a soft round black brush (**Width** *500 px*) to hide the colour correction from the background and the girl's face.

5   Select **Layer > New Adjustment Layer > HSL Adjustment**.

6   In the HSL Adjustment settings, set **Saturation Shift** to *-14%*.

The image just needs a little better composition, so let's crop the image in slightly.

7   From the **Tools Panel**, select the **Crop Tool** (C).

8   Click on the middle-top edge handle on the crop area and drag down slightly until it looks more vertically balanced. I found an image height of *2945 px* was perfect (shown on the context toolbar).

9   On the context toolbar, click **Apply**.

The Snow Queen project is now complete! I feel the finished image shows off the full double exposure effect really well.

" *In my work, the human being melts with nature; there's a balance between reality, dream and fantasy, where colour and sensitivity have a prominent role.*

Piles of tree branches, clouds forming hair, faces that blend with air and sky, human silhouettes that arise from expanses of earth and roots... this is my visionary world.

2

Pure Gold

Particle disintegration
by *Johny Åkerlund*

In this project, Johny explores this eye-catching effect
most commonly associated with motion and speed.

BEFORE YOU
GET STARTED

Resources

 You can get all the resources that are referenced in this project from:

https://affin.co/puregold

Knowledge of Affinity Photo

To get the most from undertaking this project, you will need to:

- Be familiar with the interface of Affinity Photo. You can learn more about the interface in the Interface Tour chapter, starting on p. 13.

- Follow along with example resources by navigating and viewing snapshots that are saved in your project file. Named snapshots are suggested at stages throughout the project. See p. 9.

- Have good core skills. See the skills table below to see which additional aspects of Affinity Photo you need to be confident with to complete this project:

Selections	p. 106
Masking	p. 116

PROJECT
DETAILS

This popular effect, where the subject breaks up and disperses into pieces, looks great on most subjects and is surprisingly easy to do. The effect can vary—sometimes bigger particles, sometimes smaller such as smoke or dust. I like using this effect on a subject in motion as it gives the illusion of disintegration at great speed. You may also see the effect being called Particle Dispersion.

The photographic subject used in this project is Elise Christie, Great Britain's gold-medal-winning short-track speed skater, winning 1000- and 1500-metre gold medals at the World Short Track Championships 2017 in Rotterdam, Netherlands. Go Elise!

Resource
pure_gold.afphoto (*01. Cutout* snapshot) a MH1_3032.jpg

CUT OUT

The first step is to cut out the skater from the background.

I'll make a selection that will follow the skater's outline and then refine the selection so it surrounds the skater perfectly.

Making a selection

1 From the **File Menu**, select **Open**. Navigate to, select and open a MH1_3032.jpg.

2 On the **Tools Panel**, select the **Zoom Tool** (Z) and drag right over the skates to zoom in.

3 With the **Selection Brush Tool** (**Tools Panel**), draw a selection over the boots using a small brush **Width** (*15-20 px*).

Don't worry if you have selected too much; just hold the option ⌥ key (Mac) or alt key (Win) to paint away wrongly selected areas. Also use this to deselect areas within the selection such as under the boot.

4 Continue until the entire subject is selected.

The trickiest part on this image will be the fingers on the skater's right hand which is against the blue background. Don't worry just make it good enough for now and we'll fix that next.

Refining the selection

Normally, the refine operation separates areas of differing contrast from each other easily by painting over the areas you want to refine. However, in this case, I had to 'paint' areas of the hand back in again due to the tricky background.

Mode: Add Subtract   Width: 20 px   ▾   ✓ Snap to edges   All layers   Refine...

1   With the selection in place, click **Refine** on the context toolbar.

2   In Refine settings, set the **Preview** to *White matte* to see the edges more easily, and adjust other settings to feather the edge and set a border width within which refinement will operate.

> a) To add more to your selection, click the Adjustment brush's **Foreground** button and paint from within your selection outwards to paint back in the glove edge.

> b) To subtract areas, click the **Background** button and paint from the outside and towards your selection. For example, to clean up between the middle and ring fingers.

3 When satisfied, set the **Output** to *Mask* and click **Apply**. A mask appears on the Background layer.

I created the mask as I intended to edit the selection (as a mask) later. As it happened I didn't need the mask so I just flattened to a single layer using **Layer > Rasterise**. I could have chosen the *New layer* option instead.

4 Unlock and select the background layer, then drag the skater to the right to leave some space for the next stage.

SMUDGE

Resource

pure_gold.afphoto (*02. Smudge* snapshot)

Smudging is a retouch technique where you can drag colour around your image like running your fingers through wet paint.

1 Click on the background layer and name it *Smudge*. Then from the **Layer Menu**, choose **Duplicate**. Name the new copy *Disintegrate* and hide the layer.

2 Select the Smudge layer, then from the **Tools Panel**, select the **Smudge Brush Tool**.

3 On the **Brushes Panel**, select the *Basic* category and the brush called *Round Brush 128*. Double-click the brush to set the **Size** to *400 px* and **Hardness** to *50%*. We want to get a nice smooth smudge effect so make sure the **Spacing** is also set to *1%*.

4 Now start smudging from the skater to the left. Try keeping it simple and only do one stroke in the same area.

Adjust the brush size as you paint by pressing the ctrl+option ⌥ keys (Mac) or right mouse button+alt key (Win) while dragging the mouse left and right with left mouse button pressed; for brush hardness drag up or down with the same keys pressed.

> *I chose smudging as a technique here. A popular alternative is to use Liquify tools to warp the subject; the Push Forward Tool in Liquify Persona would have given a different base image to apply the disintegrate effect to. However, smudging gave me a more natural result, especially as the skater was in motion.*

Liquify

THE DISINTEGRATE EFFECT

Resource

pure_gold.afphoto (*03. Disintegrate* snapshot)

The effect itself uses a combination of masking and painting with texture brushes.

> Remember this rule of thumb when working with masks: white reveals, black conceals.

1   On the **Swatches Panel**, set the circular colour selectors to solid black and solid white using the square lower swatches—ensure the frontmost selector (the Primary colour) is black. You can toggle the colour selectors by pressing the X key.

2   On the **Layers Panel**, select the Smudge layer, click **Mask Layer** and then choose **Edit > Fill**. As we've set the Primary colour in the **Swatches Panel** already, ensure **Primary Colour** is enabled to fill with black; this hides the entire layer for now but we'll paint it back later. Click **Apply**.

3   Now select the Disintegrate layer and make it visible. Create a **Mask Layer** for this layer too.

4   On the **Tools Panel**, select the **Paint Brush Tool**, then on the **Brushes Panel**, change to the **Painting** category and select the first brush called *Paint 1*; adjust the context toolbar settings.

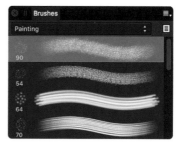

Width: 400 px ▾ Opacity: 100 % ▾ Flow: 100 % ▾ Hardness: 100 % ▾ More ⊚ Stabiliser ⌐ ⟲ Length: 35 ▾ Symmetry 1 ▾ Mirror

5 Make sure you select the mask of the top layer named Disintegrate and select the black colour. Now paint away from the left into the subject. Make sure to paint away a little on the helmet as well.

6 Select the mask on the Smudge layer and with the same brush and size set to white (not black), paint back the smudge effect. It may look too much but it's fine for the moment.

7 To fine tune, use the same brush and size with a brush colour set to black. Paint from the outer left and inwards over the smudge effect to thin it out to get a nice transition.

8 And for the final touch up, select the mask of the Disintegrate layer and with the same brush and size with white we now paint back some areas on the arm and helmet to complete the effect. Also set the Smudge layer's **Opacity** to around *70%*.

Let's add a white background to complete this section.

9 Select the Smudge layer, and from the **Toolbar**, select **Insert behind the selection**.

10 From the **Layer Menu**, choose **New Fill Layer**. The previously used white colour is used in the fill layer, which is added automatically to the bottom of the layer stack.

ADDING A NEW BACKGROUND

Resource

pure_gold.afphoto (*04. Add background* snapshot)
https://affin.co/icerink

Leaving the image with a white background gives a clean fresh look purely focused on the effect. However, the addition of an image background and some basic compositional transforms gives the subject and background a little more context.

1 Select the Disintegrate and Smudge layers and select **Arrange > Group**. Name the group *Skater* and then hide the group.

2 Select the white Fill layer and from the **File Menu**, choose **Place** and select and open the downloaded file filip-mroz-194421.jpg.

3 On the top **Toolbar**, switch on **Snapping**. This enables us to snap the image to the canvas precisely.

4 Snap the cursor to the top-left corner of the canvas, then drag down and to the right (and off the canvas) until the image snaps to the opposite canvas edge (a green vertical line appears). Reposition the image vertically so that the image's horizon is in the middle.

5 We need to remove the unwanted skater in this ice rink image so he doesn't interfere. First, rasterise the image layer using **Layer > Rasterise**.

6 On the **Tools Panel**, select the **Inpainting Brush Tool** and change your brush to a *70 px* round brush (*Basic* category) and paint over the skater.

Let's give the ice rink a blur effect that helps give the main skater a sense of motion; this complements the disintegrate effect.

1 On the **Layers Panel**, select the ice rink layer, then select **Live Filters**; from the pop-up menu, choose **Motion Blur Filter**.

2 In the Motion blur settings, check the **Preserve Alpha** box and set a **Radius** of *100 px*.

3 Select and turn on the visibility of the Skater group. Use the **Move Tool** (V) to scale and position the skater for better composition.

403

PURE GOLD

Fast as Lightning

Voila! Now the Disintegration effect is 'in the bag', I further experimented with adding some basic title text and colour adjustments to turn the project into a commercially-viable finished piece.

3

Chameleon

Swap your image's look with ready-to go macros by *Neil Ladkin*

Join Neil as he tries out some free and stylish macros for automating his workflow—multiple operations play back as a single clickable action. He'll also record his very own custom 'infrared' macro.

BEFORE YOU
GET STARTED

Resources

 You can get all the resources that are referenced in this project from:
https://affin.co/chameleon

Knowledge of Affinity Photo

To get the most from undertaking this project, you will need to:

- Be familiar with the interface of Affinity Photo. You can learn more about the interface in the Interface Tour chapter, starting on p. 13.

PROJECT
DETAILS

Macros are a recorded sequence of photo editing operations that can be stored and applied (played back) to other images.

In this project, we'll focus on pre-recorded Image Style macros that dramatically change the look and mood of your image. As some Image Style macros lend themselves more to specific image subject matter, we'll look into that too. Batch processing using a chosen macro is also used on a selected image set.

Affinity Photo also lets you record your own macros—I'll create an infrared effect and apply it to selected images.

The project's images are an assembled mix of my travel photos over the last few years. Why not try the macros out on your own shots?

INSTALLING YOUR MACRO PACK

To use the pre-recorded macros in this project, you'll have to download and install the Force Macro Pack No. 1. You'll get three .afmacros files to install into Affinity Photo.

Installing the Pack

1 If you don't have the pack already, download it using the link at the top of this page.

2 Do one of the following:

- (Mac only) From your Downloads folder (in the free-macro-pack sub-folder), double-click each afmacros file (or drag and drop the files into Affinity Photo).

- From **View > Studio**, switch on the **Library Panel.** From **Panel Preferences**, select **Import Macros** and source the files from the same location as above.

MACRO PRESETS

With Affinity Photo, preset macros are available from several categories—**Light Leaks, Image Styles** and **Distortions**. I'll focus on the **Image Styles** category exclusively for this project, which is perfect for changing the look and mood of photos.

Applying a macro

Let's load a sample image and compare the results after applying each macro in turn to the same image.

1 Select **File > Open**.

2 Navigate to, and open, the file Macro Cat.jpg.

3 From the **Library Panel**, select a macro from the expanded **Image Styles** category. I chose 'Black Beard'.

You'll see the image's look change instantly. A dialog will also pop up which lets you interact with the macro—this lets you tailor key parameters to fine-tune the results (these differ between macros).

4 Try out the other macros in the category on the same image. By clicking a new macro, the old macro is discarded.

5 Once you've chosen a macro and your preferred parameters, click **Apply**.

Once you've applied any macro, if you view the **Layers Panel**, you'll see that most of the macros involve tonal and colour adjustments and the occasional live filter.

MATCHING STYLES TO IMAGES

You'll have noticed that the macros give very different looks. In fact, some types of imagery lend themselves more to specific macro styles than others.

Hazy Day

Flat Cap

Acoustic Folk

Keyboard

The **Black Beard** macro, with its vibrance boost, brings out the coloured wood detail in an interior shot; this contrasts with the **Soft Mint** macro which gives a flatter desaturated look, perfect for stark architectural shots.

The other images benefit from macros that give subtler tone and colour shifts.

Pint of Mild

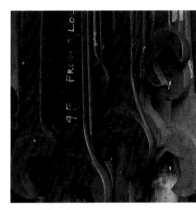

Mochachino

Black Beard

Plaid Shirt

Faded Denim

Soft Mint

BATCH PROCESSING

Instead of applying your macros image by image, macros can be applied to a whole series of images automatically by using **batch processing**—all without having to load each image in turn.

Let's pick the Black Beard macro for batch processing some landscape shots—the results should look good with the extra vibrance the macro gives.

1 Select **File > New Batch Job.**

2 From the dialog, click **Add**, then navigate to the Batch folder and select the images to process. Click **Open**.

3 I don't want to overwrite my original files, so back in the main dialog, under **Output**, enable **Save into** and choose a subfolder. I created one called *output*.

4 Check **Save as JPEG** to preserve the original file format; uncheck **Save as AFPhoto**.

5 From **Available Macros**, navigate to the **Image Styles** category, select *Black Beard*, then click **Apply**.

6 Click **OK** to run the macro against your images, boosting vibrance image by image.

With the combination of batch processing and macros, I've got some real power at my fingertips.

Resource

mother_cap_01.jpg
MyMacros.afmacros

CUSTOM MACROS

While the Force Macro Pack provides a range of macros, I want to be able to create my own macro for the photo editing operations I frequently use. Fortunately, Affinity Photo lets you create custom macros from scratch by recording any operations you make.

I'm looking for an infrared effect that will look really powerful across a range of shots.

Creating a custom category

1 On the **Library Panel**, click **Panel Preferences** and select **Create New Category**.

2 Rename the category to *MyMacros* from the **Category Options Menu** at the bottom of the panel.

Recording

1 From **View** > **Studio**, switch on the **Macro Panel**.

2 Select **File** > **Open**.

3 Navigate to, and open, the file mother_cap_01.jpg.

4 Click the **Start recording** button.

Creating the infrared effect

While recording, I'll create an infrared effect which involves applying a series of adjustments and filters to the image.

From the **Layers Panel**, apply the following in order:

1   **Invert** adjustment with a Blend Mode of *Colour*. This reverses the colour values and then blends the colour (and not luminosity) between the adjustment and underlying layer.

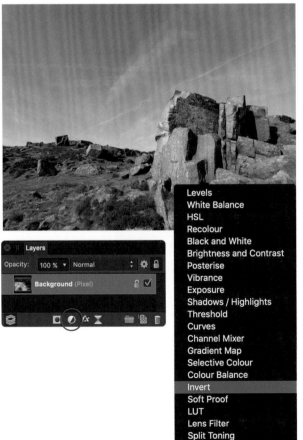

Levels
White Balance
HSL
Recolour
Black and White
Brightness and Contrast
Posterise
Vibrance
Exposure
Shadows / Highlights
Threshold
Curves
Channel Mixer
Gradient Map
Selective Colour
Colour Balance
Invert
Soft Proof
LUT
Lens Filter
Split Toning
OCIO

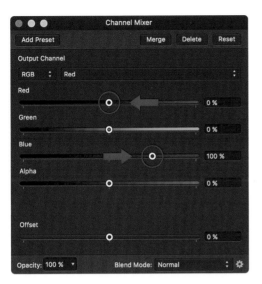

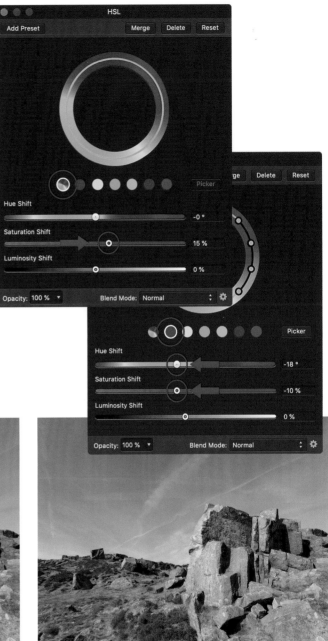

2 **Channel Mixer** adjustment with **Red** output channel set to *0% Red*, *100% Blue*; **Blue** output channel set to *100% Red*, *0% Blue*.

3 **HSL Shift** adjustment with **Saturation Shift** boost (Master channel) and a **Hue Shift** and **Saturation Shift** drop (Reds channel). For the latter, remember to swap the channel selector from *Master* to *Reds*.

4 **Diffuse Glow** live filter to give the image a dreamy look. Deselect the HSL Shift Adjustment layer by clicking **Select > Deselect Layers** before applying this filter.

5 **Brightness / Contrast** adjustment to increase the tonal contrast in the image.

Stopping recording

On the **Macro Panel**, click **Stop recording**.

The macro is created with its operations listed in chronological order in the **Macro Panel**.

Creating user interaction with the macro

As not all images will suit the same parameters, I can introduce some user interactivity with the macro once it is recorded.

In doing so, on macro playback, I can make the macro prompt for specific parameters to be adjusted to better suit the image.

1 Click the **Edit** button in the **Macro Panel**. This sets the parameters for the HSL Shift adjustment.

Remember that you can choose which (if any) operations are to be interactive.

2 From the dialog, click the **Present during playback** 'eye' button on the **Master saturation**, **Red hue** and **Red saturation** parameters to present these on playback. Rename the parameters to be *Saturation*, *Red Tone*, and *Red Intensity*, respectively.

3 Repeat for Diffuse Glow, i.e. enable **Opacity** and rename to *Diffusion*. For the Brightness / Contrast adjustment, enable both **Brightness** and **Contrast** but keep the names the same.

Now the macro is recorded and edited I can reproduce the operations by playing back the macro on other images. First, I'll need to save the macro.

What we've done here is to create a single customized dialog that prompts the user on playback, as seen on the example infrared examples opposite

Adding your macro to the Library

1 From the top of the **Macro Panel**, click **Add To Library**.

2 Select the **Category**, enter *infrared* and click **OK**.

The macro will appear in the **Library Panel** in its MyMacros category. In any session, the next time you load an image you can go to the **Library Panel** and click the infrared macro to apply it to an image. When prompted, adjust parameter sliders to suit the image.

That's all for macros and batch processing. This project should give you the skills and confidence to create your very own macros.

infrared

Saturation	16 %
Red Tone	-18 °
Red Intensity	-10 %
Diffuse	50 %
Brightness	-25 %
Contrast	130 %

Cancel   Apply

infrared

Saturation	20 %
Red Tone	100 °
Red Intensity	-50 %
Diffuse	20 %
Brightness	-25 %
Contrast	130 %

Cancel   Apply

Discovery

Pro compositing techniques
by *Neil Ladkin*

Join me as I take on the challenge of compositing images
realistically in my digital art project.

BEFORE YOU GET STARTED

Resources

 You can get all the resources that are referenced in this project from:
https://affin.co/discovery

Knowledge of Affinity Photo

To get the most from undertaking this project, you will need to:

- Be familiar with the interface of Affinity Photo. You can learn more about the interface in the Interface Tour chapter, starting on p. 13.

- Have good core skills. See the skills table below to see which additional aspects of Affinity Photo you need to be confident with to complete this project:

Adjustments	p. 100
Selections	p. 106
Masking	p. 116
Sharpening	p. 132

PROJECT DETAILS

What is compositing?

Compositing combines images from different sources into a single image, mainly for creative reasons. For professional results, the digital artist should consider each image initially and how they combine together on the page.

We've all seen composite artwork that just somehow doesn't look quite right! The images that make up the composite piece may well be of good quality but there may be a disparity between images, giving an unnatural look. Here are a few reasons why...

- Inconsistent ambient lighting

- Directional lighting varies between images

- Colour differences

- Images are 'hard edged'

- Clashes in image sharpness/blurring

In this project, I'll explore how to overcome such challenges while creating some digital art with a slightly supernatural feel.

To keep the emphasis of the project purely on compositing techniques, I've supplied the imagery as ready-to-go resources.

Resource

Discovery.afbrushes
Discovery Background.jpg

IMPORTING BRUSHES

I've supplied a few brushes that are perfect for painting and erasing—you'll need to import these first before starting the project.

- From the **Brushes Panel**'s panel preferences, select **Import Brushes**. Navigate to your resource files, select and open Discovery.afbrushes.

The brush set will be imported into the **Discovery** category in the panel.

OPENING THE BASE IMAGE

- Select **File > Open**, then navigate to, select and open Discovery background.jpg.

SCENE SPLITTING

I want to separate the base image into foreground, midground and background so I can work independently on each. This lets me introduce some depth later which will help stay focused on the main subjects of interest.

1 From the **Tools Panel**, choose the **Selection Brush Tool**.

2 Drag over the foreground to select it.

3 From the context toolbar, click **Refine** to more accurately select the division between the foreground and the rest of the image by setting **Border width**, then output as a new layer, naming it *Foreground*.

4 Repeat to create a Midground layer called *Mid* which includes the mountains and the foreground.

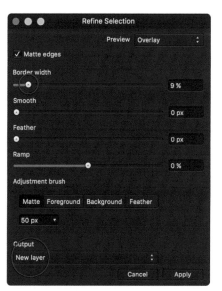

On the **Layers Panel**, switch the foreground and background layer visibility back on, so you can independently control the tones of all layers later in the project.

ADDING CONTENT

Let's add the images for compositing. They already have transparency backgrounds so they can be placed without the need to cut them out.

1 Open both Astronaut.png and Element.png as separate files.

2 Copy and paste each file into your project file, positioning and sizing each to fit the scene.

3 Name each layer *Astronaut* and *Element*, respectively.

You should now have separate layers: the background scene, the astronaut and the Element object.

TONING THE SCENE

I really want to introduce strong directional lighting that will be the major focal point in the project along with the light source itself and the astronaut. This will also challenge me to deal with how the light 'falls' on the astronaut and the surrounding ground.

The pre-designed Element object already has a light source that will flood the scene with light. My first task is to draw the light beam that somehow emanates from the Element.

Creating a light beam

1 From the **Tools Panel**, select the **Pen Tool**.

2 Click repeatedly on the page to draw a fan shape (no fill) that comes from the Element's light source and stretches to roughly the height of the astronaut. Name the created Curve layer to be *Light beam*.

3 Using the **Paint Brush Tool**, paint with a white Smoke brush over the shape. To lessen the stroke strength, drop the layer **Opacity** to *69%*.

4 On the **Layers Panel**, clip the brushed layer to the Light beam's layer by dragging. This clips the brush's strokes to the beam's outline.

> To give the smoke a more natural look, give the Light beam layer an *Overlay* blend mode and use the **Erase Brush Tool** (using the same brush) to make the smoke a little more random in appearance.

Toning down

I need to tone down the background, midground and foreground as they are a little overpowering. It will also give me the scope and opportunity to light the area under the astronaut.

For the selected Background layer:

- Add an HSL adjustment below the Mid layer, with **Saturation Shift** set to *-82%*. This strips most of the orange colour from the sky.

- To offset the grey look, use the **Rectangle Tool** to add a rectangle spanning the sky; with the **Gradient Tool**, apply a gradient fill (*RGB 0,12,43*) across the shape, falling away downwards to *0% * **Opacity**; name the layer *Tint*. This gives the sky an increasingly steely blue look toward the image edge. Lessen the layers strength with *50% * **Opacity** and a *Soft Light* blend mode.

For the selected Mid layer:

- Add another HSL Adjustment and clip it to the Mid layer by dragging; this restricts the adjustment to just this layer. The adjustment pulls down both saturation and luminance.

For the selected Foreground layer:

Repeat as for the Mid layer, but set the three sliders to *5.8°, -55%* and *-59%*, respectively.

> All adjustments are non-destructive as they are independent layers. This means I can alter my adjustments at a later time—my image layer will remain unaffected throughout.

Although the project looks overly dark at the moment, I can now bring back lighting in a very controllable way.

INTRODUCING LIGHTING

Consider light sources in your image, their direction and how any added images might be affected by light—whether from your main image or from the added image itself.

In this project, our most obvious light source comes from the Element, but also from the sun behind the mountains.

Unmasking to introduce lighting

By unmasking areas, I'll reveal more light back into the scene by erasing with a soft brush.

For the foreground area:

1 From the **Tools Panel**, select the **Erase Brush Tool**.

2 From the **Brushes Panel**, choose a Round Light Brush; from the context toolbar, reduce **Flow** to around *30%*, keeping **Hardness** to *0%*. Adjust **Opacity** to suit and choose black to erase with.

3 With the Foreground layer's Adjustment mask selected, erase away the adjustment under and in front of the astronaut to reveal the unadjusted foreground layer.

4 To bring back some colour from the sun, erase on the HSL adjustment mask directly above the background layer in a similar way.

> I changed hardness and opacity as I continued to erase. Also, keeping the Flow value low meant that I erased less when painting. This gave me more control.

More light, more colour. Less light, less colour

As I've exposed more light (and therefore colour) when erasing the foreground area, I added an HSL adjustment clipped to the Foreground layer that desaturated (*-55%*) and removed luminance (*-59%*) from just this area.

ASTRONAUT

In this project, our Astronaut looks even odder than most astronauts do on a moor. This is a good example of tonal and lighting mismatch, which can be fixed with a simple adjustment and then erasing.

Reducing uniform tone

- From **Layer > New Adjustment Layer**, select the **Brightness / Contrast Adjustment** and alter the settings to match the surrounding scene (**a**). Clip the adjustment to the Astronaut layer to affect just the astronaut.

Lighting

Using the same principle that we used for the foreground, I want to reintroduce light by erasing parts of the adjustment mask over the astronaut's spacesuit; I'll fix unwanted blue shadow tones too.

1 Select the Astronaut's Brightness / Contrast Adjustment layer.

2 With the **Erase Brush Tool**, erase the adjustment by painting in black (**b**). Concentrate on the front of the helmet, chest, legs and boots.

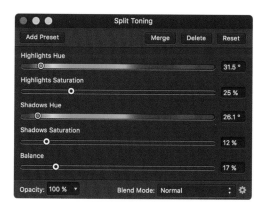

3 Duplicate the layer and continue erasing (**c**).

4 To fix the blue tone in the shadows, I applied a **Split Toning adjustment** to the Astronaut layer (**d**).

5 Paint in more highlights as separate layers (always using *Overlay* blend modes); also erase around the boots using the Grass brush (**e**) on a new Mask layer to blend the boots into the grass.

> You'll need to use erase brush strokes of varied width and opacity here. To help productivity, use the [and] shortcut keys for width control, and number keys for opacity control (e.g., 4 for *40%*).

SHADOWS AND HIGHLIGHTS

Let's now move back to the foreground to create two shadow areas cast from the Astronaut—one stronger than the other. Highlights from the Element light source can also now be added.

Adding shadows

1 With Foreground layer selected, add a new pixel layer named *Shadow1* with a *Multiply* blend mode.

2 Colour pick from the darkest grass area; press the option ⌥ key (Mac) or alt key (Win), then click-drag to sample. With the **Paint Brush Tool**, paint with a soft brush (*20-40% Opacity*; *30% Hardness*), then use the **Erase Brush Tool** with a Grass brush to paint back grass-like detail.

When painting in shadows, always avoid 100% black.

3 Repeat for a new *Shadow2* layer, but add a **Gaussian Blur** layer effect (*3.7 px*) and drop **Opacity** (*64%*) for a softer shadow.

R:18 G:13 B:7

Adding highlights

Highlights are added to the grass in front of the astronaut in two passes—first by painting and then by erasing with a Grass brush.

1 Add a new pixel layer named *Highlight* with an *Overlay* blend mode.

2 With the **Paint Brush Tool**, paint with a white *64 px* Round Light Brush to add a soft highlight around the astronaut.

3 With the **Erase Brush Tool**, paint over the soft highlight with a white *20 px* Grass brush.

4 Group the shadow and highlight layers together using **Arrange > Group**. Name this group *Shadow/highlight*.

By erasing with a grass brush, you're breaking up the uniformity of the shadows and highlights, taking advantage of the random nature of grass brush strokes.

ADDING MOOD

Nothing creates mood better than some introduced mist and smoke, for creative effect and for practically overcoming problems while compositing, e.g. to make composite images appear more seamless.

Mist

Let's soften the hard edge between the foreground and midground using some 'moody' mist.

1 With the Midground layer selected, add a new pixel layer.

2 With the **Paint Brush Tool**, paint with a white Smoke brush along the division between the foreground and midground and reduce the layer's **Opacity** to *40%*.

For greater realism, create another pixel layer inside the Foreground layer and paint along the edge again with the same brush. The two 'mist' layers should blend together well.

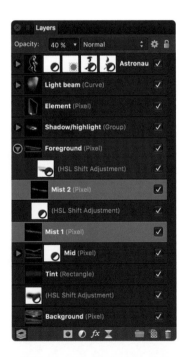

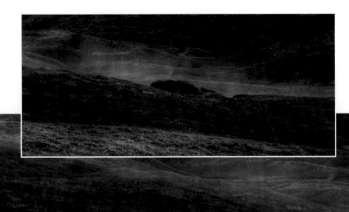

Smoke and steam

Before moving on, I'll add some more smoke around the Element object to complement and disturb the smoke in the light beam, and then add some more widespread steam emanating from around the Element.

- **Smoke**: Add a pixel layer, named *Smoke*, to the top of the layer stack. Paint with the Smoke brush, then apply a *Screen* blend mode, lessening the layer **Opacity** to suit (I chose *50%*).

- **Steam**: Create a group called Steam, placed under the Smoke layer, which should contain pixel layers containing more widespread brush strokes using the same brush, but with different layer blend modes such as *Soft Light* and *Lighter Colour*.

Diffusion

To complement the surrounding mist, the light beam needs to be more diffuse.

- Select the Light beam layer, and apply a **Gaussian Blur** layer effect (about *4 px*) from the **Effects Panel**.

The Smoke layer, Steam group and the Light beam layer's Layer Effects icon are shown in the **Layers Panel**.

FINISHING TOUCHES

Adding image depth

At the moment, the image appears slightly flat which draws the eye as much to the background as to the foreground. With the foreground layer already separate from the midground and background layers, I can now give the image a sense of depth.

- Choose **Select > Deselect Layers**, and then **Layer > New Live Filter Layer > Gaussian Blur Filter** (set to *1.2 px*). Drag the filter layer from the top of the layer stack to directly above the Mid layer.

Making stars

I'm going to introduce a blue haze under the light along with some stars—this adds a little extra atmosphere. I'll use another file that contains both haze and stars.

1 Open Stars.png in Affinity Photo.

2 Copy and paste its layer content into your project file, positioning and sizing it over the light beam.

3 Name the layer to be *Stars*, give it a *Screen* blend mode and an **Opacity** of *80%*.

4 Apply a Mask Layer and erase with the **Erase Brush Tool** and a black Smoke brush (*70%* **Flow**; *0%* **Hardness**) around the edges of the image.

I added some extra stars sparingly using our Stars brush, with a brush **Opacity** of *57%*.

Accentuating light sources

Let's add some glare to the Element's light source, particles and the sun.

1   Add new pixel layers called *Glare* and *Sun*.

2   With the **Paint Brush Tool**, paint over the sources with a white Round Soft Brush set to *0%* **Hardness**.

3   Apply an *Overlay* blend mode and lower **Opacity** to the light source and particles to soften the results.

4   Switch to the Sun layer, then with the same brush settings, paint in white over the sun.

Tonal fine-tuning

Tonal adjustments and filters applied at the top of your layer stack affect the whole composition. I often use these to marry everything together and match tones on project completion.

1 Choose **Select > Deselect Layers**.

2 From the **Layers Panel**, select **Adjustments**. From the pop-up menu, I applied the following adjustments:

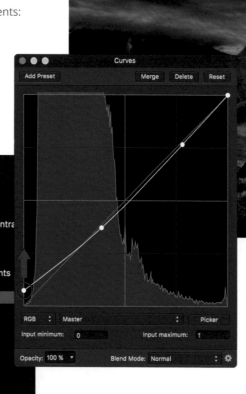

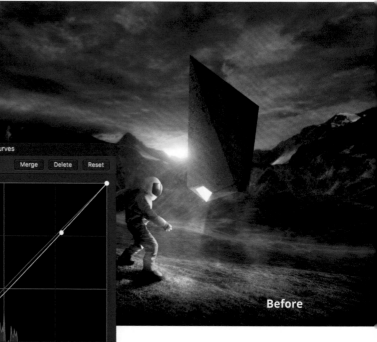

Before

Curves adjustment
Use to lighten the shadows so the image corners aren't so dark.

After

White Balance adjustment
Use to 'warm up' the image.

Split-toning adjustment

Use to stylize the image and remove colour casts; in this case, an orange cast.

Live Unsharp Mask filter

Gives a harsher look, especially noticeable on the Element's stone textures.

Apply Live filters via **Layer > New Live Filter Layer** when all other layers are deselected.

Well that completes the pro compositing project!

I hope you've seen that consideration to lighting, tone, and colour can make your compositing work reach even higher levels of quality.

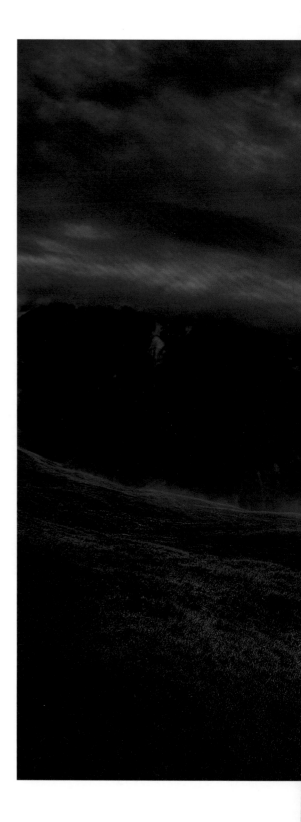

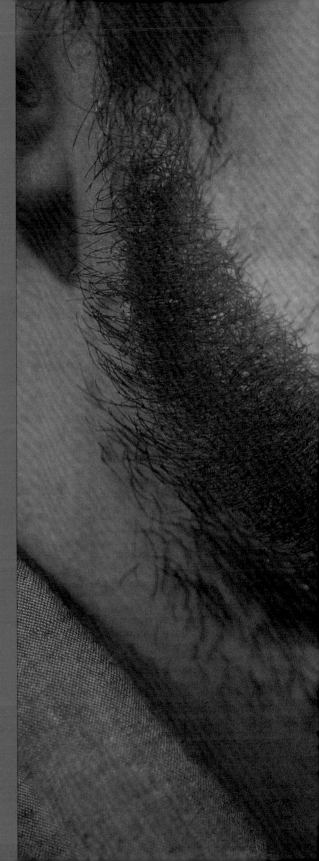

Cologne

Creating custom hair brushes by *Paolo Limoncelli*

This project, intended for a potential cologne advert, covers the workflow of creating hair brushes from a sample image, and applying them to the same image for realistic facial hair retouching. I'll also tune up brushes for use with graphics tablets or other pressure-sensitive devices.

BEFORE YOU GET STARTED

Resources

 You can get all the resources that are referenced in this project from:
https://affin.co/cologne

Knowledge of Affinity Photo

To get the most from undertaking this project, you will need to:

- Be familiar with the interface of Affinity Photo. You can learn more about the interface in the Interface Tour chapter, starting on p. 13.

PROJECT DETAILS

In this project, I want to improve the appearance of a model subject's beard while keeping results realistic.

Using Affinity Photo's powerful raster brush engine, I'll create hair brushes from traced hairs on the original subject. Each traced hair will act as a brush nozzle, which along with other nozzles, will make up my brush tip. With a built up set of brushes for different hair types, I'll be ready for some absolutely authentic hair retouching.

BRUSH TYPES

To cater for different facial hair lengths and appearance, I'll create brushes for three categories of hair:

- Long

- Short

- Out of Focus

For each category, I'll create an Intensity brush for retouching and an Image brush for filling—both created from the same nozzles.

- **Intensity brushes** use greyscale data of a specific nozzle to apply a colour or a correction (e.g., burn). Any image you use for the nozzle will be internally translated to a grey ramp resulting in an intensity map.

- **Image brushes** use pure raster data (including colour) and distribute this data sequentially.

CREATING NOZZLES

To create custom brushes, I first need to create one or more nozzles that will make up each category's Intensity and Image brush tip. Each nozzle will represent a single 'hair' on the brush tip.

Tracing

Let's start with long ones, so let's find an area suitable for this purpose, where hairs are distinct and well defined.

1 Download the image from the web address in the above Resource box. (1920x1137px without site sign-up; 5999x3555px with site sign-up.)

2 Open the image (man-2308464.jpg) in Affinity Photo using **File > Open**, then duplicate the locked background layer via right-click.

3 From the **Tools Panel**, select the **Pen Tool**.

4 From the Pen context toolbar, select a strong blue colour (*RGB 0,37,255*) for the **Stroke**. Click at one end of the hair and then, at the other end, hold down the mouse button and click-drag away from the node to bend the curve to fit. Close the curve with the esc key.

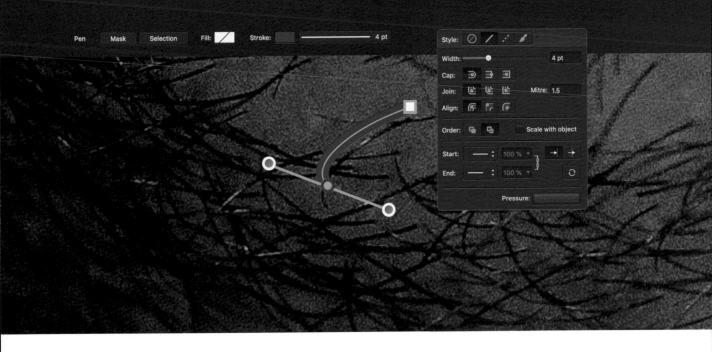

5 Change the stroke from *0 pt* to *4 pt* width on the context toolbar.

6 Repeat this process nine times, each time with a different hair of similar length.

7 From the **Layers Panel**, select all Curve layers, group together (**Arrange > Group**) and name the group *long*.

This group contains the data that will make up our first brush tip.

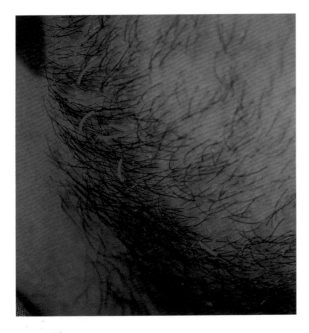

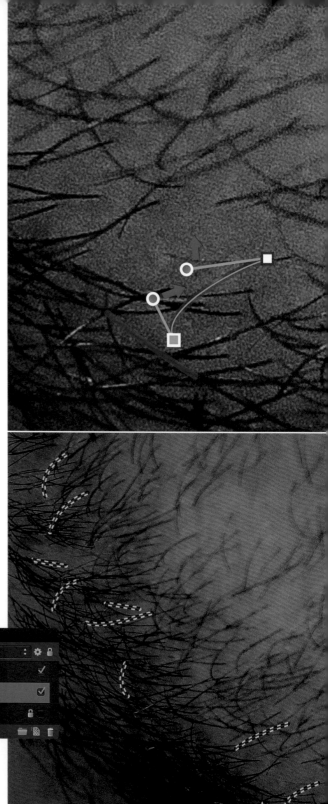

Editing strokes

Let's make the strokes a little more realistic by matching them to the underlying hair more accurately.

1   First, we'll temporarily make the hair more visible. From the **Layers Panel**, change the group's Blend Mode to *Add* and change **Opacity** to around *40%*.

2   Resize all stroke widths down to *1 pt*, then use the **Node Tool** to reposition nodes or control handles to better fit the image's hair.

Selection from layers

1   From the **Layers Panel**, change the group's Blend Mode back to *Passthrough*.

2   Click on the group thumbnail while holding the cmd ⌘ key (Mac) or ctrl key (Win). This shortcut will create a selection from the group's layer content and allows us to copy the raster data to a new layer.

3   With the selection still active, select the topmost Background layer, and **Copy** and **Paste** from the **Edit Menu** to create a new Background layer.

4 Hiding all layers, except the new Background layer, will show our traced hairs in isolation.

> For an isolated view of your work, click the new Background layer's thumbnail with the option ⌥ key (Mac) or alt key (Win) pressed.

Exporting hairs

Let's export the traced hair to make separate PNG files for each brush nozzle. In Export Persona, you can export each hair as a drawn slice in PNG format.

1 From the top **Toolbar**, select **Export Persona**.

2 From the **Tools Panel**, select the **Slice Tool** (S) and draw a marquee around each hair in turn—resize and reposition each slice if needed.

3 On the **Slices Panel**, ensure the **Export Preset** is set to *Single PNG-24* to preserve transparency.

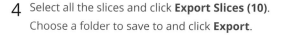

4 Select all the slices and click **Export Slices (10)**. Choose a folder to save to and click **Export**.

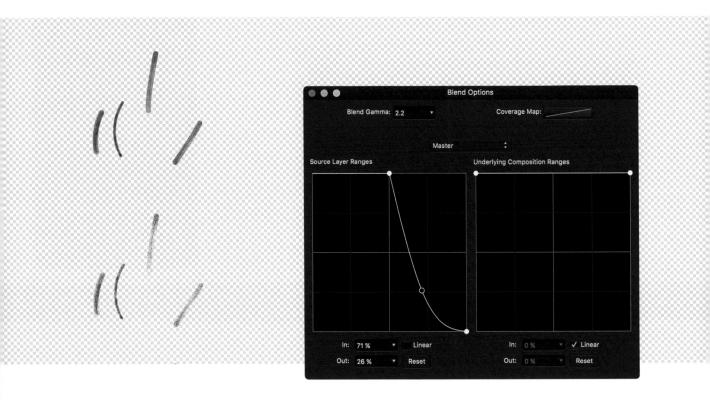

Short and out-of-focus hair

This process can be repeated for short hairs and out-of-focus ones. Just start again, tracing chosen hairs, then make a selection, copy to new layer and export slices to PNG.

For out-of-focus hair, I applied a Levels adjustment, pulling the **White Level** down (to *60%*) to lighten the hair. I also used the Blend Ranges option on the Layers Panel to lessen the stroke strength on the created raster layer.

Resource
Nozzles>short folder (slice21.png - slice30.png)

CREATING BRUSH PRESETS

Using the exported PNGs for long, short and out-of-focus hairs, you should now have all the necessary resources to create custom brushes.

Let's leave the exported long hair samples you created for the moment, and concentrate on creating short Intensity and short Image brushes. This is because the brush setup introduces a few extra settings of interest to the project.

Creating a short intensity brush

Intensity brushes will be used to retouch and fix our work using mostly Blur and Burn tools together with the Erase Brush Tool; this improves shading and volume. We'll use some short nozzles to create the brush.

1 On the **Brushes Panel**, select **Panel Preferences**, then choose **Create New Category** from the pop-up menu; rename the created Brushes category to be *Retouching Tools* from the same menu.

2 Select **New Intensity Brush** from the previous menu.

3 From your Downloads folder, browse to the nozzles > Short folder. Select all PNG files in this folder and click **Open**. Rename the new brush to be *Intensity - Short* via right-click.

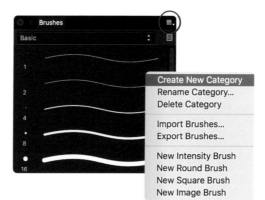

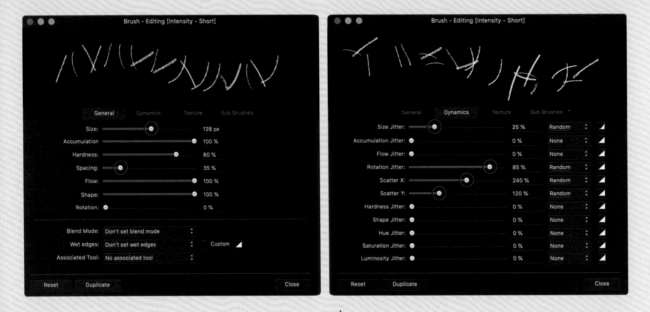

Editing brushes

> The term Jitter is a bit technical but think of these settings as how random the size, rotation and scattering will be for each brush nozzle.

1 Double-click the Intensity - Short brush entry to display the Brush - Editing settings.

In the upper preview window, the separate nozzles combine to make the brush stroke.

2 Even though randomly arranged, the nozzles are packed too closely. To improve nozzle distribution, increase **Size** to *128 px* and **Spacing** to *35%*.

3 Click the **Dynamics** tab. This tab lets us randomize nozzle behaviour by increasing **Size Jitter**, **Rotation Jitter** and **Scatter Jitter** and setting the Controller setting to *Random*.

Long and out-of-focus hair

This process can be repeated for long hair and out-of-focus hair. For long hair, use your exported files from p. 455 or those in the nozzles > Long folder in your downloaded resources for practice.

For out-of-focus brushes, trace chosen hairs, then select, copy and export to PNG. For these brush presets, I switched off **Rotation Jitter** and chose **Flow Jitter** instead to give me a subtler result.

Repeat the same steps for all remaining nozzles to complete the creation of Intensity brushes.

Image brushes

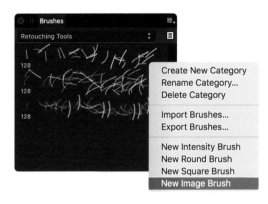

Image brushes contain real sampled colour data, so they tend to be designed for specific images; however, when used with equivalent Intensity brushes they can be used more globally.

Creating Image brushes

Use the same procedure (p. 457) as described for Intensity brushes but with a few differences:

- On the **Brushes Panel**, select **New Image Brush** (instead of New Intensity Brush).

- On nozzle import, the nozzle preview window will show nozzles in colour (not greyscale).

- We'll boost randomness so Jitter values are a bit different.

Here are my Jitter settings (Dynamics tab) for all my created Intensity and Image brushes so far:

Brush Name	Size Jitter	Flow Jitter	Rotation Jitter	Scatter X	Scatter Y
Intensity - Short	25 Random	0	85 Random	240 Random	120 Random
Intensity - Long	32 Random	45 Random	0	400 Random	220 Random
Intensity - Out of Focus	35 Random	50 Random	0	35 Random	75 Random
Image - Short	40 Random	0	4 Random	120 Random	80 Random
Image - Long	32 Random	0	100 Random	56 Random	150 Random
Image - Out of Focus	45 Random	60 Random	0	50 Random	125 Random

All other Jitter settings are assumed to be set to 0%.

DIRECTIONAL AND PRESSURE-SENSITIVE BRUSHES

The Intensity and Image brush set gives me a good core set of brushes for retouching. However, I wanted to expand the set to introduce brushes whose nozzles follow the direction of the brush stroke; I also needed some brushes that respond to pressure sensitivity when using a graphics tablet.

Rather than create brushes from scratch I can duplicate existing brushes and modify them.

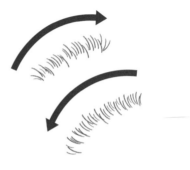

Directional brushes

Randomized nozzles are great for blocking, but facial hair tends to grow in the same direction. To create directional brushes to simulate this, we're going to make a couple of directional brushes to follow our mouse/pen direction.

1. On the **Brushes Panel**, double-click the Image - Short brush, then click **Duplicate** in the dialog. Select the duplicated brush in the panel.

2. In the **Texture** tab, delete every nozzle in the **Brush Nozzles** window except the second one. We'll base the brush on this single nozzle that will repeat along the brush stroke.

3 In the **General** tab, drop brush **Size** to *96 pt* and **Spacing** to *15 pt*.

4 In the **Dynamics** tab, adjust **Size Jitter** and both **Scatter Jitter** values, but more importantly, increase **Rotation Jitter** to *100%* and set the controller to *Direction*. This aligns the nozzle to the brush direction.

5 Rename the brush (via right-click in the panel) to *Image - Short Directional*.

6 Follow these steps to create directional versions of the Intensity - Short, Image - Long and Intensity - Long brushes.

My final Jitter settings (Dynamics tab) for my Directional brushes were as follows:

Brush Name	Size Jitter	Flow Jitter	Rotation Jitter	Scatter X	Scatter Y
Image - Short Directional	40 Random	0	100 Direction	35 Random	75 Random
Intensity - Short Directional	40 Random	0	100 Direction	35 Random	45 Random
Image - Long Directional	32 Random	0	100 Direction	25 Random	100 Random
Intensity - Long Directional	32 Random	25 Random	100 Direction	45 Random	80 Random

Pressure-sensitive brushes

For graphics tablet users, I created pressure-sensitive brushes duplicated from short directional brushes (p. 460). The key settings for these brushes, named Image - Short Dynamic and Intensity - Short Dynamic, include increased **Size Jitter** values, changing controllers from *Direction* to *Pressure* and advanced pressure ramp control.

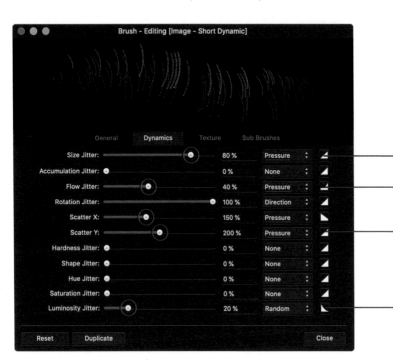

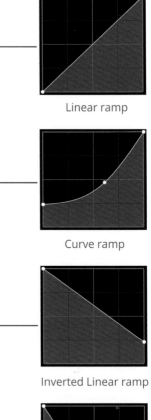

Linear ramp

Curve ramp

Inverted Linear ramp

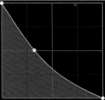

Inverted Curve ramp

> Your brush strokes should immediately become pressure sensitive as soon as you change the controllers to Pressure.

How does it work?

Essentially, the more you press your stylus on the tablet, the greater the variance of size, flow, and scattering of nozzles.

- **Size Jitter** linearly increase the nozzle size as you press.

- **Flow Jitter** lays down more nozzles as you press according to an exponential curve ramp.

- **Scatter Jitter** normally spreads out nozzles with increasing stylus pressure. In fact, I wanted the reverse, where nozzles are condensed more with increased pressure. To do this, I inverted the linear ramp (as indicated).

- **Luminosity Jitter** applies a random light variance to the nozzles with pressure. An inverted ramp, will give occasional light hairs amongst dark ones; the ramp is curved to exponentially introduce light hairs.

> To experiment, try setting all jitter settings to *0%* apart from one. As you press on the tablet, you'll see, in isolation, how that jitter setting affects the brush stroke when varying pressure.

Resource
Retouching Tools.afbrushes
cologne.afphoto (*01. Blocking* snapshot)

RETOUCHING

My core retouching objective is to improve the beard's appearance, while trying to keep the result as natural as possible. The beard isn't as tidy as I'll need for some potential advertising work.

The retouch work assumes the bigger sample image (5999 x 3555px) is downloaded. If you chose to download the smaller sample image to avoid site sign up, you may have to reduce your brush sizes to work best with the image.

Brush import

If you haven't created the brush sets yourself, you can use my completed retouch brushes. Simply double-click the downloaded Retouching Tools.afbrushes file to import to the **Brushes Panel**.

Along with the brushes described previously, I've supplied a few softened intensity and image long brushes to experiment with.

Blocking

To block in the beard area, we'll apply our first level of hairs, focussing on the cheek.

1 Create a new empty pixel layer named *Facial Hairs - Blocking* with a layer **Opacity** of *80%*.

2 From the **Tools Panel**, select the **Paint Brush Tool** and choose the Image - Out Of Focus brush from the Retouching Tools category of the **Brushes Panel**. Set the brush **Opacity** to *20%* on the context toolbar, then roughly paint the cheek area.

3 Paint some more using an Image - Long brush (**Opacity** *80%*) to lay down long hairs.

For an isolated view of your brush work, click the Blocking layer's thumbnail with the option ⌥ key (Mac) or alt key (Win) pressed.

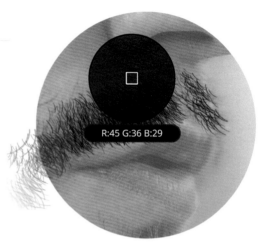

Resource
cologne.afphoto (*02. Directional brushing* snapshot)

Directional brush retouching

Now let's thicken the beard naturally by applying directional brushes.

1 Create a new layer called *Facial Hairs - Directional*.

2 Paint with the Image - Long Directional brush, following the direction of existing beard hair.

3 Swap to the Image - Short Directional variant and use a brush **Opacity** of *40%*.

To improve the moustache:

4 Select the Intensity - Short Directional brush and sample a moustache hair colour by pressing the option ⌥ key (Mac) or alt key (Win) while holding the mouse button down. Continue painting the moustache until you're satisfied.

Erasing

With the **Erase Brush Tool**, paint with a basic Soft Round brush (**Hardness** *0%*; **Opacity** *40%*) on both layers again to either erase overly strong painted areas or gradually blend away hairs from out-of-focus areas.

> At this point, I also blocked in more of the beard and moustache and continued to selectively erase using the same brushes as before.

Resource
cologne.afphoto (*03. BurnBlur* snapshot)
cologne.afphoto (*04. CleanUp* snapshot)

Burning and blurring

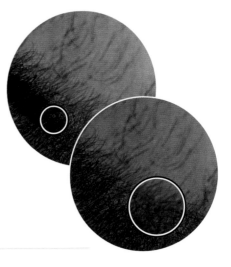

1   Switch to the **Burn Brush Tool**, and select *Midtones* from the context
toolbar. Paint on both Directional and Blocking layers with the
Intensity - Short Directional brush to darken the lower cheek area; this
improves the shading.

2   With the **Blur Brush Tool**, use a basic Soft Round brush on both layers
to blur areas and harmonise out-of-focus areas with sharper ones.

Changing opacity

While the results are looking good, I think the beard's appearance is a little too strong. I can
fix this by dropping the **Opacity** of the Facial Hair - Directional layer from *100%* down to *80%*.

Clean up

To finish off, I'll clean up areas around the cheek and some small hairs
just below the nostril and mouth.

1   From the **Layers Panel**, create a new empty pixel layer called
Inpainting.

2   From the **Tools Panel**, select the **Inpainting Brush Tool** and ensure
the context toolbar is set to *50 px* **Width** and *Current Layer & Below*
is set. Start brushing away stray hairs and unsightly imperfections.

With a difficult subject like this, due to the out of focus areas and
differing hair characteristics, I think the retouching is looking realistic
thanks to some custom brush design and some restrained brush
control.

My retouch work came in useful when I used the finished image in a
commercial advertising piece.

Experiment with the extra dynamic
and softened brushes available in
the Retouching Tools brush set.

WITHOUT COMPROMISE

CMYK

Eau de Cologne

INDEX

Mac

AFFINITY Photo

PHOTO PERSONA SHORTCUTS

PHOTO PERSONA SHORTCUTS

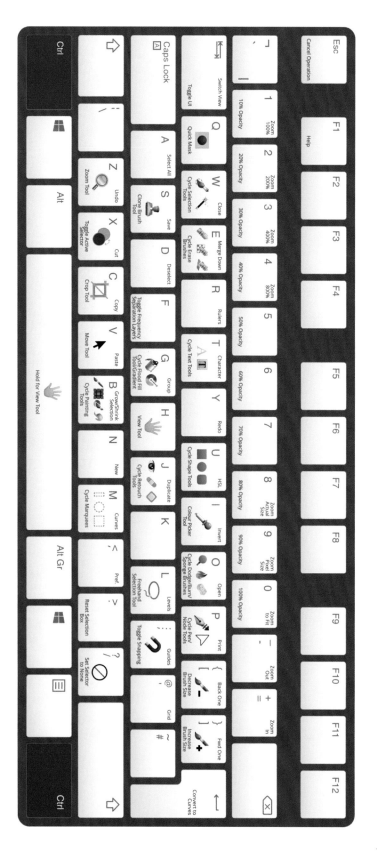

AFFINITY
Photo

Windows

LIQUIFY PERSONA SHORTCUTS

LIQUIFY PERSONA SHORTCUTS

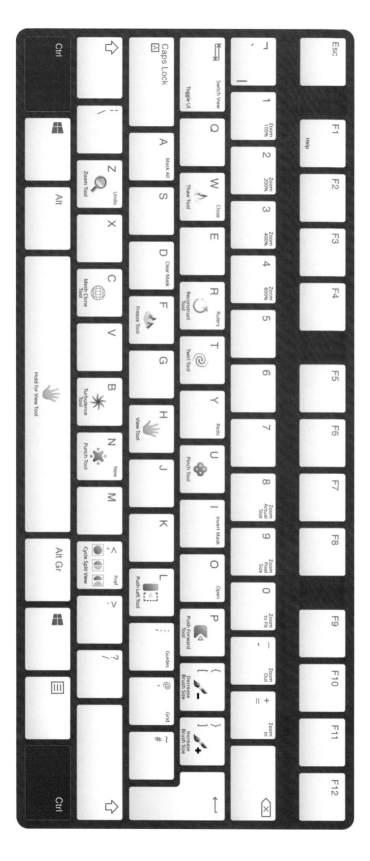

AFFINITY Photo

Windows

AFFINITY
Photo

Mac

DEVELOP PERSONA SHORTCUTS

DEVELOP PERSONA SHORTCUTS

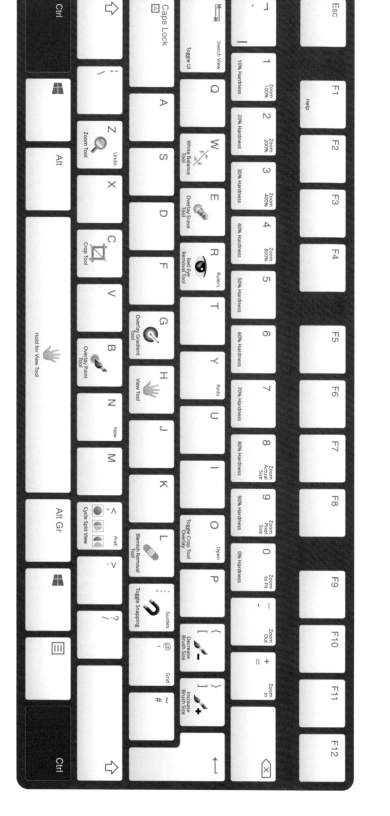

AFFINITY
Photo

Windows

AFFINITY **Photo**

 Mac

GESTURES

Zooming

Alt

Alt

Panning

Alt

Scrolling

Vertical

Horizontal

Shift ⇧

EXPRESSIONS

For use in input boxes in the Transform panel (and other areas of the UI)

W: 120 px
H: 150 px

W

H

Original

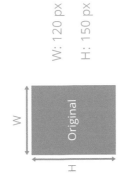

W: =75%	= 90 px
W: h+30	= 180 px
W: h-5	= 145 px
W: 2*h	= 300 px
W: h/2	= 75 px
W: gr*h	= 242.7 px

W: 118+55	= 173 px
W: 37*4	= 148 px
W: +80	= 200 px
W: −20	= 100 px
W: *=2	= 240 px
W: /=2	= 60 px
W: *=1.4	= 168 px

ADVANCED TEXT

Press buttons for various actions
Alt ⌥   Cmd ⌘   Shift ⇧   Ctrl ^

↓

Line Break ↵

⇧

ctrl

Decrease Leading ◄

Increase Leading ►

Loosen Spacing ▲

+ ≡

⇧ Super-script

◄

alt

Tighten Spacing ▼

− En Dash
⇧ Em Dash
^ Subscript

}
]

⌥

cmd ⌘

^ Spelling Options

/
\

?
¿

⇧ Bigger

∨.

P

∨.

⇧ Smaller

O

Non-Breaking Space

^ Emoji & Symbols

L

K

⌘ + T   Character Panel
⇧ ⌘ + T   Typography Dialog

(Add ⌘ to increase step size   ◄ & ▲)
(Add ⌘ to decrease step size   ◄ & ▼)

AFFINITY
Photo

Windows

ADVANCED TEXT

Press buttons for various actions

Ctrl   Alt   Shift ⇧

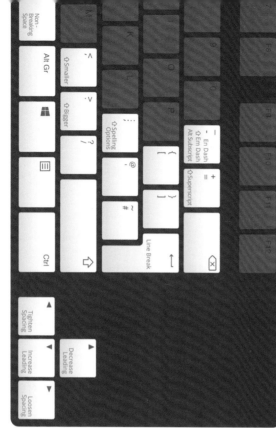

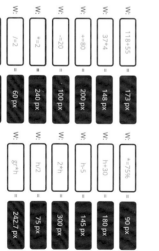

Non-Breaking Space

Alt Gr

⇧Smaller `

⇧Bigger ´

?

⟨▦⟩

Ctrl

⇧Spelling Options ∴

@ ·

ʒ

– En Dash
– ⇧ Em Dash
Alt Subscript

⇧Superscript

[{

] }

Line Break

⟨⌫⟩

⇧

↑

Tighten Spacing ▲

Decrease Leading ▶

Increase Leading ◀

Loosen Spacing ▼

Ctrl   + T   Character Panel
Ctrl+⇧ + T   Typography Dialog

Alt + ⇧ + ▲   Tighten Spacing More
Alt + ⇧ + ▼   Loosen Spacing More
Ctrl + ⇧ + ◀   Precise Increase Leading
Ctrl + ⇧ + ▶   Precise Decrease Leading

EXPRESSIONS

For use in input boxes in the Transform panel (and other areas of the UI)

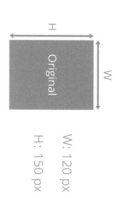

Original

W: 120 px
H: 150 px

W:	118+55	=	173 px
W:	37*4	=	148 px
W:	+=80	=	200 px
W:	–=20	=	100 px
W:	*=2	=	240 px
W:	/=2	=	60 px
W:	*=1.4	=	168 px

W:	*=75%	=	90 px
W:	h+30	=	180 px
W:	h-5	=	145 px
W:	2*h	=	300 px
W:	h/2	=	75 px
W:	gr*h	=	242.7 px

MODIFIERS & LAYER CONTROL

Clone, Healing & Liquify Mesh Clone	Option	Select a source
Dodge/Burn & Blur/Sharpen tools	Option	Temporarily switches to the opposite tool
Freehand Selection Tool	Shift Shift Drag	Temporarily switches to Polygonal from Freehand Temporarily switches between Polygonal and Magnetic Temporarily switches to Freehand from Polygonal or Magnetic
General	Shift Cmd Option Ctrl	Reverses aspect ratio constraint on scaling Scales from the centre of selection Ignores snapping during operation Rotates from opposite corner of layer
Layers Panel	☐ Layer 1 ☑ Layer 1 ☑ ☑ Layer 1 ☑ Layer 1	Double-click = Change layer name Double-click = Zoom to layer Alt + Click = Show selected only Cmd + Click = Pixel selection from layer
Liquify tools	Shift Option	Reduces rate of application of the effect Switches to the opposite of the default effect

Painting	Shift Option + Drag Ctrl + Option + Drag	Draws straight line connecting two strokes Temporarily switches to the colour picker Left-right changes width, up-down changes hardness of brush
Pixel selections	Shift Cmd Ctrl Option	Constrains marquee to square or circle Moves underlying layer with selection Adds to selection Removes from selection
Pixel Tool	Cmd	Erases from the current layer or objects
Selecting	Shift Option Drag + Ctrl Option + Drag	Selects multiple layers Selects layer behind current selection Ignores initial layer below cursor Selects layers partially encompassed
Vector drawing tools	Shift Option Cmd	Constrains node position and handle angles Sets node to Sharp (for creating cusps) Temporarily switches to Node editing (from Pen)
White Balance Tool	Shift Option + Drag	Creates an average of multiple sampled points Creates a sample from a marquee
Zoom Tool	Option + Click Option + Drag	Zooms out Zoom to marquee

MODIFIERS & LAYER CONTROL

Category	Modifier	Description
Clone, Healing & Liquify Mesh Clone	Alt	Select a source
Dodge/Burn & Blur/Sharpen tools	Alt	Temporarily switches to the opposite tool
Freehand Selection Tool	Shift	Temporarily switches to Polygonal from Freehand
	Shift	Temporarily switches between Polygonal and Magnetic
	Drag	Temporarily switches to Freehand from Polygonal or Magnetic
General	Shift	Reverses aspect ratio constraint on scaling
	Ctrl	Scales from the centre of selection
	Alt	Ignores snapping during operation
	Right button down	Rotates from opposite corner of layer
Layers Panel	Double-click = Change layer name	
	Double-click = Zoom to layer	
	Alt + Click = Show selected only	
	Ctrl + Click = Pixel selection from layer	
	☐ Layer 1	
	◤◢ Layer 1	
	◤◢◤ Layer 1	
Liquify tools	Shift	Reduces rate of application of the effect
	Alt	Switches to the opposite of the default effect

Category	Modifier	Description
Painting	Shift	Draws straight line connecting two strokes
	Alt + Drag	Temporarily switches to the colour picker
	Alt + Right button down + Drag	Left-right changes width, up-down changes hardness of brush
Pixel selections	Shift	Constrains marquee to square or circle
	Ctrl	Moves underlying layer with selection
	Alt	Removes from selection
	Right button down + Drag	Adds to selection
Pixel Tool	Ctrl	Erases from the current layer or objects
Selecting	Shift	Selects multiple layers
	Alt	Selects layer behind current selection
	Alt + Drag	Ignores initial layer below cursor
	Right button down + Drag	Selects layers partially encompassed
Vector drawing tools	Shift	Constrains node position and handle angles
	Alt	Sets node to Sharp (for creating cusps)
	Ctrl	Temporarily switches to Node editing (from Pen)
White Balance Tool	Shift	Creates an average of multiple sampled points
	Alt + Drag	Creates a sample from a marquee
Zoom Tool	Alt + Click	Zooms out
	Alt + Drag	Zoom to marquee

AFFINITY
Photo

Windows